美 国 人 文 系 列

美国经典外交
文 献 选 读

王 波 / 主编

SELECTED READINGS OF
AMERICAN CLASSIC
DIPLOMATIC DOCUMENTS

北京大学出版社
PEKING UNIVERSITY PRESS

图书在版编目(CIP)数据

美国经典外交文献选读：英文 / 王波主编. —北京：北京大学出版社，2019.6
（美国人文系列）
ISBN 978-7-301-30541-6

Ⅰ.①美… Ⅱ.①王… Ⅲ.①英语—阅读教学—高等学校—教材 ②外交—文献—汇编—美国　Ⅳ.①H319.4：D

中国版本图书馆CIP数据核字（2019）第096634号

书　　　名	美国经典外交文献选读 MEIGUO JINGDIAN WAIJIAO WENXIAN XUANDU
著作责任者	王　波　主编
责任编辑	李　娜
标准书号	ISBN 978-7-301-30541-6
出版发行	北京大学出版社
地　　　址	北京市海淀区成府路205号　100871
网　　　址	http://www.pup.cn　新浪微博：@北京大学出版社
电子信箱	345014015@qq.com
电　　　话	邮购部 010-62752015　发行部 010-62750672　编辑部 010-62759634
印刷者	三河市博文印刷有限公司
经销者	新华书店
	730毫米×980毫米　16开本　11印张　326千字 2019年6月第1版　2019年6月第1次印刷
定　　　价	42.00元

未经许可，不得以任何方式复制或抄袭本书之部分或全部内容。
版权所有，侵权必究
举报电话：010-62752024　电子信箱：fd@pup.pku.edu.cn
图书如有印装质量问题，请与出版部联系，电话：010-62756370

前　言

《美国经典外交文献选读》既是一部英文教材，也是一部关于美国外交思想史的文献汇编。它以不同历史时期美国主流外交思想为主线，精选了从美国建国到第二次世界大战时期具有代表性的美国外交文献作为研读文本。希望通过阅读这些原汁原味的英文外交文献，读者能够了解和熟悉美国外交思想的历史发展和演变过程，深刻领悟美国历史上重要外交思想的内涵、意义及相关背景，并对美国外交思想和对外政策的历史根源有比较深入的研究。

这部教材包括导言在内共7章。导言是对美国不同历史时期外交思想的一个综述，旨在让读者对美国外交思想的全貌有一个比较清晰的了解和认识。其余6章以不同历史时期美国外交思想为线索进行编写。每章根据不同历史时期美国外交思想的主题酌情选编了数篇英文外交文献，包括以下内容：阅读思考（Pre-reading questions）、作者简介（About the author）、文本（Text）、词汇表（Vocabulary）、讨论题（Questions for discussion）、背景材料（Background）、扩展阅读（Further reading）等。

背景材料旨在助力读者阅读，让读者在特定的历史文化语境中深刻理解文献内涵，同时熟悉相关的中英文表达。扩展阅读可以帮助读者扩充相应的背景知识，帮助读者深入研究相关文献和相应的外交思想主题。教材对文献中一些重点及难点句子、词组或知识点作了一些注释或翻译，以方便读者使用。早期的英文文献存在少量语法或语言错误，为保持文献原貌，教材未作修改，特此说明。

这部教材可供英语专业、国际关系专业、外交专业和世界史专业（尤其是美国史方向）本科高年级学生以及其他相关专业研究生作为专业课教材使用，或供希望通过研读原汁原味美国外交文献来提高英语技能、了解美国外交历史演变脉络、洞察美国外交思想深刻内涵的读者使用。在教学过程中，使用者可根据需要酌情采用精读和泛读相结合的方法阅读文本，课前阅读尤为重要，这是课堂讨论的前提和基础。要以了解文献的相关历史文化背景知识作为学习的重点，以准确理解文献的主要内容，包括文献重要历史意义作为学习的目标。每篇文献要放置在文献所处特定时代大背景下去深刻剖析、解读、思考、讨论，避免以偏概全或孤立地理解单个文本，同时，要注意写作者的政治立场。

准确地说，这部教材只是提供了一个视角，一个方向，一点参考，为使用者系统、全面研读美国外交思想、探究美国历史发展推开了一扇窗，打开了一扇门。

教材主编王波教授长期从事美国研究的教学和科研，曾在北京大学出版社出版美国人文系列，包括：《美国重要历史文献导读：从殖民时期到十九世纪》（2002）、《美国重要历史文献导读：二十世纪》（2001）、《美国历史与文化选读》（2004）。本教材由王波教授设计体例，撰写导言，编写部分章节，对书稿进行修改、润色，并已多次在硕士和博士研究生中使用教材的自编讲义开设"美国外交思想"的专业方向选修课程。

教材编写过程中，叶建军、武媛媛、尚洁、杨超、花爱萍、魏丽、袁飞等老师帮助编写了部分章节，在此表示深深的谢意。虽然贡献有大小，但是每个人的作用都是不可或缺的。

此外，教材中的英文背景材料和中文背景材料，部分选编自一些中外文学术期刊、著作或网站，考虑到作为教材使用，没有一一加以注释，在此对这些相关成果的研究者和编译者表示诚挚的感谢！

教材中肯定存在不妥之处，请教材使用者批评指正。

主编

2018年6月于南京

目 录

导言　如何解读美国外交 …………………………………………………………… 1

Chapter 1　Isolationism（孤立主义） ………………………………………… 1
　Text 1　Farewell Address ……………………………………………………… 2
　Text 2　First Inaugural Address ……………………………………………… 17

Chapter 2　Monroe Doctrine（门罗主义） …………………………………… 25
　Text 1　Seventh Annual State of the Union Address to Congress ………… 26
　Text 2　Second Annual Address ……………………………………………… 30

Chapter 3　Manifest Destiny & Imperialism（天定命运论与帝国主义）…… 44
　Text 1　The Great Nation of Futurity ………………………………………… 46
　Text 2　Annexation …………………………………………………………… 51
　Text 3　The March of the Flag ……………………………………………… 57
　Text 4　America's Destiny …………………………………………………… 64

Chapter 4　Open Door Policy（门户开放）…………………………………… 75
　Text 1　The First Open Door Note …………………………………………… 76
　Text 2　Communications Between Mr. Choate and Lord Salisbury ……… 80
　Text 3　The Second Open Door Note ………………………………………… 83

Chapter 5　Wilsonism（威尔逊主义）………………………………………… 88
　Text 1　The World Must Be Made Safe for Democracy …………………… 90
　Text 2　Fourteen Points ……………………………………………………… 98
　Text 3　In Favour of the League of Nations ………………………………… 104

Chapter 6　Four Freedoms（四大自由）……………………………………… 124
　Text 1　The Four Freedoms Speech ………………………………………… 126
　Text 2　Atlantic Charter ……………………………………………………… 136
　Text 3　The United Nations Fight for the Four Freedoms ………………… 138

参考书目 ………………………………………………………………………… 157

导言　如何解读美国外交

美国两百多年的发展历程见证了这个超级大国从无到有、从小到大、由弱到强、由强到霸的成长过程。它的外交主旋律呈现出一个弱小的共和国到全球帝国的扩张过程。从18世纪末北美13个殖民地到建国之初的13个州，从南北战争之前北方资本主义和南方种植园农奴制两种经济体制并存的分裂国家到19世纪末的一个地区资本主义强国，从20世纪两次世界大战的参与者、战胜国到美苏冷战时代的霸权主义国家以及苏联解体后的唯一超级大国，美国快速地成长壮大。作为局外人，我们必须以一种客观的眼光去审视、解读美国的成长历程和发展模式，从而更深刻地认识这个国家。

美国在短短两百多年的时间，能一跃成为世界上最具影响力的国家之一，原因无疑是多方面的。但是，我们尤其要关注的是，它的外交政策是"产生这种影响的最直接和极为重要的形式"[①]。因此，研究美国外交史意义重大。

如何解读美国外交史？美国的学者们莫衷一是。传统美国外交史学主要有三大学派。第一个学派被称为传统学派，也就是国家主义学派。这一学派的学者都是理想主义者，他们认为外交史曾经是美国史学很小的一部分，到了20世纪30年代美国才真正产生了外交史。换言之，弱国无外交是颠扑不破的真理。随着美国国际地位发生重大变化，美国必须有自己独特的外交史，向海外倡导美国式的民主制度、思想和价值观。国家主义者往往对美国的外交充满了自豪。

第二个学派被称为现实主义学派。这一学派的学者基本都是第一次世界大战之后一群对美国理想破灭的人。他们目睹了20世纪30年代的法西斯主义，目睹了第二次世界大战中集体安全体系的破灭，第二次世界大战后又出现美苏争霸世界的局面。于是，他们中的一些人开始重新检讨美国的外交政策，发现美国的外交政策理想主义色彩太浓，道德感太重。于是，他们强调外交的现实性，强调外交要面对现实，主张强权政治，觉得美国对世界干预得太多，认为美国的利益主要是在欧洲，主张美国要集中精力关注欧洲的问题。

第三个学派是新左派。他们对美国政府的政策持批评的态度，认为美国外交基本上是失败的，他们中有的学者对美国外交做了经济解释，思想上接受了马克思主义的

[①] 贾庆国：《美国外交思想与实践》，袁明主编：《美国文化与社会十五讲》，北京：北京大学出版社，2003年，第237页。

成分，认为美国追求的是经济利益、商业扩张，实际上这是一场大悲剧。这一派学者的思想来源是20世纪初的进步主义思想，认为美国试图用经济手段来解决美国国内问题，否认外交决策过程中的舆论影响力，认为一小批政治精英控制了舆论，表面上是为了追求美国的利益，实则损害了美国的国家利益。

20世纪70年代以来，美国的外交史学发生了一些变化，以前一般不提及外部事物的反应，70年代开始重视外部事物的反应。美国大学的"美国外交"课程更名为"美国国际关系史"，破除外交单向发生的关系，寻找外交的国际根源。随着经济全球化不断深入，外交不仅被看作是政府之间的事情，也认为有其他各种因素对美国外交政策发挥了作用：移民、传教士、农场主、跨国公司等。美国外交史学研究开始和其他学科结合并产生各种联系，外交史学研究领域得到了较大的拓展。

中国学者应该如何去认识和解读美国外交？仁者见仁，智者见智，这里不一一去回顾了。本书认为，无论用什么学派去阐释美国的外交历程，都必须重视不同历史时期美国独特的外交思想和传统。它们的连续性、稳定性以及随着时代变迁发生的变化奠定了不同历史时期美国外交政策的主旋律。这些外交思想为美国建国后的迅速崛起奠定了和平发展的环境，让这个北美小国得以在一个相对和平的环境中迅速发展壮大，成为地跨两洋的超级大国。

美国有哪些外交思想？它们如何发挥作用？美国外交思想就是"美国的历史、文化以及它和外部的世界关系相互作用的结果"①。因此，美国外交思想是一个动态的、变化的概念。但是总的来说，理想主义和现实主义的互动是美国外交思想演变的基本主线。理想主义和现实主义外交思想体现在不同时期一个个具体的外交实践和主流思想中。无论从什么视角去解读美国外交史，只要抓住这些主流外交思想的演变，就抓住了美国外交史发展演变的主线，就可以清晰地看出美国外交历程中理想主义和现实主义的深层互动，以及它的本质。

孤立主义是美国现实主义和理想主义互动的最初形式和结果。"美国是在反对英国殖民统治斗争中诞生的国家，具有反殖民主义与孤立主义传统。"② 无论是1776年宣布独立后，还是从1789年正式建立联邦制开始，美国这个地区小国在建国初期，国内不稳定，周边不安全，英、法、西、俄等欧洲殖民主义国家对这个未完全开发的美洲大陆虎视眈眈。联邦政府第一任总统乔治·华盛顿韬光养晦，高瞻远瞩，在其第二任的告别演说中提出了以中立政策为核心的孤立主义思想作为美国外交政策的基础和核心，为建国初期美国的繁荣与稳定奠定了政治和外交基础。孤立主义思想成为美国

---

① 贾庆国：《美国外交思想与实践》，袁明主编：《美国文化与社会十五讲》，北京：北京大学出版社，2003年，第239页。
② 李庆余：《美国外交史——从独立战争至2004年》，济南：山东画报出版社，2008年，第1页。

从建国开始一直到第二次世界大战坚持了一个半世纪的外交主原则。

随着美国国力逐步增强,清教徒理想让美国人的扩张主义思想初显端倪。美国人试图扩充自己的领土,扩大自己的影响力,但那个时候美国还没有实力去干涉美洲以外的事务,门罗主义成为最佳选择。表面上门罗主义是美国人主动关切美洲人民的独立和尊严,维护美洲人民的利益与安全,事实上是美国不希望欧洲列强干涉美洲大陆,于是美洲冠冕堂皇成了美国人的美洲。

门罗主义的本质是把孤立主义思想扩展为美洲孤立的思想,是美国反殖民主义传统的延续。它是理想主义和现实主义结合的又一结果。门罗主义为美国的国家发展创造了一个相对安全的周边环境。同时,门罗主义也为美国未来在美洲甚至全球实行单边主义扩张政策提供了一定的依据和借口,创造了一个有利于美国和平发展的地区安全环境。

19世纪的美国经历了西进运动、南北战争、工业化、城市化等一系列声势浩大的历史事件。从清教徒的使命意识延伸而来的天定命运思想驱使美国人不断向西开拓,向西移民,通过收购领土、对外战争,最终完成了北美大陆扩张,在19世纪末初步完成了工业化和城市化,成为当时世界的主要经济大国之一。这种天定命运的思想是不安分的,它驱使美国人开始向海外扩张,逐渐走向帝国主义道路。

崛起的美国开始放眼世界,试图确立自己在世界政治舞台上的身份,但这个时候的世界已被欧洲列强瓜分殆尽。1898年美西战争的爆发给了美国海外扩张的正当理由和天赐良机。即便美国依然有反殖民主义的倾向,它还是在战后第一次拥有了自己的海外殖民地。

"美西战争标志着美国进入世界大国行列,也标志着美国从孤立主义开始向国际主义转变。"[①]从此,美国走上了帝国主义道路。虽然孤立主义和门罗主义依然是影响美国外交政策决策的主要依据,但是国际主义者越来越有影响力。美国外交中的现实主义成分越来越浓厚。

门户开放是美国帝国主义政策的一个初步表现。20世纪初,亚洲已被欧洲列强瓜分殆尽,成为它们的势力范围。于是,门户开放成为美国最明智的选择。美国打着门户开放、利益均沾的幌子,把触角伸到亚洲,开始关注美洲以外的事务。美国政府向列强的两次门户开放照会,形成了美国对华政策的雏形,成为美国对华政策的指导性原则。

由于帝国主义列强之间的深刻矛盾无法解决,一场世界大战难以避免。美国最终也未能幸免,于1917年宣布作为同盟国加入第一次世界大战。"历史进展到第一次世

---

① 李庆余:《美国外交史——从独立战争至2004年》,济南:山东画报出版社,2008年,第1页。

界大战时,美国已大体完成了从美国到美洲、从美洲到亚洲的跳跃,终于从大国体系的边缘艰难地挤进国际政治舞台,进入争霸世界的行列。在新的历史条件下,美国再次扩大了门罗主义的范围。"① 战争为美国扩大在世界的影响力提供了机会。美国不满足于成为战争的一个简单赢家,试图通过战后重建在世界发挥更大的影响力,威尔逊总统提出用十四点计划来重建欧洲和世界,彻底向世人表明了美国试图主导世界的野心。

事实上,威尔逊倡导的以正义原则为基础的道义外交思想(即威尔逊主义)是19世纪末20世纪初美国进步主义思想在外交领域的具体表现。

以中产阶级为主导的进步主义运动虽然在美国国内是一场轰轰烈烈的社会改良运动,但在外交领域的运用并不成功。孤立主义依旧是美国国内一股强劲的传统思想,左右着外交决策。威尔逊总统未能得到国会的大力支持,最终国会没有批准美国加入国际联盟(简称"国联")。没有美国加入的国联成了一个无力维护世界和平的虚弱的国际组织,集体安全体系无法建立。威尔逊的道义外交彻底失败了。欧洲的问题依然没有得到彻底解决,于是第二次世界大战顺理成章地成为第一次世界大战的延续,它的爆发是早晚的事情。这表明,虽然美国的扩张主义和国际思想越来越强烈,但孤立主义思想依旧是美国国内占据主导地位的思想,它决定了当时的美国外交政策。不过,值得关注的是,威尔逊主义,特别是他的"十四点计划","并不是对具体安排的设想,而是美国着眼于世界全局,由美国牵头、与欧洲列强共同维持世界秩序的一个总框架",它的重要性不在于当时是否有效,而在于它"先于现实提出了美国外交的走向"。②

第一次世界大战结束后,美国人再次把注意力转移到国内。孤立主义再次成为美国外交的主旋律。但是,孤立只是暂时的。20世纪20年代末突如其来的一场席卷整个资本主义世界的经济危机打破了美国人的平静生活。经济危机的爆发和大萧条的出现让提出全球主义的政治家和决策者无力关心美洲以外的事务,不得不先处理国内事务。

第二次世界大战爆发前,"主张参与乃至干涉国际事务的声音曾一次次被孤立主义的主旋律淹没"③。第二次世界大战爆发后,情况发生了重大变化。美国的中立地位受到挑战,它的国家利益特别是商业利益受到战争影响。美国政府如果不采取强有力的措施,就无法保护它的全球商业利益。罗斯福总统意识到,美国参战是迟早的事

---

① 陈乐民主编:《西方外交思想史》,北京:中国社会科学出版社,1995年,第189页。
② 同上书,第188页。
③ 贾庆国:《美国外交思想与实践》,袁明主编:《美国文化与社会十五讲》,北京:北京大学出版社,2003年,第242页。

情,但是美国的国防动员和战争准备还远远不够,不足以打赢这场战争。于是,罗斯福在其国情咨文中呼吁国会授权和拨款,呼吁全民动员,通过《租借法案》这一创举,让美国成为西方民主国家的兵工厂。因此,美国虽还未宣战,却已用实际行动表明了自己的立场。罗斯福总统野心勃勃地勾画着世界的未来。

罗斯福总统的四大自由演说勾画出美国主导的战后世界蓝图。它虽是一篇国情咨文,但却阐明了美国的立场,阐明了罗斯福总统的外交思想,它既是现实主义的,也是美国式的理想主义的。最终,珍珠港事件的爆发让美国迅速参战。第二次世界大战彻底改变了美国的历史,也部分改变了世界历史。第二次世界大战"彻底打破了孤立主义对美国外交的影响,为美国政府全面参与国际事务铺平了道路"[①]。

第二次世界大战结束后,美苏爆发冷战。美国把触角伸向世界上每一个角落,试图建立美国主导的国际体系,遏制成为冷战时代美国外交思想的主旋律。1991年苏联解体,美国步入了后冷战外交时代。"后冷战外交是在全球化、多极化与美国成为独一无二的超级大国这一时代语境下展开的。"[②]

美国经历了近一个世纪的国际参与和竞争后,继续奉行全球主义,妄图独霸世界。但是,美国的决策者发现,冷战后的世界战略格局发生了巨大变化,以中国为首的第三世界已经崛起,它们奉行独立自主的外交政策。美国的传统盟友日本、欧洲等国在政治上日趋独立,世界多极化趋势不可抵挡,美国虽是唯一的超级大国,但它试图一统天下的野心再也无法实现了。

从务实的孤立主义思想到初显端倪暴露扩张野心的门罗主义政策,从打着天赋使命旗帜的地区扩张主义到以门户开放为借口的全球主义,随着国力的增强,美国从建国开始一直到20世纪初基本上都奉行的孤立传统被逐渐放弃,美国开始进行海外扩张,卷入欧洲的事务,开始寻求世界大国地位的确立。无论是威尔逊倡导的道义外交,还是罗斯福提出以四大自由构建世界秩序,都表明美国人在不断寻求在世界上发挥主导作用和领导地位,试图把美国式的理想主义和现实世界相结合。第二次世界大战结束后,美国彻底摆脱了孤立主义外交传统,全方位卷入世界事务,试图在各个领域发挥主导作用,建立美国主导的霸权世界,但是始终未能如愿。

抓住不同时期美国外交思想的主旋律,可以深刻认识美国外交的历史演变过程,从而对美国外交史有一个全面系统的把握和深刻的认识。鉴于此,本书各章围绕美国从建国到第二次世界大战时期外交思想的主旋律,选编了一些重要的外交文献或体现外交主旋律的文章,通过研读,读者可对当时代的美国外交思想有深刻的认识和把

---

① 贾庆国:《美国外交思想与实践》,袁明主编:《美国文化与社会十五讲》,北京:北京大学出版社,2003年,第245页。
② 李庆余:《美国外交史——从独立战争至2004年》,济南:山东画报出版社,2008年,第341页。

握。希望对美国外交感兴趣的读者通过阅读这些经典文献，深入认识相关政策的时代背景，深刻解读美国的外交历程，客观把握美国外交政策的演变脉络，特别是美国外交政策的本质。

"大国或强国的外交有两重任务：一是尽量保护自己的利益；二是尽可能地扩大自己的影响。"[①] 长期以来，美国对外政策尤其是其对华政策对中国的国家安全和社会经济发展影响巨大。中国政府一贯奉行独立自主的和平外交政策。改革开放以来，随着中国国力的进一步提升，对外关系的日益扩大，美国外交政策对中国的影响"有增无减"，因此，深入了解和全面认识美国外交政策的历史，对于中国政府制定符合中国利益的对外政策具有"十分重要的理论和现实意义"[②]。鉴于此，我们必须认真研读不同历史时期的美国外交思想，做到知己知彼，合作共赢。

---

① 陈乐民主编：《西方外交思想史》，北京：中国社会科学出版社，1995年，第6页。
② 贾庆国：《美国外交思想与实践》，袁明主编：《美国文化与社会十五讲》，北京：北京大学出版社，2003年，第237页。

Chapter 1

Isolationism

（孤立主义）

Pre-reading questions

1. What is the policy of isolationism? Did George Washington mention the word *isolationism* in his Farewell Address?
2. Do you think the isolationist policy was the best choice for the United States in Washington's time? Why?

About the author

George Washington was the first President of the United States (1789—1797) and one of the founding fathers. He served as Commander in Chief of the Continental Army during the American Revolution. Born in 1732 into a Virginia planter family, he learned the morals, manners, and body of knowledge requisite for an 18th century Virginia gentleman. He had two intertwined interests: military arts and western expansion. Commissioned a lieutenant colonel in 1754, he fought the first skirmishes of what grew into the French and Indian War. The next year, he escaped injury although four bullets ripped his coat and two horses were shot from under him.

From 1759 to the outbreak of the American Revolution, Washington managed his lands around Mount Vernon and served in the Virginia House of Burgesses. Married to a widow, Martha Dandridge Custis, he had a busy and happy life. But like his fellow planters, Washington felt himself exploited by British merchants and hampered by British regulations. As the quarrel with the mother country grew acute, he moderately but firmly voiced his resistance to the restrictions.

Washington, as a Virginia delegate, was elected Commander in Chief of the Continental Army, when the Second Continental Congress assembled in Philadelphia in May 1775. On July 3, 1775, at Cambridge, Massachusetts, he took command of his ill-trained troops and embarked upon a war that was to last six grueling years. Finally, in 1781 with the aid of French allies — Washington forced the surrender of Cornwallis at Yorktown.

Washington had long expected to retire. But he realized that the nation under its Articles of Confederation did not function well, so he became a prime mover in the steps leading to the Constitutional Convention at Philadelphia in 1787. When the new Constitution was ratified, the Electoral College unanimously elected him President.

When in office, foreign policy became preponderantly a big concern. When the French Revolution led to a major war between France and England, Washington refused to accept entirely the recommendations of either his Secretary of State Thomas Jefferson, who was pro-French, or his Secretary of the Treasury Alexander Hamilton, who was pro-British. Instead, he insisted upon a neutral course until the United States could grow stronger.

Washington did not like party politics. However, to his great disappointment, two parties were developing by the end of his first term. Wearied of politics, feeling old, he retired at the end of his second term. In his Farewell Address, he urged his countrymen to forswear excessive party spirit and geographical distinctions. In foreign affairs, he warned against long-term alliances. This has been known as the beginning of American isolationist tradition of foreign policy.

After less than three years of retirement at Mount Vernon, Washington died of a throat infection on December 14, 1799.

 Text 1

Farewell Address
George Washington, September 19, 1796

Friends and Fellow-Citizens:

1 The period for a new election of a citizen, to administer the executive government of the United States, being not far distant, and the time actually arrived, when your thoughts must be employed in designating the person, who is to be clothed with that important trust, it appears to me proper, especially as it may conduce to a more distinct expression of the public voice, that I should now apprise you of the resolution I have formed, to decline being considered among the number of those, out of whom a choice is to be made.①

2 I beg you, at the same time, to do me the justice to be assured, that this resolution has not been taken, without a strict regard to all the considerations appertaining to the relation, which binds a dutiful citizen to his country — and that, in withdrawing the tender of service which silence in my situation might imply, I am influenced by no diminution of zeal for your future interest, no deficiency of grateful respect for your past kindness; but am supported by a full conviction that the step is compatible with both.

3 The acceptance of, and continuance hitherto in, the office to which your suffrages have

---

① 建国初期，美国宪法对总统任期没有具体限制。华盛顿总统已连任两届，决定退休，不再连任。

twice called me, have been a uniform sacrifice of inclination to the opinion of duty, and to a deference for what appeared to be your desire. I constantly hoped that it would have been much earlier in my power, consistently with motives, which I was not at liberty to disregard, to return to that retirement, from which I had been reluctantly drawn. The strength of my inclination to do this, previous to the last election, had even led to the preparation of an address to declare it to you;① but mature reflection on the then perplexed and critical posture of our affairs with foreign nations, and the unanimous advice of persons entitled to my confidence, impelled me to abandon the idea.②

4   I rejoice, that the state of your concerns, external as well as internal, no longer renders the pursuit of inclination incompatible with the sentiment of duty, or propriety; and am persuaded whatever partiality may be retained for my services, that in the present circumstances of our country, you will not disapprove my determination to retire.

5   The impressions, with which, I first undertook the arduous trust, were explained on the proper occasion. In the discharge of this trust, I will only say, that I have, with good intentions, contributed towards the organization and administration of the government, the best exertions of which a very fallible judgment was capable. Not unconscious, in the outset, of the inferiority of my qualifications, experience in my own eyes, perhaps still more in the eyes of others, has strengthened the motives to diffidence of myself; and every day the increasing weight of years admonishes me more and more, that the shade of retirement is as necessary to me as it will be welcome. Satisfied that if any circumstances have given peculiar value to my services, they were temporary, I have the consolation to believe, that while choice and prudence invite me to quit the political scene, patriotism does not forbid it.

6   In looking forward to the moment, which is intended to terminate the career of my public life, my feelings do not permit me to suspend the deep acknowledgment of that debt of gratitude which I owe to my beloved country, for the many honors it has conferred upon me; still more for the steadfast confidence with which it has supported me; and for the opportunities I have thence enjoyed of manifesting my inviolable attachment, by services faithful and persevering, though in usefulness unequal to my zeal. If benefits have resulted to our country from these services, let it always be remembered to your praise, and as an instructive example in our annals, that, under circumstances in which the passions agitated in every direction were liable to mislead, amidst appearances sometimes dubious, vicissitudes of fortune③ often discouraging, in situations in which not infrequently want of success has countenanced the spirit of criticism, the constancy of your support was the essential prop of the efforts, and a guarantee of the plans by which they were effected. Profoundly penetrated with this idea, I shall carry it with me to my grave, as a strong incitement to unceasing vows that Heaven may continue to you the choicest tokens of its beneficence — that your Union

---

① 华盛顿总统在第一个任期结束时曾起草过一份告别演说，由于连任，那份告别演说就搁置不用了。
② 这充分说明，华盛顿第一个任期结束时，美国面临着对外关系的严峻考验，只有他才是最合适领导美国的人选。
③ vicissitudes of fortune: 命运的变迁。

and brotherly affection may be perpetual — that the free constitution, which is the work of your hands, may be sacredly maintained — that its administration in every department may be stamped with wisdom and virtue — that, in fine, the happiness of the people of these states, under the auspices of liberty, may be made complete, by so careful a preservation and so prudent a use of this blessing as will acquire to them the glory of recommending it to the applause, the affection — and adoption of every nation which is yet a stranger to it.

7   Here, perhaps, I ought to stop. But a solicitude for your welfare, which cannot end but with my life, and the apprehension of danger, natural to that solicitude, urge me on an occasion like the present, to offer to your solemn contemplation, and to recommend to your frequent review, some sentiments; which are the result of much reflection, of no inconsiderable observation, and which appear to me all important to the permanency of your felicity as a people.① These will be offered to you with the more freedom as you can only see in them the disinterested warnings of a parting friend, who can possibly have no personal motive to bias his counsel. Nor can I forget, as an encouragement to it, your indulgent reception of my sentiments on a former and not dissimilar occasion.

8   Interwoven as is the love of liberty with every ligament of your hearts, no recommendation of mine is necessary to fortify or confirm the attachment.

9   The unity of government which constitutes you one people is also now dear to you. It is justly so; for it is a main pillar in the edifice of your real independence, the support of your tranquility at home; your peace abroad; of your safety; of your prosperity; of that very liberty which you so highly prize.② But as it is easy to foresee, that from different causes and from different quarters, much pains will be taken, many artifices employed, to weaken in your minds the conviction of this truth; as this is the point in your political fortress against which the batteries of internal and external enemies will be most constantly and actively (though often covertly and insidiously) directed, it is of infinite moment, that you should properly estimate the immense value of your national union to your collective and individual happiness; that you should cherish a cordial, habitual and immovable attachment to it; accustoming yourselves to think and speak of it as of the Palladium③ of your political safety and prosperity; watching for its preservation with jealous anxiety; discountenancing whatever may suggest even a suspicion that it can in any event be abandoned, and indignantly frowning upon the first dawning of every attempt to alienate any portion of our country from the rest, or to enfeeble the sacred ties which now link together the various parts.

10   For this you have every inducement of sympathy and interest. Citizens by birth or choice, of a common country, that country have a right to concentrate your affections. The name of American, which belongs to you, in your national capacity, must always exalt the just

---

① 华盛顿总统希望在退休之际分享个人对国家治理的思考，因为这事关"美利坚民族的福祉的永恒"。
② "政府的统一使你们结合成一个民族，现在也被你们所珍视。这是理所当然的，因为它是支撑你们真正独立的主要支柱，也是保证你们国内安定、国外和平、安全、繁荣以及你们所珍惜的自由的基石。"
③ Palladium：（希腊神话中的智慧女神）雅典娜的神像。

pride of Patriotism, more than any appellation derived from local discriminations. With slight shades of difference, you have the same religion, manners, habits and political principles. You have in a common cause fought and triumphed together — The independence and liberty you possess are the work of joint councils, and joint efforts — of common dangers, sufferings and successes.

11 But these considerations, however powerfully they address themselves to your sensibility are greatly outweighed by those who apply more immediately to your interest. Here every portion of our country finds the most commanding motives for carefully guarding and preserving the Union of the whole.

12 The North, in an unrestrained intercourse with the South, protected by the equal laws of a common government, finds in the productions of the latter, great additional resources of maritime and commercial enterprise and — precious materials of manufacturing industry. The South in the same intercourse, benefiting by the agency of the North, sees its agriculture grow and its commerce expand. Turning partly into its own channels the seamen of the North, it finds its particular navigation invigorated; and while it contributes, in different ways, to nourish and increase the general mass of the national navigation, it looks forward to the protection of a maritime strength, to which itself is unequally adapted. The East, in a like intercourse with the West, already finds, and in the progressive improvement of interior communications, by land and water, will more and more find a valuable vent for the commodities which it brings from abroad, or manufactures at home. The West derives from the East supplies requisite to its growth and comfort — and what is perhaps of still greater consequence, it must of necessity owe the secure enjoyment of indispensable outlets for its own productions to the weight, influence, and the future maritime strength of the Atlantic side of the Union, directed by an indissoluble community of Interest as one nation. Any other tenure by which the West can hold this essential advantage, whether derived from its own separate strength, or from an apostate and unnatural connection with any foreign power, must be intrinsically precarious.

13 While then every part of our country thus feels an immediate and particular interest in Union, all the parts combined cannot fail to find in the united mass of means and efforts greater strength, greater resource, proportionably greater security from external danger, a less frequent interruption of their peace by foreign nations; and, what is of inestimable value![①] They must derive from Union an exemption from those broils and wars between themselves, which so frequently afflict neighboring countries, not tied together by the same government; which their own rivalships alone would be sufficient to produce, but which opposite foreign alliances, attachments and intrigues would stimulate and imbitter. Hence likewise they will avoid the necessity of those overgrown military establishments, which under any form of government are inauspicious to liberty, and which are to be regarded as particularly hostile to Republican liberty: In this sense it is, that your union ought to be considered as a main prop of

---

① 华盛顿总统强调联合起来力量更大，只有联合起来，才能确保美国的长治久安和国家发展。

your liberty, and that the love of the one ought to endear to you the preservation of the other.

14 These considerations speak a persuasive language to every reflecting and virtuous mind, and exhibit the continuance of the Union as a primary object of patriotic desire. Is there a doubt, whether a common government can embrace so large a sphere? Let experience solve it. To listen to mere speculation in such a case were criminal. We are authorized to hope that a proper organization of the whole, with the auxiliary agency of governments for the respective Subdivisions, will afford a happy issue to the experiment. This is well worth a fair and full experiment. With such powerful and obvious motives to Union, affecting all parts of our country, while experience shall not have demonstrated its impracticability, there will always be reason, to distrust the patriotism of those, who in any quarter may endeavor to weaken its bands.

15 In contemplating the causes which may disturb our Union, it occurs as matter of serious concern, that any ground should have been furnished for characterizing parties by geographical discriminations — Northern and Southern — Atlantic and Western; whence designing men may endeavor to excite a belief that there is a real difference of local interests and views. One of the expedients of party to acquire influence, within particular districts, is to misrepresent the opinions and aims of other districts. You cannot shield yourselves too much against the jealousies and heart burnings which spring from these misrepresentations. They tend to render alien to each other those who ought to be bound together by fraternal affection. The inhabitants of our Western country have lately had a useful lesson on this head. They have seen, in the negotiation by the Executive, and in the unanimous ratification by the Senate, of the Treaty with Spain, and in the universal satisfaction at that event, throughout the United States, a decisive proof how unfounded were the suspicions propagated among them of a policy in the General Government and in the Atlantic States unfriendly to their interests in regard to the Mississippi. They have been witnesses to the formation of two Treaties, that with Great Britain and that with Spain, which secure to them every thing they could desire, in respect to our foreign relations, towards confirming their prosperity. Will it not be their wisdom to rely for the preservation of these advantages on the Union by which they were procured? Will they not henceforth be deaf to those advisers, if such there are, who would sever them from their brethren and connect them with aliens?

16 To the efficacy and permanency of your Union, a government for the whole is indispensable.① No alliances however strict between the parts can be an adequate substitute. They must inevitably experience the infractions and interruptions which all alliances in all times have experienced. Sensible of this momentous truth, you have improved upon your first essay, by the adoption of a Constitution of Government, better calculated than your former for an intimate Union, and for the efficacious management of your common concerns. This government, the offspring of our own choice uninfluenced and unawed, adopted upon full

---

① 华盛顿总统再次强调解散邦联制政府体制、建立联邦政府的现实必要性，那就是"提高国家的效力，让合众国永存"。

investigation and mature deliberation, completely free in its principles, in the distribution of its powers, uniting security with energy, and containing within itself a provision for its own amendment, has a just claim to your confidence and your support. Respect for its authority, compliance with its laws, acquiescence in its measures, are duties enjoined by the fundamental maxims of true liberty. The basis of our political systems is the right of the people to make and to alter their constitutions of government. But the Constitution which at any time exists, 'till changed by an explicit and authentic act of the whole people, is sacredly obligatory upon all. The very idea of the power and the right of the people to establish government presupposes the duty of every Individual to obey the established government.

17 All obstructions to the execution of the laws, all combinations and associations, under whatever plausible character, with the real design to direct, control counteract, or awe the regular deliberation and action of the constituted authorities are destructive of this fundamental principle and of fatal tendency. They serve to organize faction, to give it an artificial and extraordinary force — to put in the place of the delegated will of the nation, the will of a party; often a small but artful and enterprising minority of the community; and, according to the alternate triumphs of different parties, to make the public administration the mirror of the ill concerted and incongruous projects of faction, rather than the organ of consistent and wholesome plans digested by common councils and modified by mutual interests. However combinations or associations of the above description may now and then answer popular ends, they are likely, in the course of time and things, to become potent engines, by which cunning, ambitious and unprincipled men will be enabled to subvert the power of the people, and to usurp for themselves the reins of government; destroying afterwards the very engines which have lifted them to unjust dominion.

18 Towards the preservation of your government and the permanency of your present happy state, it is requisite, not only that you steadily discountenance irregular oppositions to its acknowledged authority, but also that you resist with care the spirit of innovation upon its principles however specious the pretexts. One method of assault may be to effect, in the forms of the constitution, alterations which will impair the energy of the system, and thus to undermine what cannot be directly overthrown. In all the changes to which you may be invited, remember that time and habit are at least as necessary to fix the true character of governments, as of other human institutions — that experience is the surest standard, by which to test the real tendency of the existing constitution of a country — that facility in changes upon the credit of mere hypotheses and opinion exposes to perpetual change, from the endless variety of hypotheses and opinion: and remember, especially, that for the efficient management of your common interests, in a country so extensive as ours, a government of as much vigor as is consistent with the perfect security of liberty is indispensable — liberty itself will find in such a government, with powers properly distributed and adjusted, its surest guardian. It is indeed little else than a name, where the government is too feeble to withstand the enterprises of faction, to confine each member of the society within the limits prescribed by the laws and to maintain all in the secure and tranquil enjoyment of the rights of person and property.①

19　I have already intimated to you the danger of parties in the state, with particular reference to the founding of them on geographical discriminations.② Let me now take a more comprehensive view, and warn you in the most solemn manner against the baneful effects of the spirit of party, generally.

20　This spirit, unfortunately, is inseparable from our nature, having its root in the strongest passions of the human mind. It exists under different shapes in all governments, more or less stifled, controlled, or repressed; but in those of the popular form it is seen in its greatest rankness and is truly their worst enemy.

21　The alternate domination of one faction over another, sharpened by the spirit of revenge natural to party dissention, which in different ages and countries has perpetrated the most horrid enormities, is itself a frightful despotism. But this leads at length to a more formal and permanent despotism. The disorders and miseries, which result, gradually incline the minds of men to seek security and repose in the absolute power of an individual: and sooner or later the chief of some prevailing faction more able or more fortunate than his competitors, turns this disposition to the purposes of his own elevation, on the ruins of public liberty.

22　Without looking forward to an extremity of this kind (which nevertheless ought not to be entirely out of sight) the common and continual mischiefs of the spirit of party are sufficient to make it the interest and the duty of a wise people to discourage and restrain it.

23　It serves always to distract the public councils and enfeeble the public administration. It agitates the community with ill founded jealousies and false alarms, kindles the animosity of one part against another, foments occasionally riot and insurrection. It opens the door to foreign influence and corruption, which find a facilitated access to the government itself through the channels of party passions. Thus the policy and the will of one country are subjected to the policy and will of another.

24　There is an opinion that parties in free countries are useful checks upon the administration of the government and serve to keep alive the spirit of liberty. This within certain limits is probably true — and in governments of a monarchical cast patriotism may look with indulgence, if not with favor, upon the spirit of party. But in those of the popular character, in governments purely elective, it is a spirit not to be encouraged. From their natural tendency, it is certain there will always be enough of that spirit for every salutary purpose. And there being constant danger of excess, the effort ought to be, by force of public opinion, to mitigate and assuage it. A fire not to be quenched; it demands a uniform vigilance to prevent its bursting into a flame, lest instead of warming it should consume.

---

① 这里，华盛顿总统着重强调了宪法、法制和自由对政府治理的重要性。
② 华盛顿总统开始讨论政党的危害，指出政党的形成主要是因为不同地区的利益差异导致。华盛顿总统关于党派问题的看法，是他《告别演说》的主要内容之一。华盛顿总统虽然反对建立政党，但是由于自己的立场，不知不觉中，华盛顿总统已成为联邦党人。

25   It is important, likewise, that the habits of thinking in a free country should inspire caution in those entrusted with its administration, to confine themselves within their respective constitutional spheres; avoiding in the exercise of the powers of one department to encroach upon another. The spirit of encroachment tends to consolidate the powers of all the departments in one, and thus to create whatever the form of government, a real despotism. A just estimate of that love of power, and proneness to abuse it, which predominates in the human heart, is sufficient to satisfy us of the truth of this position. The necessity of reciprocal checks in the exercise of political power; by dividing and distributing it into different depositories, and constituting each the guardian of the public weal against invasions by the others, has been evinced by experiments ancient and modern; some of them in our country and under our own eyes. To preserve them must be as necessary as to institute them. If in the opinion of the people, the distribution or modification of the constitutional powers be in any particular wrong, let it be corrected by an amendment in the way which the Constitution designates. But let there be no change by usurpation; for though this, in one instance, may be the instrument of good, it is the customary weapon by which free governments are destroyed. The precedent must always greatly overbalance in permanent evil any partial or transient benefit which the use can at any time yield.

26   Of all the dispositions and habits which lead to political prosperity, religion and morality are indispensable supports.① In vain would that man claim the tribute of patriotism, who should labor to subvert these great pillars of human happiness, these firmest props of the duties of men and citizens. The mere politician, equally with the pious man ought to respect and to cherish them. A volume could not trace all their connections with private and public felicity. Let it simply be asked where is the security for property, for reputation, for life, if the sense of religious obligation deserts the oaths, which are the instruments of investigation in courts of justice? And let us with caution indulge the supposition, that morality can be maintained without religion. Whatever may be conceded to the influence of refined education on minds of peculiar structure — reason and experience both forbid us to expect that national morality can prevail in exclusion of religious principle.

27   This is substantially true, that virtue or morality is a necessary spring of popular government. The rule indeed extends with more or less force to every species of free government. Who that is a sincere friend to it, can look with indifference upon attempts to shake the foundation of the fabric.

28   Promote then as an object of primary importance, institutions for the general diffusion of knowledge. In proportion as the structure of a government gives force to public opinion, it is essential that public opinion should be enlightened.

29   As a very important source of strength and security, cherish public credit. One method of preserving it is to use it as sparingly as possible: avoiding occasions of experience by cultivating peace, but remembering also that timely disbursements to prepare for danger

---

① 华盛顿总统强调了宗教和道德的作用。

frequently prevent much greater disbursements to repel it — avoiding likewise the accumulation of debt, not only by shunning occasions of experience, but by vigorous exertions in time of peace to discharge the debts which unavoidable wars may have occasioned, not ungenerously throwing upon posterity the burthen① which we ourselves ought to bear. The execution of these maxims belongs to your Representatives, but it is necessary that public opinion should cooperate. To facilitate to them the performance of their duty, it is essential that you should practically bear in mind, that towards the payment of debts there must be revenue — that to have revenue there must be taxes — that no taxes can be devised which are not more or less inconvenient and unpleasant — that the intrinsic embarrassment inseparable from the selection of the proper objects (which is always a choice of difficulties) ought to be a decisive motive for a candid construction of the conduct of the government in making it, and for a spirit of acquiescence in the measures for obtaining revenue which the public exigencies may at any time dictate.

30 Observe good faith and justice towards all Nations. Cultivate peace and harmony with all — religion and morality enjoin this conduct;② and can it be that good policy does not equally enjoin it? It will be worthy of a free, enlightened, and, at no distant period, a great nation, to give to mankind the magnanimous and too novel example of a people always guided by an exalted justice and benevolence. Who can doubt that in the course of time and things the fruits of such a plan would richly repay any temporary advantages which might be lost by a steady adherence to it? Can it be, that Providence has not connected the permanent felicity of a nation with its virtue? The experiment, at least, is recommended by every sentiment which ennobles human Nature. Alas! is it rendered impossible by its vices?

31 In the execution of such a plan nothing is more essential than that permanent inveterate antipathies against particular nations and passionate attachments for others should be excluded; and that in place of them just and amicable feelings towards all should be cultivated. The nation, which indulges towards another a habitual hatred, or a habitual fondness, is in some degree a slave. It is a slave to its animosity or to its affection, either of which is sufficient to lead it astray from its duty and its interest. Antipathy in one nation against another — disposes each more readily to offer insult and injury, to lay hold of③ slight causes of umbrage, and to be haughty and intractable, when accidental or trifling occasions of dispute occur. Hence frequent collisions, obstinate envenomed and bloody contests. The nation, prompted by ill will and resentment sometimes impels to war the government, contrary to the best calculations of policy. The government sometimes participates in the national propensity, and adopts through passion what reason would reject; at other times, it makes the animosity of the nation subservient to projects of hostility instigated by pride, ambition and other sinister and pernicious motives. The peace often, sometimes perhaps the liberty, of nations has been

---

① burthen:（古）burden.
② "与所有国家和平、和谐相处——通过宗教和道义来规范这一行为。"
③ lay hold of: 紧紧抓住。

the victim.

32   So likewise, a passionate attachment of one nation for another produces a variety of evils.① Sympathy for the favorite nation, facilitating the illusion of an imaginary common interest, in cases where no real common interest exists, and infusing into one the enmities of the other, betrays the former into a participation in the quarrels and wars of the latter, without adequate inducement or justification: It leads also to concessions to the favorite nation of privileges denied to others, which is apt doubly to injure the nation making the concessions — by unnecessarily parting with what ought to have been retained — and by exciting jealousy, ill will, and a disposition to retaliate, in the parties from whom equal privileges are withheld: And it gives to ambitious, corrupted, or deluded citizens (who devote themselves to the favorite Nation) facility to betray, or sacrifice the interests of their own country, without odium, sometimes even with popularity; gilding with the appearances of a virtuous sense of obligation a commendable deference for public opinion, or a laudable zeal for public good, the base or foolish compliances of ambition corruption or infatuation.

33   As avenues to foreign influence in innumerable ways, such attachments are particularly alarming to the truly enlightened and independent patriot. How many opportunities do they afford to tamper with domestic factions, to practice the arts of seduction, to mislead public opinion, to influence or awe the public Councils! Such an attachment of a small or weak, towards a great and powerful nation, dooms the former to be the satellite of the latter.

34   Against the insidious wiles of foreign influence②, (I conjure you to believe me fellow citizens,) the jealousy of a free people ought to be constantly awake; since history and experience prove that foreign influence is one of the most baneful foes of Republican government. But that jealousy to be useful must be impartial; else it becomes the instrument of the very influence to be avoided, instead of a defense against it. Excessive partiality for one foreign nation and excessive dislike of another, cause those whom they actuate to see danger only on one side, and serve to veil and even second the arts of influence on the other. Real patriots, who may resist the intrigues of the favorite, are liable to become suspected and odious; while its tools and dupes usurp the applause and confidence of the people, to surrender their interests.

35   The great rule of conduct for us, in regard to foreign nations is in extending our commercial relations to have with them as little political connection as possible.③ So far as we have already formed engagements let them be fulfilled with perfect good faith. Here let us stop.

36   Europe has a set of primary interests, which to us have none, or a very remote relation. Hence she must be engaged in frequent controversies, the causes of which are essentially

---

① 华盛顿总统不断强调反对建立联盟，保持外交的独立性。
② "要提防外国势力的阴谋诡计。"
③ "我们处理外国事务最重要的原则就是，在与他们发展贸易关系时，尽量避免与他们发生政治联系。"由此可见，华盛顿总统的孤立主义政策是相对的，它鼓励发展商业关系，反对发展政治关系。

foreign to our concerns. Hence therefore it must be unwise in us to implicate ourselves, by artificial ties, in the ordinary vicissitudes of her politics①, or the ordinary combinations and collisions of her friendships, or enmities.

37 Our detached and distant situation invites and enables us to pursue a different course.② If we remain one people, under an efficient government, the period is not far off, when we may defy material injury from external annoyance; when we may take such an attitude as will cause the neutrality we may at any time resolve upon to be scrupulously respected; when belligerent nations, under the impossibility of making acquisitions upon us, will not lightly hazard the giving us provocation; when we may choose peace or war, as our interest guided by justice shall counsel.

38 Why forego the advantages of so peculiar a situation? Why quit our own to stand upon foreign ground? Why, by interweaving our destiny with that of any part of Europe, entangle our peace and prosperity in the toils of European ambition, rivalship, interest, humor or caprice?

39 This is our true policy to steer clear of permanent alliances, with any portion of the foreign world.③ So far, I mean, as we are now at liberty to do it, for let me not be understood as capable of patronizing infidelity to existing engagements. I hold the maxim no less applicable to public than to private affairs, that honesty is always the best policy. I repeat it therefore, let those engagements be observed in their genuine sense. But in my opinion, it is unnecessary and would be unwise to extend them.

40 Taking care always to keep ourselves, by suitable establishments, on a respectably defensive posture, we may safely trust to temporary alliances for extraordinary emergencies.④

41 Harmony, liberal intercourse with all nations, are recommended by policy, humanity and interest. But even our commercial policy should hold an equal and impartial hand: neither seeking nor granting exclusive favors or preferences; consulting the natural course of things; diffusing and diversifying by gentle means the streams of commerce, but forcing nothing; establishing with powers so disposed — in order to give to trade a stable course, to define the rights of our merchants, and to enable the government to support them — conventional rules of intercourse; the best that present circumstances and mutual opinion will permit, but temporary, and liable to be from time to time abandoned or varied, as experience and circumstances shall dictate; constantly keeping in view, that 'tis folly in one nation to look for disinterested favors from another — that it must pay with a portion of its Independence for whatever it may accept under that character — that by such acceptance, it may place itself in

---

① vicissitudes of her politics: 政治兴衰。
② 美国远离欧洲大陆，这种地理上的独特优势和当时相对落后的交通、通讯手段使美国建国后很长时间一直未受到欧洲列强的纷扰。这给了美国迅速发展的巨大机会。
③ "远离永久联盟，不与任何外国结盟，这是我们真正要遵循的政策。"这是典型的美国实用主义。事实上，后来美国不断与一些利益攸关的国家结盟，建立了一系列有利于自己的联盟。
④ "我们必须总是保持受人尊敬的防御姿态，我们可以在紧急情况下，信任一个临时性的盟友。"这里充分体现了美国的实用主义，即便华盛顿总统反对建立联盟，但在紧急情况下，他并不反对这么做。

the condition of having given equivalents for nominal favors and yet of being reproached with ingratitude for not giving more. There can be no greater error than to expect, or calculate upon real favors from nation to nation. This is an illusion which experience must cure, which a just pride ought to discard.

42　　In offering to you, my countrymen, these counsels of an old and affectionate friend, I dare not hope they will make the strong and lasting impression,① I could wish — that they will control the usual current of the passions, or prevent our nation from running the course which has hitherto marked the destiny of nations: But if I may even flatter myself, that they may be productive of some partial benefit, some occasional good; that they may now and then recur to moderate the fury of party spirit, to warn against the mischiefs of foreign Intrigue, to guard against the Impostures of pretended patriotism — this hope will be a full recompense for the solicitude for your welfare, by which they have been dictated.

43　　How far in the discharge of my official duties, I have been guided by the principles which have been delineated, the public records and other evidences of my conduct must witness to you and to the world. To myself, the assurance of my own conscience is, that I have at least believed myself to be guided by them.

44　　In relation to the still subsisting war in Europe, my Proclamation of the 22nd of April 1793 is the index to my plan. Sanctioned by your approving voice and by that of your Representatives in both Houses of Congress, the spirit of that measure has continually governed me; uninfluenced by any attempts to deter or divert me from it.

45　　After deliberate examination with the aid of the best lights I could obtain I was well satisfied that our country, under all the circumstances of the case, had a right to take, and was bound in duty and interest, to take a neutral position. Having taken it, I determined, as far as should depend upon me, to maintain it, with moderation, perseverance and firmness.

46　　The considerations, which respect the right to hold this conduct, it is not necessary on this occasion to detail. I will only observe, that according to my understanding of the matter, that right, so far from being denied by any of the belligerent powers has been virtually admitted by all.

47　　The duty of holding a neutral conduct may be inferred, without anything more, from the obligation which justice and humanity impose on every nation, in cases in which it is free to act, to maintain inviolate the relations of peace and amity towards other nations.

48　　The inducements of interest for observing that conduct will best be referred to your own reflections and experience. With me, a predominant motive has been to endeavor to gain time to our country to settle and mature its yet recent institutions, and to progress without interruption, to that degree of strength and consistency, which is necessary to give it, humanly speaking, the command of its own fortunes.

49　　Though in reviewing the incidents of my Administration, I am unconscious of intentional error — I am nevertheless too sensible of my defects not to think it probable that

---

① 华盛顿总统强调他的政策只适用于当时美国所处的国内外环境，再次充分说明了美国的实用主义和现实主义。

I may have committed many errors. Whatever they may be I fervently beseech the Almighty to avert or mitigate the evils to which they may tend. I shall also carry with me the hope that my country will never cease to view them with indulgence; and that after forty five years of my life dedicated to its service, with an upright zeal, the faults of incompetent abilities will be consigned to oblivion, as myself must soon be to the mansions of rest.①

50　Relying on its kindness in this as in other things, and actuated by that fervent love towards it, which is so natural to a man, who views in it the native soil of himself and his progenitors for several generations; I anticipate with pleasing expectation that retreat, in which I promise myself to realize, without alloy, the sweet enjoyment of partaking, in the midst of my fellow citizens, the benign influence of good laws under a free government — the ever favorite object of my heart, and the happy reward, as I trust, of our mutual cares, labors and dangers.

Vocabulary

suffrage (para. 3)	*n.* the right to vote in national elections
diffidence (para. 5)	*n.* the quality of lacking belief in one's quality or confidence
admonish (para. 5)	*v.* to counsel against; caution
consolation (para. 5)	*n.* the comforting in time of grief, defeat, or trouble
vicissitudes (para. 6)	*n.* one of the many changes and problems in a situation or in one's life that
beneficence (para. 6)	*n.* a charitable act or gift; kindness
auspice (para. 6)	*n.* protection or support; authority
contemplation (para. 7)	*n.* thoughtful observation; meditation
ligament (para. 8)	*n.* connection or unifying bond
edifice (para. 9)	*n.* a building of imposing appearance or size; structure
discountenance (para. 9)	*v.* refuse to approve of sth.
alienate (para. 9)	*v.* to cause to become unfriendly; exclude
auxiliary (para. 14)	*adj.* giving assistance or support; supplementary
propagate (para. 15)	*v.* to cause to spread to a large number of people
acquiescence (para. 16)	*n.* acceptance without protest
maxim (para. 16)	*n.* a short saying that express general truth
incongruous (para. 17)	*adj.* strange or surprising to the surrounding
baneful (para. 19)	*adj.* harmful
despotism (para. 21)	*n.* political system with one in absolute power; oppression
animosity (para. 23)	*n.* bitter hatred; hostility

---

① "我也将怀着一种希望，愿我的国家永远宽恕这些错误，我秉持正直的热忱，报效国家已 45 载，我希望因为我的能力不足导致的过失，会随着我不久以后长眠地下而湮没无闻。"

mitigate (para. 24)	*v.* to lessen the seriousness of it
assuage (para. 24)	*v.* make (an unpleasant feeling) less intense
encroach (para. 25)	*v.* to advance beyond proper limits; intrude
weal (para. 25)	*n.* the welfare of the community; welfare
evince (para. 25)	*v.* to show clearly or convincingly; demonstrated
usurpation (para. 25)	*n.* to take power for oneself illegally
magnanimous (para. 30)	*adj.* to show generous qualities
Providence (para. 30)	*n.* God
inveterate (para. 31)	*adj.* (of habits or feelings) long established and unlikely to change
antipathy (para. 31)	*n.* a feeling of strong dislike towards someone or something
umbrage (para. 31)	*n.* a feeling of anger caused by being offended
haughty (para. 31)	*adj.* behaving in a proud unfriendly way
intractable (para. 31)	*adj.* having a strong will and difficult to control
pernicious (para. 31)	*adj.* very harmful or evil, often in a way that you do not notice easily
retaliate (para. 32)	*v.* to do something bad to someone who has done something bad already
laudable (para. 32)	*adj.* deserving praise
conjure (para. 34)	*v.* ask for or request earnestly
dupe (para. 34)	*n.* someone who is tricked, especially into becoming involved in something illegal
provocation (para. 37)	*n.* a reason to take action
patronize (para. 39)	*v.* to behave towards someone as if one were better or more important
imposture (para. 42)	*n.* the action of deceiving someone
recompense (para. 42)	*n.* compensation, payment or reward
delineated (para. 43)	*adj.* depicted in words or gestures; outlined
beseech (para. 49)	*v.* to eagerly and anxiously ask someone for something
mitigate (para. 49)	*v.* to lessen the seriousness of
consigned (para. 49)	*adj.* turned over to another's charge; delivered
oblivion (para. 49)	*n.* the state of being completely forgotten
progenitor (para. 50)	*n.* ancestor

Questions for discussion

1. What were the main concerns of George Washington expressed to his countrymen in his Farewell Address?
2. According to Washington, why was the unity of government very important?
3. How did Washington view political parties?

4. According to Washington, what kind of foreign policy should the United States pursue at that time? Why did Washington suggest it? Was it the only choice for America then?
5. "Observe good faith and justice towards all Nations." (para. 30)
   Please make some comments.
6. "Taking care always to keep ourselves, by suitable establishments, on a respectably defensive posture, we may safely trust to temporary alliances for extraordinary emergencies." (para. 40)
   Please make some comments.

About the author

Thomas Jefferson, the third President of the United States (1801—1809), was the principal author of *The Declaration of Independence* (1776), and one of the most influential Founding Fathers for his promotion of the ideals of republicanism and democracy in the United States. Major events during his presidency include the Louisiana Purchase (1803) and the Lewis and Clark Expedition (1804—1806). Jefferson served as the wartime Governor of Virginia (1779—1781), first United States Secretary of State (1789—1793), and second Vice President (1797—1801).

As a political philosopher, Jefferson was a man of the enlightenment and knew many intellectual leaders in Britain and France. He idealized the independent yeoman farmer as exemplar of republican virtues, distrusted cities and financiers, and favored states' rights and a strictly limited federal government. Jefferson supported the separation of church and state and was the author of *Virginia Statute for Religious Freedom*. He was the eponym of Jeffersonian democracy and the co-founder and leader of the Democratic-Republican Party, which dominated American politics for a quarter-century. He was a supreme partisan and he fought three remarkable adversaries, John Adams, Alexander Hamilton and John Marshall, in contests so stirring that historians today still cannot describe them dispassionately.

A polymath, Jefferson achieved distinction as, among other things, a horticulturist, statesman, architect, archaeologist, paleontologist, inventor, and founder of the University of Virginia. President Abraham Lincoln thought that all honor should be given to Jefferson to the man, in the concrete pressure of a struggle for national independence by a single people, had the coolness, forecast and capacity to introduce into a merely revolutionary document, an abstract truth, applicable to all men and all time. When President John F. Kennedy welcomed forty-nine Nobel Prize winners to the White House in 1962 he said, "I think this is the most extraordinary collection of talent and of human knowledge that has ever been gathered together at the White House — with the possible exception of when Thomas Jefferson dined alone." Jefferson has been consistently ranked by scholars as one of the greatest of U.S. presidents.

 Text 2

First Inaugural Address
Thomas Jefferson, March 4, 1801

Friends & Fellow Citizens,

1   Called upon to undertake the duties of the first Executive office of our country, I avail myself of the presence of that portion of my fellow citizens which is here assembled to express my grateful thanks for the favor with which they have been pleased to look towards me, to declare a sincere consciousness that the task is above my talents, and that I approach it with those anxious and awful presentiments which the greatness of the charge, and the weakness of my powers so justly inspire. A rising nation, spread over a wide and fruitful land, traversing all the seas with the rich productions of their industry, engaged in commerce with nations who feel power and forget right, advancing rapidly to destinies beyond the reach of mortal eye[①]; when I contemplate these transcendent objects, and see the honor, the happiness, and the hopes of this beloved country committed to the issue and the auspices of this day, I shrink from the contemplation and humble myself before the magnitude of the undertaking. Utterly indeed should I despair, did not the presence of many, whom I here see, remind me, that, in the other high authorities provided by our constitution, I shall find resources of wisdom, of virtue, and of zeal, on which to rely under all difficulties. To you, then, gentlemen, who are charged with the sovereign functions of legislation, and to those associated with you, I look with encouragement for that guidance and support which may enable us to steer with safety the vessel in which we are all embarked, amidst the conflicting elements of a troubled world.

2   During the contest of opinion through which we have past, the animation of discussions and of exertions has sometimes worn an aspect which might impose on strangers unused to think freely, and to speak and to write what they think; but this being now decided by the voice of the nation, announced according to the rules of the constitution all will of course arrange themselves under the will of the law, and unite in common efforts for the common good. All, too, will bear in mind this sacred principle, that though the will of the majority is in all cases to prevail, that will, to be rightful, must be reasonable; that the minority possess their equal rights, which equal laws must protect, and to violate would be oppression. Let us then, fellow citizens, unite with one heart and one mind, let us restore to social intercourse

---

① "一个新兴的国家，在一片广阔而物产富饶的土地上成长，带着其丰富的工业产品横渡大洋，与那些只知强权忘了正义的国家进行交易，正在迅速奔向人类无法预见的命运。"

that harmony and affection without which liberty, and even life itself, are but dreary things. And let us reflect that having banished from our land that religious intolerance under which mankind so long bled and suffered, we have yet gained little if we countenance a political intolerance, as despotic, as wicked, and capable of as bitter and bloody persecutions. During the throes and convulsions of the ancient world, during the agonizing spasms of infuriated man, seeking through blood and slaughter his long lost liberty, it was not wonderful that the agitation of the billows should reach even this distant and peaceful shore; that this should be more felt and feared by some and less by others; and should divide opinions as to measures of safety; but every difference of opinion is not a difference of principle. We have called by different names brethren of the same principle. We are all republicans: we are all federalists.① If there be any among us who would wish to dissolve this Union, or to change its republican form, let them stand undisturbed as monuments of the safety with which error of opinion may be tolerated, where reason is left free to combat it. I know indeed that some honest men fear that a republican government cannot be strong; that this government is not strong enough. But would the honest patriot, in the full tide of successful experiment, abandon a government which has so far kept us free and firm, on the theoretic and visionary fear, that this government, the world's best hope, may, by possibility, want energy to preserve itself? I trust not. I believe this, on the contrary, the strongest government on earth. I believe it the only one, where every man, at the call of the law, would fly to the standard of the law, and would meet invasions of the public order as his own personal concern. — Sometimes it is said that man cannot be trusted with the government of himself. Can he then be trusted with the government of others? Or have we found angels, in the form of kings, to govern him? Let history answer this question.

3 Let us, then, with courage and confidence, pursue our own federal and republican principles; our attachment to union and representative government. kindly separated by nature and a wide ocean from the exterminating havoc of one quarter of the globe; too high minded to endure the degradations of the others, possessing a chosen country, with room enough for our descendants to the thousandth and thousandth generation, entertaining a due sense of our equal right to the use of our own faculties, to the acquisitions of our own industry, to honor and confidence from our fellow citizens, resulting not from birth, but from our actions and their sense of them, enlightened by a benign religion, professed indeed and practiced in various forms, yet all of them inculcating honesty, truth, temperance, gratitude and the love of man, acknowledging and adoring an overruling providence, which by all its dispensations proves that it delights in the happiness of man here, and his greater happiness hereafter; with all these blessings, what more is necessary to make us a happy and a prosperous people? Still

---

① 美国在讨论联邦宪法制定和建立联邦制国家初期，尤其是在华盛顿总统任内，首任国务卿杰斐逊被认为是反联邦党人之首（anti-federalist）。实际上，当时绝大多数联邦党人或反联邦党人，都热爱新成立的美国，他们的分歧主要集中体现在联邦政府应该拥有多大权力的问题上。杰斐逊不主张政府权力过大，因此他才被称为反联邦党人。他自称联邦党人，充分说明他热爱新成立的联邦制国家。

one thing more, fellow citizens, a wise and frugal government, which shall restrain men from injuring one another, shall leave them otherwise free to regulate their own pursuits of industry and improvement, and shall not take from the mouth of labor the bread it has earned. This is the sum of good government; and this is necessary to close the circle of our felicities.

4   About to enter, fellow citizens, on the exercise of duties which comprehend every thing dear and valuable to you, it is proper you should understand what I deem the essential principles of our government, and consequently those which ought to shape its administration. I will compress them within the narrowest compass they will bear, stating the general principle, but not all its limitations. — Equal and exact justice to all men, of whatever state or persuasion, religious or political: — peace, commerce, and honest friendship with all nations, entangling alliances with none①: — the support of the state governments in all their rights, as the most competent administrations for our domestic concerns, and the surest bulwarks against anti-republican tendencies: — the preservation of the general government in its whole constitutional vigor, as the sheet anchor of our peace at home, and safety abroad: a jealous care of the right of election by the people, a mild and safe corrective of abuses which are lopped by the sword of revolution where peaceable remedies are unprovided: — absolute acquiescence in the decisions of the majority, the vital principle of republics, from which is no appeal but to force, the vital principle and immediate parent of the despotism: — a well disciplined militia, our best reliance in peace, and for the first moments of war, till regulars may relieve them: — the supremacy of the civil over the military authority: — economy in the public expense, that labor may be lightly burthened: — the honest payment of our debts and sacred preservation of the public faith: — encouragement of agriculture, and of commerce as its handmaid: — the diffusion of information, and arraignment of all abuses at the bar of the public reason: — freedom of religion; freedom of the press; and freedom of person, under the protection of the Habeas Corpus② — and trial by juries impartially selected. These principles form the bright constellation, which has gone before us and guided our steps through an age of revolution and reformation. The wisdom of our sages, and blood of our heroes have been devoted to their attainment: — they should be the creed of our political faith; the text of civic instruction, the touchstone by which to try the services of those we trust; and should we wander from them in moments of error or of alarm, let us hasten to retrace our steps, and to regain the road which alone leads to peace, liberty and safety.

5   I repair then, fellow citizens, to the post you have assigned me. With experience enough in subordinate offices to have seen the difficulties of this the greatest of all, I have learnt to expect that it will rarely fall to the lot of imperfect man to retire from this station with the reputation, and the favor, which bring him into it. Without pretensions to that high confidence you reposed in our first and greatest revolutionary character, whose preeminent services had entitled him to the first place in his country's love, and destined for him the fairest page in the

---

① 杰斐逊总统不建议与任何国家建立联盟关系，他的政策可看作是华盛顿孤立主义外交政策的延续。
② Habeas Corpus: 人身保护令。

volume of faithful history, I ask so much confidence only as may give firmness and effect to the legal administration of your affairs. I shall often go wrong through defect of judgment. When right, I shall often be thought wrong by those whose positions will not command a view of the whole ground. I ask your indulgence for my own errors, which will never be intentional; and your support against the errors of others, who may condemn what they would not if seen in all its parts. The approbation implied by your suffrage, is a great consolation to me for the past; and my future solicitude will be, to retain the good opinion of those who have bestowed it in advance, to conciliate that of others by doing them all the good in my power, and to be instrumental to the happiness and freedom of all.

6   Relying then on the patronage of your good will, I advance with obedience to the work, ready to retire from it whenever you become sensible how much better choices it is in your power to make.① And may that infinite power, which rules the destinies of the universe, lead our councils to what is best, and give them a favorable issue for your peace and prosperity.

Vocabulary

presentiment (para. 1)	*n.* an intuitive feeling about the future, especially one of foreboding
transcendent (para. 1)	*adj.* surpassing the ordinary; exceptional
auspice (para. 1)	*n.* a divine or prophetic token
animation (para. 2)	*n.* the state of being full of life or vigor; liveliness
intercourse (para. 2)	*n.* communications or dealings between individuals or groups
banish (para. 2)	*v.* to force to leave or drive away
convulsion (para. 2)	*n.* a violent social or political upheaval
brethren (para. 2)	*n.* people belonging to a particular group
exterminate (para. 3)	*v.* to destroy completely
havoc (para. 3)	*n.* great confusion or disorder
inculcate (para. 3)	*v.* to instill (an idea or attitude) by persistent instruction
temperance (para. 3)	*n.* abstinence from alcoholic drinks
dispensation (para. 3)	*n.* permission to be exempted
compress (para. 4)	*v.* express in a shorter form or abridge
compass (para. 4)	*n.* the range of scope of something
bulwark (para. 4)	*n.* a person, an institution or principle which acts as a defense
lop (para. 4)	*v.* remove something unnecessary
acquiescence (para. 4)	*n.* to accept something reluctantly but without protest
supremacy (para. 4)	*n.* the state of being superior to all others in authority, power or status
handmaid (para. 4)	*n.* a subservient partner or element
arraignment (para. 4)	*n.* a legal document calling someone to a court to answer a criminal charge or an indict ment

---

① 暗指美国人民有权根据他们的喜好通过选举更换总统。

constellation (para. 4)	*n.* a group of associated or similar people or things
touchstone (para. 4)	*n.* a standard or criteria by which something is judged or recognized
pretension (para. 5)	*n.* an aspiration or claim to a certain status or quality
approbation (para. 5)	*n.* (*formal*) approval or praise
conciliate (para. 5)	*v.* stop someone being angry or discontented; placate or pacify
patronage (para. 6)	*n.* the power to control appointments to office or the right to privileges

Questions for discussion

1. According to the speech, what was Jefferson's principle in dealing with the interplay of equality and liberty?
2. Why did Thomas Jefferson say his government was the strongest government on earth?
3. What were the federal and republican principles which could help the public attach to union and representative government?

Background

Isolationism, or non-interventionism, the diplomatic policy whereby a nation seeks to avoid alliances with other nations in order to avoid being drawn into wars not related to direct territorial self-defense, has had a long history in the United States. It refers to America's longstanding reluctance to become involved in European alliances and wars. Isolationists held the view that America's perspective on the world was different from that of European societies and that America could advance the cause of freedom and democracy by means other than war. American isolationism did not mean disengagement from the world stage. Isolationists were not averse to the idea that the United States should be a world player and even further its territorial, ideological and economic interests, particularly in the Western Hemisphere.

Isolationist perspective dates back to the colonial period. Thomas Paine is generally credited with instilling the first Isolationism ideas into the American body politic; his work *Common Sense* contains many arguments in favor of avoiding alliances. These ideas introduced by Paine took such a firm foothold that the Second Continental Congress struggled against forming an alliance with France and only agreed to do so when it was apparent that the American Revolutionary War could be won in no other manner.

George Washington's Farewell Address is often regarded as laying the foundation for a tradition of American non-interventionism. President Thomas Jefferson extended Washington's ideas in his March 4th, 1801 inaugural address. "peace, commerce, and honest friendship with all nations, entangling alliances with none." In 1823, President James Monroe articulated what would come to be known as the Monroe Doctrine which some have interpreted as non-interventionist in intent: "In the wars of the European powers, in matters relating to themselves, we have never taken part, nor does it comport with our policy, so to do. It is only when our rights are invaded, or seriously menaced that we resent injuries, or make preparations for our defense." The Monroe Doctrine in essence was another name for isolationism. It was the extension of Washington's isolationist policy which could be regarded as the isolation of American continent.

The United States' policy of isolationism was maintained throughout most of the 19th century and the beginning of the 20th century. America did not give up the policy until America's involvement in World War II. Historians have attributed the fact to a geographical position at once separate and far removed from Europe.

Washington's Farewell Address was printed by David C. Claypoole's *American Daily Advertiser* (Philadelphia) on 19 September 1796. Neither the proof sheet that Claypoole made for Washington's examination nor the copy that Claypoole worked from in making the proof sheet has been found. The New York Public Library owns Washington's final manuscript of the Farewell Address as well as drafts made by James Madison and Alexander Hamilton and a number of letters relating to the preparation of those drafts.

美国建国时只有13个州。这13个州也是英国在北美的13个殖民地。美国是在反对英国殖民统治的斗争中诞生的，具有反殖民主义的传统。建国初期，美国国力弱小，加之远离欧洲，以中立之名采取的孤立主义政策成为美国外交政策的最佳选择，也成为美国外交政策的传统。总的来说，孤立主义作为一种外交政策主张，以尽量避免对外国承担政治和军事义务的同盟关系方式来维护和拓展美国的国家利益，它不鼓励发展政治、军事和外交关系，而在经济和文化等方面并不限制与外界的交往。正如华盛顿总统在告别演说中鼓励美国保持并发展与欧洲的贸易关系。

独立战争前，殖民地人民受到英国的压迫。长达一个多世纪欧洲大国的竞争是美国外交思想形成的历史大背景。美国对欧洲战争的基本方针在1796年华盛顿的告别演说中得到完整、准确的表达，他强调："在扩大我们贸易关系时，美国应该尽量少与外国发生政治上的牵连"，"我们正确的政策是避免同外部世界任何地方建立永久同盟"。华盛顿总统的告别演说是美国外交史上最重要的文献之一，为美国外交确立了"重大准则"。这一外交准则在欧洲战争期间由亚当斯、杰斐逊与麦迪逊继续加以贯彻。1800年，杰斐逊当选为总统，他在就职演说中重申："我们都是联邦党人，我们都是共和党人……同所有地方贸易，但不同任何人结盟。"

由华盛顿提出的坚持不与任何国家（主要为欧洲列强）结盟、不卷入列强纷争、完全独立地处理国际事务的孤立主义外交原则，其精髓是美国为自己行动，不为别人行动。孤立主义原则对日后美国的单边主义外交实践，即推行不受他国和国际机构的影响，不建立和依靠联盟，完全独立依靠本国实力处理国际事务的外交政策具有重大而深远的影响。正是由于孤立主义与单边主义的这种紧密关系，自华盛顿确立孤立主义外交原则之后直至1914年第一次世界大战爆发，美国的外交实践始终以单边主义为主导，始终坚持不与任何国家（主要为欧洲列强）结盟，不卷入列强纷争，独立地处理外交和国际事务。

孤立主义实际上是美国统治集团在某种条件下推行扩张政策的一种韬光养晦的方式，它长期存在于美国的外交实践中，并在相当程度上左右或影响着美国建国以后的各种外交活动。20世纪30年代，孤立主义思潮的泛滥以及由此在外交政策中采取的所谓"中立"立场，不仅危害了和平，也损害了美国的利益。第二次世界大战的爆发，特别是珍珠港事件的发生，最终使美国摒弃了传统的孤立主义思想，从此走上霸权主义道路，真正成为一个世界大国。应该说，孤立主义是美国建国后持续了将近一个半世纪的外交政策主旋律。

Further reading

Crutchfield, James A., *George Washington: First in War, First in Peace*, New York: Forge Books, 2005.

Doenecke, Justus D., "American Isolationism, 1939—1941", *Journal of Libertarian Studies*, Summer/Fall 1982, 6 (3), pp.201—216.

Grackel, Theodore, *The Papers of George Washington*, Charlottesville: University of Virginia Press, 2006.

Henriques, Peter R., *Realistic Visionary: A Portrait of George Washington*, Charlottesville: University of Virginia Press, 2006.

Paterson, Thomas G., J., Garry Clifford & Kenneth J. Hagan, *American Foreign Relation* (5th Edition), Boston: Houghton Mifflin, 2000.

保罗·约翰逊：《乔治·华盛顿传》，李蔚超译，南京：译林出版社，2016年。

亨利·基辛格：《大外交》，顾淑馨等译，海口：海南出版社，1998年。

华盛顿·欧文：《华盛顿传》，吉灵娟译，武汉：长江文艺出版社，2016年。

黄安年：《美国的崛起》，北京：中国社会科学出版社，1992年。

贾庆国：《美国外交思想与实践》，袁明主编：《美国文化与社会十五讲》，北京：北京大学出版社，2003年。

克里斯托弗·希钦斯：《托马斯·杰斐逊传》，彭娟等译，南京：译林出版社，2014年。

李庆余编著：《美国外交——从孤立主义到全球主义》，南京：南京大学出版社，1990年。

李庆余等：《美国外交传统及其缔造者》，北京：商务印书馆，2010年。

乔伊斯·亚普雷拜：《美国民主的先驱：托马斯·杰斐逊传》，彭小娟译，叶桂革校，合肥：安徽教育出版社，2005年。

S. F. 比米斯：《美国外交史》（第一分册），叶笃义译，北京：商务印书馆，1985年。
汪凯：《从亚当斯到杰克逊——美国早期精英政治的兴衰》，北京：中央编译出版社，2016年。
王晓德：《美国外交的奠基时代（1776—1860）》，北京：中国社会科学出版社，2013年。
杨生茂主编：《美国外交政策史：1775—1989》，北京：人民出版社，1991年。
余志森：《华盛顿评传》，北京：中国社会科学出版社，1990年。

Chapter 2

Monroe Doctrine

（门罗主义）

Pre-reading questions

1. Was America powerful enough to protect Latin American countries in Monroe's era?
2. To what extent did Monroe Doctrine relate to Washington's isolationist policy?

About the author

James Monroe, whose most recognized accomplishment was the Monroe Doctrine, was born on April 28, 1758 in Virginia, and was the 5th President of the United States. He attended the College of William & Mary before serving in the Continental Army. He was very experienced in military service. His service in the military was highlighted by a wound he received in Trenton. Later in 1777 he was commissioned as a Major, and later as an Aide-de-camp to William Alexander, Lord Sterling. He resigned from the army in 1778.

In 1780, Monroe returned to Virginia to study law under Thomas Jefferson, who eventually became his mentor. He was subsequently elected to the House of Delegates in 1782 and was involved in the Congress under the *Articles of Confederation*. Although Monroe was a good friend of Madison and Jefferson, he sided with George Mason and Patrick Henry in terms of speaking against the ratification of the Constitution as he believed it gave too much power to a central government. Later, Monroe was chosen to be a Senator and continued to work closely with Madison and Jefferson to organize the Republican Party. And along with Thomas Jefferson, he helped to negotiate the Louisiana Purchase. After the War of 1812, Monroe served two full terms as President of the United States — from 1817 to 1825.

Monroe was very exceptional and he was very much a man who believed in balance and consensus. He was capable of pulling in people from all walks of life and he tried to implement plans that were best for all involved. At the time, many of the biggest parties had died out or split, leaving one largely joint Democratic-Republican Party. Many called the time the "era of good feelings", though those good feelings did not last very long. Economic depression, the rejection of Missouri as a Union state and a large struggle over slavery marred

Monroe's presidency as a tumultuous time fraught with conflict and infighting.

Monroe presented the Monroe Doctrine to Congress in 1823 — proclaiming that America should be self-sustaining and free from European interests, colonization and interference. He further proclaimed that the United States would stay neutral between European superpowers.

Monroe's ongoing quest to bring peace and unity to the United States was often expressed through his "for the good of the people" statement, "The best form of government is that which is most likely to prevent the greatest sum of evil." His terms as President were remarkable because he ran virtually uncontested in his re-election bid — such was his level of support during the election process. A man of compromise and consensus, he was often reluctant to increase the power of the federal government. Monroe was called by many the father of modern libertarianism. He died on July 4, 1831.

 Text 1

Seventh Annual State of the Union Address to Congress
James Monroe, December 2, 1823

President Monroe's seventh annual message to Congress① put "European Powers" on notice that American continents were off limits② to European colonization and that any attempts to interfere with American lands would be considered the "manifestation of an unfriendly disposition toward the United States".

1　At the proposal of the Russian Imperial Government, made through the minister of the Emperor residing here, a full power and instructions have been transmitted to the minister of the United States at St. Petersburg to arrange by amicable negotiation the respective rights and interests of the two nations on the northwest coast of this continent③. A similar proposal has been made by His Imperial Majesty to the Government of Great Britain, which has likewise been acceded to. The Government of the United States has been desirous by this friendly proceeding of manifesting the great value which they have invariably attached to the friendship of the Emperor and their solicitude to cultivate the best understanding with his Government. In the discussions to which this interest has given rise and in the arrangements by which they may terminate the occasion has been judged proper for asserting, as a principle in which the rights and interests of the United States are involved, that the American continents, by the free and independent condition which they have assumed and maintain, are

---

① annual message to Congress: 总统每年向国会做年度国情咨文, 通报情况, 提出政策建议。
② off limits: 范围外。
③ 1821 年 9 月, 沙俄宣布把北纬 51 度线以北的北太平洋中的俄属岛屿和海岸附近 115 英里之内的海域作为俄国内海, 其他国家船只未经许可不得驶入。美国就此和沙俄谈判。

henceforth not to be considered as subjects for future colonization by any European powers.

2   It was stated at the commencement of the last session that a great effort was then making in Spain and Portugal to improve the condition of the people of those countries, and that it appeared to be conducted with extraordinary moderation. It need scarcely be remarked that the results have been so far very different from what was then anticipated. Of events in that quarter of the globe, with which we have so much intercourse and from which we derive our origin, we have always been anxious and interested spectators.① The citizens of the United States cherish sentiments the most friendly in favor of the liberty and happiness of their fellow-men on that side of the Atlantic. In the wars of the European powers in matters relating to themselves we have never taken any part, nor does it comport with② our policy to do so. It is only when our rights are invaded or seriously menaced that we resent injuries or make preparation for our defense. With the movements in this hemisphere we are of necessity more immediately connected, and by causes which must be obvious to all enlightened and impartial observers. The political system of the allied powers is essentially different in this respect from that of America. This difference proceeds from that which exists in their respective Governments; and to the defense of our own, which has been achieved by the loss of so much blood and treasure, and matured by the wisdom of their most enlightened citizens, and under which we have enjoyed unexampled felicity, this whole nation is devoted.③ We owe it, therefore, to candor and to the amicable relations existing between the United States and those powers to declare that we should consider any attempt on their part to extend their system to any portion of this hemisphere as dangerous to our peace and safety. With the existing colonies or dependencies of any European power we have not interfered and shall not interfere. But with the Governments who have declared their independence and maintain it, and whose independence we have, on great consideration and on just principles, acknowledged, we could not view any interposition for the purpose of oppressing them, or controlling in any other manner their destiny, by any European power in any other light than as the manifestation of an unfriendly disposition toward the United States. In the war between those new Governments and Spain we declared our neutrality at the time of their recognition, and to this we have adhered, and shall continue to adhere, provided no change shall occur which, in the judgment of the competent authorities of this Government, shall make a corresponding change on the part of the United States indispensable to their security.

3   The late events in Spain and Portugal show that Europe is still unsettled. Of this important fact no stronger proof can be adduced than that the allied powers should have thought it proper, on any principle satisfactory to themselves, to have interposed by force in the internal concerns of Spain. To what extent such interposition may be carried, on the same

---

① 门罗总统明确指出，美国作为一个移民国家，割裂不了与欧洲的各种密切联系。
② comport with: to correspond to, to adapt to 与……一致，适合。
③ "我们的政府经历了流血牺牲、耗费了大量财力才得以建立，之后开明人士的智慧又使之成熟完善。正是在这个政府之下，我们享受了史无前例的幸福。我们举国上下全心全意保卫自己的政府。"

principle, is a question in which all independent powers whose governments differ from theirs are interested, even those most remote, and surely none of them more so than the United States. Our policy in regard to Europe, which was adopted at an early stage of the wars which have so long agitated that quarter of the globe, nevertheless remains the same, which is, not to interfere in the internal concerns of any of its powers; to consider the government de facto① as the legitimate government for us; to cultivate friendly relations with it, and to preserve those relations by a frank, firm, and manly policy, meeting in all instances the just claims of every power, submitting to injuries from none②. But in regard to those continents circumstances are eminently and conspicuously different. It is impossible that the allied powers should extend their political system to any portion of either continent without endangering our peace and happiness; nor can anyone believe that our southern brethren, if left to themselves, would adopt it of their own accord. It is equally impossible, therefore, that we should behold such interposition in any form with indifference. If we look to the comparative strength and resources of Spain and those new Governments, and their distance from each other, it must be obvious that she can never subdue them. It is still the true policy of the United States to leave the parties to themselves, in hope that other powers will pursue the same course.

Vocabulary

amicable (para. 1)	*adj.* done or achieved in a polite or friendly way and without quarrelling
solicitude (para. 1)	*n.* anxious care for sb's comfort, health or happiness 渴望，挂念
cultivate (para. 1)	*v.* to develop an attitude, a way of talking or behaving, etc.
colonization (para. 1)	*n.* the act of colonizing; the establishment of colonies
moderation (para. 2)	*n.* the quality of being reasonable and not being extreme
intercourse (para. 2)	*n.* communication and exchange between people, countries, etc.
invade (para. 2)	*v.* to enter a country, town, etc. using military force in order to take control of it; or to enter a place in large numbers, especially in a way that causes damage or confusion
felicity (para. 2)	*n.* great happiness 幸福，福祉
candor (para. 2)	*n.* ability to make judgments free from discrimination or dishonesty; or the quality of being honest and straightforward in attitude and speech
interfere (para. 2)	*v.* to get involved in and try to influence a situation that does not

---

① de facto: 事实上（的），实际上（的）。
② "在欧洲遭受连年战祸之初，我们就已制定出一贯的对欧政策，那就是：不干涉任何欧洲国家的内政；承认事实上的政府为合法政府；培养同该政府的友好关系，为了维持友好关系而采取坦诚、坚定和果断的政策，在任何情况下都满足它们的正当要求，同时绝不屈服于对我们权益的损害。"

	concern you, in a way that annoys other people
disposition (para. 2)	*n.* an attitude of mind especially one that favors one alternative over others
interpose (para. 3)	*v.* to place sth. between two people or things 干预
agitate (para. 3)	*v.* to make sb. feel angry, anxious or nervous
legitimate (para. 3)	*adj.* allowed and acceptable according to the law
subdue (para. 3)	*v.* to bring sb. / sth. under control, especially by using force

Questions for discussion

1. According to Monroe, was American political system similar to or very different from that of the allied powers?
2. What was Monroe's attitude towards those European powers?
3. According to Monroe, what kinds of polices did America adopt towards those newly independent countries in the American continent?
4. Were there any implications in Monroe's message that the United States was claiming its interests in the American continent?
5. What kind of impacts did the Monroe Doctrine have upon the American diplomacy?

About the author

John Quincy Adams (1767—1848) was the sixth President of the United States from March 4, 1825 to March 4, 1829. He was also an American diplomat and served in both the Senate and House of Representatives. He was a member of the Federalist, Democratic-Republican, National Republican, and later Anti-Masonic and Whig parties. As a diplomat, he was involved in many international negotiations, and helped formulate the Monroe Doctrine as Secretary of State.

Adams served as Secretary of State in the Cabinet of President James Monroe from 1817 until 1825, a tenure during which he was instrumental in the acquisition of Florida. Typically, his views concurred with those espoused by Monroe. As Secretary of State, he negotiated the Adams-Onís Treaty and wrote the Monroe Doctrine, which warned European nations against meddling in the affairs of the Western Hemisphere. Adams' interpretation of neutrality was so strict that he refused to cooperate with Great Britain in suppressing the slave trade. On Independence Day 1821, in response to those who advocated American support for Latin America's independence movement from Spain, Adams gave a speech in which he said that

American policy was moral support for but not armed intervention on behalf of independence movements, stating that America "goes not abroad in search of monsters to destroy."

Adams is regarded as one of the greatest diplomats in American history, and during his tenure as Secretary of State he was one of the designers of the Monroe Doctrine. During his term as president, however, Adams achieved little of consequence in foreign affairs. A reason for this was the opposition he faced in Congress, where his rivals prevented him from succeeding. Among the few diplomatic achievements of his administration were treaties of reciprocity with a number of nations, including Denmark, Mexico, the Hanseatic League, the Scandinavian countries, Prussia and Austria. However, thanks to the successes of Adams' diplomacy during his previous eight years as Secretary of State, most of the foreign policy issues he would have faced had been resolved by the time he became President.

 Text 2

Second Annual Address
John Quincy Adams, December 5, 1826

Fellow citizens of the Senate and of the House of Representatives:

1 The assemblage of the representatives of our Union in both Houses of the Congress at this time occurs under circumstances calling for the renewed homage of our grateful acknowledgments to the Giver of All Good①. With the exceptions incidental to the most felicitous condition of human existence, we continue to be highly favored in all the elements which contribute to individual comfort and to national prosperity. In the survey of our extensive country we have generally to observe abodes of health and regions of plenty. In our civil and political relations we have peace without and tranquility within our borders. We are, as a people, increasing with unabated rapidity in population, wealth, and national resources, and whatever differences of opinion exist among us with regard to the mode and the means by which we shall turn the beneficence of Heaven to the improvement of our own condition, there is yet a spirit animating us all which will not suffer the bounties of Providence to be showered upon us in vain, but will receive them with grateful hearts, and apply them with unwearied hands to the advancement of the general good.

2 Of the subjects recommended to Congress at their last session, some were then definitively acted upon. Others, left unfinished, but partly matured, will recur to your attention without needing a renewal of notice from me. The purpose of this communication will be to present to your view the general aspect of our public affairs at this moment and the measures which have been taken to carry into effect the intentions of the legislature as signified by the

---

① the Giver of All Good: 上帝。

laws then and heretofore enacted.

3   In our intercourse with the other nations of the earth we have still the happiness of enjoying peace and a general good understanding, qualified, however, in several important instances by collisions of interest and by unsatisfied claims of justice, to the settlement of which the constitutional interposition of the legislative authority may become ultimately indispensable.

4   By the decease of the Emperor Alexander of Russia, which occurred contemporaneously with the commencement of the last session of Congress, the United States have been deprived of a long tried, steady, and faithful friend. Born to the inheritance of absolute power and trained in the school of adversity, from which no power on earth, however absolute, is exempt, that monarch from his youth had been taught to feel the force and value of public opinion and to be sensible that the interests of his own government would best be promoted by a frank and friendly intercourse with this Republic, as those of his people would be advanced by a liberal intercourse with our country. A candid and confidential interchange of sentiments between him and the government of the U.S. upon the affairs of Southern America took place at a period not long preceding his demise, and contributed to fix that course of policy which left to the other governments of Europe no alternative but that of sooner or later recognizing the independence of our southern neighbors, of which the example had by the United States already been set.

5   The ordinary diplomatic communications between his successor, the Emperor Nicholas, and the United States have suffered some interruption by the illness, departure, and subsequent decease of his minister residing here, who enjoyed, as he merited, the entire confidence of his new sovereign, as he had eminently responded to that of his predecessor. But we have had the most satisfactory assurances that the sentiments of the reigning Emperor toward the United States are altogether conformable to those which had so long and constantly animated his imperial brother, and we have reason to hope that they will serve to cement that harmony and good understanding between the two nations which, founded in congenial interests, cannot but result in the advancement of the welfare and prosperity of both.

6   Our relations of commerce and navigation with France are, by the operation of the convention of 1822-06-24, with that nation, in a state of gradual and progressive improvement. Convinced by all our experience, no less than by the principles of fair and liberal reciprocity which the United States have constantly tendered to all the nations of the earth as the rule of commercial intercourse which they would universally prefer, that fair and equal competition is most conducive to the interests of both parties, the United States in the negotiation of that convention earnestly contended for a mutual renunciation of discriminating duties[①] and charges in the ports of the two countries. Unable to obtain the immediate recognition of this principle in its full extent, after reducing the duties of discrimination so far as was found attainable it was agreed that at the expiration of two years from 1822-10-01, when the

---

① 差别关税。

convention was to go into effect, unless a notice of six months on either side should be given to the other that the convention itself must terminate, those duties should be reduced one-fourth, and that this reduction should be yearly repeated, until all discrimination should cease, while the convention itself should continue in force. By the effect of this stipulation three-fourths of the discriminating duties which had been levied by each party upon the vessels of the other in its ports have already been removed; and on the first of next October, should the convention be still in force, the remaining one-fourth will be discontinued. French vessels laden with French produce will be received in our ports on the same terms as our own, and ours in return will enjoy the same advantages in the ports of France.

7 By these approximations to an equality of duties and of charges not only has the commerce between the two countries prospered, but friendly dispositions have been on both sides encouraged and promoted. They will continue to be cherished and cultivated on the part of the United States. It would have been gratifying to have had it in my power to add that the claims upon the justice of the French government, involving the property and the comfortable subsistence of many of our fellow citizens, and which have been so long and so earnestly urged, were in a more promising train of adjustment than at your last meeting; but their condition remains unaltered.

8 With the government of the Netherlands the mutual abandonment of discriminating duties had been regulated by legislative acts on both sides. The act of Congress of 1818-04-20①, abolished all discriminating duties of impost and tonnage upon the vessels and produce of the Netherlands in the ports of the United States upon the assurance given by the government of the Netherlands that all such duties operating against the shipping and commerce of the United States in that Kingdom had been abolished. These reciprocal regulations had continued in force several years when the discriminating principle was resumed by the Netherlands in a new and indirect form by a bounty of 10 percent in the shape of a return of duties to their national vessels, and in which those of the United States are not permitted to participate. By the act of Congress of 1824-01-07②, all discriminating duties in the United States were again suspended, so far as related to the vessels and produce of the Netherlands, so long as the reciprocal exemption should be extended to the vessels and produce of the United States in the Netherlands. But the same act provides that in the event of a restoration of discriminating duties to operate against the shipping and commerce of the United States in any of the foreign countries referred to therein the suspension of discriminating duties in favor of the navigation of such foreign country should cease and all the provisions of the acts imposing discriminating foreign tonnage and impost duties in the United States should revive and be in full force with regard to that nation.

---

① The act outlines the ban on importing slaves, the forfeiture of ships built for such a purpose, and the penalties for involvement in the slave trade. The date was the day Monroe approved the act.
② The Tariff of 1824 was a protective tariff in the United States designed to protect American industry in the face of cheaper British commodities, especially iron products, wool and cotton textiles, and agricultural goods.

9   In the correspondence with the government of the Netherlands upon this subject they have contended that the favor shown to their own shipping by this bounty upon their tonnage is not to be considered a discriminating duty; but it cannot be denied that it produces all the same effects. Had the mutual abolition been stipulated by treaty, such a bounty upon the national vessels could scarcely have been granted consistent with good faith. Yet as the act of Congress of 1824-01-07 has not expressly authorized the Executive authority to determine what shall be considered as a revival of discriminating duties by a foreign government to the disadvantage of the United States, and as the retaliatory measure① on our part, however just and necessary, may tend rather to that conflict of legislation which we deprecate than to that concert to which we invite all commercial nations, as most conducive to their interest and our own, I have thought it more consistent with the spirit of our institutions to refer to the subject again to the paramount authority of the Legislature to decide what measure the emergency may require than abruptly by proclamation to carry into effect the minatory provisions② of the act of 1824.

10   During the last session of Congress treaties of amity, navigation, and commerce were negotiated and signed at this place with the government of Denmark, in Europe, and with the federation of Central America, in this hemisphere. These treaties then received the constitutional sanction③ of the Senate, by the advice and consent to their ratification. They were accordingly ratified on the part of the U.S., and during the recess of Congress have been also ratified by the other respective contracting parties. The ratifications have been exchanged, and they have been published by proclamations, copies of which are herewith communicated to Congress.

11   These treaties have established between the contracting parties the principles of equality and reciprocity in their broadest and most liberal extent, each party admitting the vessels of the other into its ports, laden with cargoes the produce or manufacture of any quarter of the globe, upon the payment of the same duties of tonnage and impost that are chargeable upon their own. They have further stipulated that the parties shall hereafter grant no favor of navigation or commerce to any other nation which shall not upon the same terms be granted to each other, and that neither party will impose upon articles of merchandise the produce or manufacture of the other any other or higher duties than upon the like articles being the produce or manufacture of any other country. To these principles there is in the convention with Denmark an exception with regard to the colonies of that Kingdom in the arctic seas, but none with regard to her colonies in the West Indies.

12   In the course of the last summer the term to which our last commercial treaty with Sweden was limited has expired. A continuation of it is in the contemplation of the Swedish government, and is believed to be desirable on the part of the United States. It has been

---

① retaliatory measure: 报复性行为。
② minatory provisions: 威胁性条款。
③ constitutional sanction: 宪法批准。

proposed by the King of Sweden that pending the negotiation of renewal the expired treaty should be mutually considered as still in force, a measure which will require the sanction of Congress to be carried into effect on our part, and which I therefore recommend to your consideration.

13   With Prussia, Spain, Portugal, and, in general, all the European powers between whom and the United States relations of friendly intercourse have existed their condition has not materially varied since the last session of Congress. I regret not to be able to say the same of our commercial intercourse with the colonial possessions of Great Britain in America. Negotiations of the highest importance to our common interests have been for several years in discussion between the two governments, and on the part of the United States have been invariably pursued in the spirit of candor and conciliation. Interests of great magnitude and delicacy had been adjusted by the conventions of 1815 and 1818, while that of 1822, mediated by the late Emperor Alexander, had promised a satisfactory compromise of claims which the government of the U.S., in justice to the rights of a numerous class of their citizens, was bound to sustain.

14   But with regard to the commercial intercourse between the United States and the British colonies in America, it has been hitherto found impracticable to bring the parties to an understanding satisfactory to both. The relative geographical position and the respective products of nature cultivated by human industry had constituted the elements of a commercial intercourse between the United States and British America, insular and continental, important to the inhabitants of both countries; but it had been interdicted by Great Britain upon a principle heretofore practiced upon by the colonizing nations of Europe, of holding the trade of their colonies each in exclusive monopoly to herself.

15   After the termination of the late war this interdiction had been revived, and the British government declined including this portion of our intercourse with her possessions in the negotiation of the convention of 1815. The trade was then carried on exclusively in British vessels 'til the act of Congress, concerning navigation, of 1818 and the supplemental act of 1820 met the interdict by a corresponding measure on the part of the United States. These measures, not of retaliation, but of necessary self defense, were soon succeeded by an act of Parliament opening certain colonial ports to the vessels of the United States coming directly from them, and to the importation from them of certain articles of our produce burdened with heavy duties, and excluding some of the most valuable articles of our exports. The United States opened their ports to British vessels from the colonies upon terms as exactly corresponding with those of the act of Parliament as in the relative position of the parties could be made, and a negotiation was commenced by mutual consent, with the hope on our part that a reciprocal spirit of accommodation and a common sentiment of the importance of the trade to the interests of the inhabitants of the two countries between whom it must be carried on would ultimately bring the parties to a compromise with which both might be satisfied. With this view the government of the United States had determined to sacrifice something of that entire reciprocity which in all commercial arrangements with foreign powers they are entitled to demand, and to acquiesce in some inequalities disadvantageous to ourselves rather than to forego the benefit of a final and permanent adjustment of this interest to the satisfaction of Great Britain herself. The negotiation, repeatedly suspended by accidental circumstances, was, however, by mutual agreement and express assent, considered as pending and to be speedily resumed.

16 In the meantime another act of Parliament, so doubtful and ambiguous in its import as to have been misunderstood by the officers in the colonies who were to carry it into execution, opens again certain colonial ports upon new conditions and terms, with a threat to close them against any nation which may not accept those terms as prescribed by the British government①. This act, passed 1825-07, not communicated to the government of the U.S., not understood by the British officers of the customs in the colonies where it was to be enforced, was never the less submitted to the consideration of Congress at their last session. With the knowledge that a negotiation upon the subject had long been in progress and pledges given of its resumption at an early day, it was deemed expedient to await the result of that negotiation rather than to subscribe implicitly to terms the import of which was not clear and which the British authorities themselves in this hemisphere were not prepared to explain.

17 Immediately after the close of the last session of Congress one of our most distinguished citizens was dispatched as envoy extraordinary and minister plenipotentiary② to Great Britain, furnished with instructions which we could not doubt would lead to a conclusion of this long controverted interest upon terms acceptable to Great Britain. Upon his arrival, and before he had delivered his letters of credence③, he was bet by an order of the British council excluding from and after the first of December now current the vessels of the United States from all the colonial British ports excepting those immediately bordering on our territories. In answer to his expostulations upon a measure thus unexpected he is informed that according to the ancient maxims of policy of European nations having colonies their trade is an exclusive possession of the mother country; that all participation in it by other nations is a boon or favor not forming a subject of negotiation, but to be regulated by the legislative acts of the power owning the colony; that the British government therefore declines negotiating concerning it, and that as the U.S. did not forthwith accept purely and simply the terms offered by the act of Parliament of 1825-07, Great Britain would not now admit the vessels of the United States even upon the terms on which she has opened them to the navigation of other nations.

18 We have been accustomed to consider the trade which we have enjoyed with the British colonies rather as an interchange of mutual benefits than as a mere favor received; that under

---

① "同时，英国议会的另一则法案意义含混，令人充满疑惑，以至于在殖民地执行该法案的官员也产生了误读。他们根据新法案的条款再次开放一些港口，如果其他国家不接受这些由英国政府预设的条款就威胁关闭这些港口。"

② minister plenipotentiary: 特命全权公使。

③ letters of credence:（外交官向派驻国呈递的）到任国书。

every circumstance we have given an ample equivalent. We have seen every other nation holding colonies negotiate with other nations and grant them freely admission to the colonies by treaty, and so far are the other colonizing nations of Europe now from refusing to negotiate for trade with their colonies that we ourselves have secured access to the colonies of more than one of them by treaty. The refusal, however, of Great Britain to negotiate leaves to the United States no other alternative than that of regulating or interdicting altogether the trade on their part, according as either measure may effect the interests of our own country, and with that exclusive object I would recommend the whole subject to your calm and candid deliberations.

19   It is hoped that our unavailing exertions to accomplish a cordial good understanding on this interest will not have an unpropitious effect upon the other great topics of discussion between the two governments. Our northeastern and northwestern boundaries are still unadjusted. The commissioners under the seventh article of the Treaty of Ghent[①] have nearly come to the close of their labors; nor can we renounce the expectation, enfeebled as it is, that they may agree upon their report to the satisfaction or acquiescence of both parties. The commission for liquidating the claims for indemnity for slaves carried away after the close of the war has been sitting, with doubtful prospects of success. Propositions of compromise have, however, passed between the two governments, the result of which we flatter ourselves may yet prove unsatisfactory. Our own dispositions and purposes toward Great Britain are all friendly and conciliatory; nor can we abandon but with strong reluctance the belief that they will ultimately meet a return, not of favors, which we neither as nor desire, but of equal reciprocity and good will.

20   With the American governments of this hemisphere we continue to maintain an intercourse altogether friendly, and between their nations and ours that commercial interchange of which mutual benefit is the source of mutual comfort and harmony the result is in a continual state of improvement. The war between Spain and them since the total expulsion of the Spanish military force from their continental territories has been little more than nominal, and their internal tranquility, though occasionally menaced by the agitations which civil wars never fail to leave behind them, has not been affected by any serious calamity.

21   The congress of ministers from several of those nations which assembled at Panama, after a short session there, adjourned to meet again at a more favorable season in the neighborhood of Mexico. The decease of one of our ministers on his way to the Isthmus, and the impediments of the season, which delayed the departure of the other, deprived United States of the advantage of being represented at the first meeting of the Congress. There is, however, no reason to believe that any transactions of the congress were of a nature to affect

---

① 《根特条约》，1814年为结束英美战争（1812—1814）而缔结的条约。1814年12月24日在佛兰芒人的根特城签订了和约。条约规定互相归还侵占的领土和遣返战俘。双方同意建立帕萨马阔迪湾岛屿归属委员会，停止对印第安人的军事行动，采取措施制止贩卖奴隶。条约确认美国的独立，但没能彻底解决引起英美战争的争端问题。

injuriously the interests of the United States or to require the interposition of our ministers had they been present. Their absence has, indeed, deprived United States of the opportunity of possessing precise and authentic information of the treaties which were concluded at Panama; and the whole result has confirmed me in the conviction of the expediency to the United States of being represented at the congress. The surviving member of the mission, appointed during your last session, has accordingly proceeded to his destination, and a successor to his distinguished and lamented associate will be nominated to the Senate. A treaty of amity, navigation, and commerce has in the course of the last summer been concluded by our minister plenipotentiary at Mexico with the united states of that Confederacy, which will also be laid before the Senate for their advice with regard to its ratification.

....

22   In closing this communication I trust that it will not be deemed inappropriate to the occasion and purposes upon which we are here assembled to indulge a momentary retrospect, combining in a single glance the period of our origin as a national confederation with that of our present existence, at the precise interval of half a century from each other. Since your last meeting at this place the 50th anniversary of the day when our independence was declared has been celebrated throughout our land, and on that day, while every heart was bounding with joy and every voice was tuned to gratulation, amid the blessings of freedom and independence which the sires of a former age had handed down to their children, two of the principal actors in that solemn scene — the hand that penned the ever memorable Declaration[①] and the voice that sustained it in debate — were by one summons, at the distance of 700 miles from each other, called before the Judge of All to account for their deeds done upon earth. They departed cheered by the benedictions of their country, to whom they left the inheritance of their fame and the memory of their bright example.

23   If we turn our thoughts to the condition of their country, in the contrast of the first and last day of that half century, how resplendent and sublime is the transition from gloom to glory! Then, glancing through the same lapse of time, in the condition of the individuals we see the first day marked with the fullness and vigor of youth, in the pledge of their lives, their fortunes, and their sacred honor to the cause of freedom and of mankind; and on the last, extended on the bed of death, with but sense and sensibility left to breathe a last aspiration to Heaven of blessing upon their country, may we not humbly hope that to them too it was a pledge of transition from gloom to glory, and that while their mortal vestments were sinking into the clod of the valley their emancipated spirits were ascending to the bosom of their God!

---

① 指美国的《独立宣言》。

Vocabulary

assemblage (para. 1)	*n.* gathering, assembly
collision (para. 3)	*n.* a strong disagreement between two people or between opposing ideas, opinions, etc.
interposition (para. 3)	*n.* interference, the action of interposing someone or something.
decease/demise (para. 4)	*n.* (*formal or Law*) death
cement (para. 5)	*v.* (*figurative*) settle or establish firmly
reciprocity (para. 6)	*n.* the practice of exchanging things with others for mutual benefit, especially privileges granted by one country or organization to another
renunciation (para. 6)	*n.* formal rejection of something, typically a belief, claim, or course of action
stipulation (para. 6)	*n.* demand or specify (a requirement), typically as part of a bargain or agreement
interdiction (para. 15)	*n.* an authoritative prohibition, in particular
compromise (para. 15)	*n.* an agreement or settlement of a dispute that is reached by each side making concessions
expedient (para. 16)	*adj.* convenient and practical although possibly improper or immoral
subscribe (para. 16)	*v.* approve, agree
expostulation (para. 17)	*n.* strong disapproval or disagreement
deliberation (para. 18)	*n.* long and careful consideration or discussion
expulsion (para. 20)	*n.* the process of forcing someone to leave a place, especially a country
agitation (para. 20)	*n.* the action of arousing public concern about an issue and pressing for action on it
impediment (para. 21)	*n.* hindrance or obstruction in doing something
transaction (para. 21)	*n.* published reports of proceedings at the meetings
sire (para. 22)	*n.* father or other male forebear

Questions for discussion

1. In this address, which points showed the spirit of the Monroe Doctrine?
2. Did John Quincy Adams develop the Monroe Doctrine? If the answer is positive, how did he do that?
3. How did the Monroe Doctrine influence the diplomatic relations between the U.S. and the European countries, and the Latin America?

Chapter 2　Monroe Doctrine（门罗主义）

Background

Monroe Doctrine was initiated on December 2, 1823. It proclaimed that European powers should no longer colonize or interfere with the affairs of the nations of the Americas. The United States planned to stay neutral in wars between European powers and its colonies. However, if these latter types of wars were to occur in the Americas, the United States would view such action as hostile. President James Monroe first stated the doctrine during his seventh annual State of the Union Address to Congress, a defining moment in the foreign policy of the United States.

At that time, the United Kingdom was torn between monarchical principle and a desire for new markets; South America as a whole constituted a much larger market for British goods than the United States. When Russia and France proposed that Britain join in helping Spain regain her New World colonies, Britain vetoed the idea. The United States was also negotiating with Spain to purchase Florida, and once that treaty was ratified, the Monroe administration began to extend recognition to the new Latin American republics — Argentina, Chile, Colombia and Mexico were all recognized in 1822.

In 1823, France invited Spain to restore the Bourbons to power, and there was talk of France and Spain warring upon the new republics with the backing of the Holy Alliance (Russia, Prussia and Austria). This news appalled the British government — all the work of James Wolfe, William Pitt and other eighteenth-century British statesmen to get France out of the New World would be undone, and France would again be a power in the Americas.

British Foreign Minister George Canning proposed that the US and the UK join to warn off France and Spain from intervention. Both Thomas Jefferson and James Madison urged Monroe to accept the offer, but John Quincy Adams was more suspicious. Adams also was quite concerned about Russia and Mexico's efforts to extend their influence over the joint British-American claimed territory of Oregon Country. At the Cabinet meeting of November 7, 1823, Adams argued against Canning's offer, and declared, "It would be more candid, as well as more dignified, to avow our principles explicitly to Russia and France, than to come in as a cockboat in the wake of the British man-of-war." He argued and finally won over the Cabinet to an independent policy. In Monroe's Annual Message to Congress on December 2, 1823, he delivered what we have come to call the Monroe Doctrine. Essentially, the United States was informing the powers of the Old World that the Americas were no longer open to European colonization, and that any effort to extend European political influence into the New World would be considered by the United States "as dangerous to our peace and safety." The United States would not interfere in European wars or internal affairs, and expected Europe to stay out of the affairs of the New World.

The Monroe Doctrine states three major ideas. First, it conveys that European countries cannot colonize in any of the Americas: North, Central, or South. Second, it enforces

Washington's rule of foreign policy, in which the U.S. will only be involved in European affairs if America's rights are disturbed. Third, the U.S. will consider any attempt at colonization a threat to its national security. Roosevelt added to the doctrine, and summed up his additions with the statement, "Speak softly and carry a big stick."

The Monroe Doctrine, combined with the support of the British navy, put an end to all plans for intervention in Latin America by European powers. By 1824 the United States negotiated with Russia a treaty by which Russia withdrew any territorial claims on the Oregon Territory, and in 1867 the U.S. acquisition of Alaska ended Russian colonization in North America.

The Monroe Doctrine was extended in 1905 by Secretary of State Richard Olney, who asserted that existing European colonies in the Americas were "unnatural and inexpedient," that "the United States is practically the sovereign on this continent, and its fiat is law upon the subjects to which it confines its interposition." He further argued that to disregard the Monroe Doctrine would be a violation of international law, that it would require arbitration between European colonies and Latin American nations, and that refusal to adhere to the Monroe Doctrine would be grounds for war.

Some allege that, in practice, the Monroe Doctrine has functioned as a declaration of hegemony and a right of unilateral intervention over the nations of the Western Hemisphere — limited only by prudence, as in the case of British possessions. They point to the U.S. military interventions in Latin America and Haiti since 1846. Some critics also point to the work of mercenaries such as William Walker, who briefly installed himself as president of Nicaragua, as inspired by the Monroe Doctrine. Some Latin Americans have come to resent Monroe Doctrine, which has been summarized there in the phrase: "America for the Americans," translated into Spanish ironically as "América para los americanos." The irony lies in the fact that the Spanish term "americano" is used to name the inhabitants of the whole continent. However, in English, the term "American" is related almost exclusively to the nationals of the United States, although this wasn't always the case. Thus, while "America for the Americans" sounds very much like a call to share a common destiny, it becomes apparent that it could really imply: America (the continent) for the United States. At the turn of the century popular resentment in Latin America gave rise to a series of left of center leaders who questioned Washington's sincerity.

Chapter 2　Monroe Doctrine（门罗主义）

门罗总统向内阁成员宣讲"门罗主义"

　　1823年12月2日，美国总统詹姆斯·门罗在国会发表由国务卿约翰·昆西·亚当斯草拟的《国情咨文》，咨文中有关外交方面的陈述被称为《门罗宣言》。宣言主要包括三个基本原则，即美洲体系原则、美欧两洲互不干涉原则以及非殖民原则。《门罗宣言》成为美国用来反对美洲以外国家干涉美洲事务的有力工具，它阻止并进一步排斥欧洲列强在西半球的政治影响，使美洲和欧洲暂时脱离密切联系，从而为美国崛起后在西半球的扩张扫除了障碍。

　　19世纪初，拉美独立运动蓬勃发展，"门罗主义"的提出与当时拉美独立运动有着重要联系，并很好地回应了拉美独立运动。老牌殖民主义国家西班牙在欧洲神圣同盟支持下，妄图恢复美洲殖民地，英国和神圣同盟各国积极插手拉美事务。门罗以防止欧洲各国干涉拉美事务为理由，发表《国情咨文》。他在《咨文》中宣称，"同盟各国把它们的政治制度扩张到美洲的任何地方而不危害我们的和平与幸福是不可能的；也没有人会相信我们南方各兄弟国家的人民，如果不加援助，能够建立符合他们心愿的政治制度，所以让我们坐视欧洲列强对他们进行任何方式的干涉而不加过问，也同样是不可能的"，门罗大胆提出"美洲是美洲人的美洲"口号。门罗的外交政策，主要是为了制止欧洲列强对拉美的侵略，使拉美各国的独立得到巩固。同时，应该看到，这个宣言也为美国未来干涉和侵略拉美国家制造了借口，成为美国在拉美建立"后院"的工具。

　　总的来说，当时的美国对拉美独立运动非常同情，在1810年到1826年拉美独立运动期间，美国一直允许拉美独立地区与美国通商，南美船只不论挂何种旗帜都可进入美国的港口，美国也接纳拉美各独立组织的外交代表，允许他们在美国购置军火，有些美国人还作为志愿者参加了拉美独立运动。美国的态度得到了拉美各独立运动组织的高度评价。当时，许多美国的政治家和老百姓都支持拉美革命，许多人参与了墨西哥、智利、秘鲁和阿根廷的战争。1812年第二次英美战争之后，空置的美国武装民船也都被用于一些勇敢的活动，追捕和破坏西班牙的船只。19世纪20年代，随着佛罗里达问题的解决，美国国内要求承认拉美各独立政权的呼声日益高涨，不少政治家纷纷建议政府给予拉美独立政权完全的外交承认。在他们的推动下，美国相继承认了哥伦比亚、墨西哥、智利、巴西、秘鲁等国，对拉美独立战争的胜利起了积极作用。与美国相比，欧洲神圣同盟诸国积极支持西班牙镇压拉美独立运动，对拉美独立运动最同情的英国也迟迟不肯承认各独立国家。

1822年10月，欧洲协调体各国召开会议，会上俄、普、奥达成协议，决定授权法国出兵镇压西班牙本土革命运动，计划得手后去镇压西属美洲革命运动。逃到国外的西班牙国王斐迪南七世表示，只要法国帮助西班牙镇压革命运动，西班牙愿以土地相酬，神圣同盟的计划受到与会英国代表威灵顿公爵的坚决反对。英国的态度意味着1815年以来欧洲协调体的解体，也使神圣同盟诸国大为忌惮，毕竟英国控制着海上霸权。1822年到1823年，法国多次与西班牙、俄国、奥地利等谋划干涉西属美洲革命运动。这种情况，引起了拉美独立诸国和英美两国的不安。1823年10月到11月间发生的两件事加速了《门罗宣言》的出笼。10月16日到11月17日，沙俄政府两次照会美国，声言不承认拉美国家的独立并对共和制度大加指责。这件事加大了美国对沙俄干涉美洲事务的疑虑。而坎宁在获得法方在《波林雅克备忘录》中提出的保证后，搁置了英美联合行动的建议。美国对英国的行动大感不解，担心英国与神圣同盟合流，或者打算单独行动，于是决定尽快表态。1823年12月，门罗总统在《国情咨文》中阐明了美国的立场，即著名的《门罗宣言》。

《门罗宣言》主要包括三个方面：一、**美洲体系原则**。强调"美洲是美洲人的美洲"，神圣同盟各国的政治制度同美洲的政治制度大不相同，反对神圣同盟将君主专制制度延伸到西半球。由于政体不同，美洲应有独立于欧洲的发展道路，新大陆与旧世界应保持明确界限。二、**美欧两洲互不干涉原则**。包括：（1）欧洲列强不得干涉美洲事务，任何此类干预，将被视为"对美国不友好的表现"；（2）美国不干涉欧洲事务。这是美国建国后一直延续的外交方针，也是华盛顿孤立主义外交政策的主要内容。而欧洲国家"如企图把它们的制度扩展到西半球的任何地区，则会危及我们的和平与安全。我们不曾干涉过任何欧洲国家的现存殖民地或属地，而且将来也不会干涉。但对于那些已宣布独立并维持独立的……（美洲）国家，任何欧洲国家为了压迫它们或以其他方式控制它们的命运而进行的任何干涉，我们只能视为对合众国不友好的表现"。这一明确表态受到担心列强干涉的拉美新兴国家欢迎。三、**非殖民化原则**。强调"美洲大陆处于它们已取得并保持的独立和自由状态，今后任何欧洲强国不得再把它们当作未来殖民的对象"。这一宣言的内容没有限制美国的对外扩张，但在当时的历史条件下，这一表态对拉美国家提供了政治保护，在众多列强争相抢夺殖民地的时代，具有进步意义。

"门罗主义"对神圣同盟来说，是一个沉重打击，而对年轻的美国来说，是一个胜利，对拉美各国也极为有利，因为它们处在虎视眈眈的列强中间，"门罗主义"给了它们一种保护。未来，日益强大的美国利用"门罗主义"对外扩张，但对当时历史的积极意义应该得到高度肯定。

Further reading

Gilderhus, Mark T., "The Monroe Doctrine: Meanings and Implications", *Presidential Studies Quarterly*, Blackwell Publishing Ltd., 2006.

Lewis, James E., Jr. *John Quincy Adams: Policymaker for the Union,* Scholarly Resources, 2001.

May, Ernest R, *The Making of the Monroe Doctrine*, Cambridge, Mass.: Harvard University Press, 1975.

Preston, Daniel (ed.), *The Papers of James Monroe*, Westport, Connecticut: Greenwood Press, 2003.

Remini, Robert V., *John Quincy Adams,* New York: Times Books, 2002.

哈尔·马科维奇：《詹姆斯·门罗》，席娟译，北京：现代教育出版社，2005年。

理查德·霍夫施塔特：《美国政治传统及其缔造者》，崔永禄等译，北京：商务印书馆，1994年。

罗伯特·V.雷明尼：《雄辩老将：约翰·昆西·亚当斯传》，饶涛等译，合肥：安徽教育出版社，2006年。

王晓德：《美国外交的奠基时代（1776—1860）》，北京：中国社会科学出版社，2013年。

杨卫东：《扩张与孤立——约翰·昆西·亚当斯外交思想研究》，北京：中国社会科学出版社，2006年。

杨卫东：《约翰·昆西·亚当斯与美国"大陆帝国"的构建》，《东北师范大学学报》2006年第1期。

钟月强：《美国"门罗主义"外交政策实践研究》，《人民论坛》2015年第36期。

Chapter 3
Manifest Destiny & Imperialism
（天定命运论与帝国主义）

Pre-reading questions

1. How much do you know about the term "Manifest Destiny"?
2. What's the relationship between the doctrine of Manifest Destiny and American imperialism?

About the author

John Louis O'Sullivan (1813—1895) was an American columnist and editor who was noted for the coinage of the term "Manifest Destiny" in 1845 to promote the annexation of Texas and the Oregon Country to the United States. He was an influential political writer and advocate for the Democratic Party at that time, but faded from prominence soon thereafter. He was rescued from obscurity in the 20th century after the famous phrase "Manifest Destiny" was traced back to him.

O'Sullivan was born on a British warship at Gibraltar when his father was U.S. Consul to the Barbary states. He attended the military school of Lorize, France, and the Westminster School at London, and later graduated from Columbia College in New York City in 1831. O'Sullivan then practiced law in New York until 1837, when he turned to journalism and co-founded and served as editor for *The United States Magazine and Democratic Review* (generally called the *Democratic Review*). The magazine featured political essays — many of them penned by O'Sullivan. In 1841, at 27 years of age, O'Sullivan was elected to the New York State Assembly. In office, he gained a reputation as an advocate for abolition of the death penalty. He also championed other reforms, such as rights for women and working people, and religious toleration. However, his agenda met much resistance in the Assembly, and he did not seek reelection after the end of the 1842 term.

Being a Democrat, O'Sullivan worked tirelessly to promote James K. Polk in the 1844 presidential campaign. Among his services in Polk's campaign were the establishment of the *Daily News* in connection with Samuel J. Tilden, on July 13, 1844, and the creation of *The New York Morning News*, soon before the election of 1844 to promote the Democratic Party particularly among working class people in New York City. O'Sullivan's efforts helped Polk carry New York State. Had Polk lost New York, he would have lost the presidency. This led some people to claim that O'Sullivan may have single-handedly won the election for Polk.

The year 1845 witnessed the highlight of O'Sullivan's life. In the July-August 1845 issue of the *Democratic Review*, O'Sullivan published an essay entitled "Annexation", which called on the U.S. to admit the Republic of Texas into the Union. O'Sullivan argued in the essay that the United States had a divine mandate to expand throughout North America, writing of "our manifest destiny to overspread the continent allotted by Providence for the free development of our yearly multiplying millions." This was O'Sullivan's first usage of the phrase "Manifest Destiny". His second use of the phrase became extremely influential when O'Sullivan addressed the ongoing boundary dispute with Great Britain in the Oregon Country in a column in the *New York Morning News* on December 27, 1845. The term "Manifest Destiny" soon became a catch phrase which provided a label for expansionist sentiments particularly popular during the 1840s.

O'Sullivan's editorial career was abruptly brought to an end at the peak of his fame and influence at the time of the "Manifest Destiny" articles. In May 1846, O'Sullivan was fired by the investors of the *New York Morning News* due to his poor financial management of the newspaper. Around the same time, O'Sullivan sold the *Democratic Review*, although he would still occasionally write for the magazine. Five months later, O'Sullivan married Susan Kearny Rodgers and went to Cuba. The year before, his sister Mary married Cuban planter and revolutionary Cristobal Madan. O'Sullivan thereafter became involved in a movement to have Cuba annexed to the United States. He assisted General Narciso Lopez in organizing two filibuster invasions of Cuba to liberate the island from Spanish rule, and as a result, was charged with other conspirators in federal court in New Orleans in 1850 and in New York in 1851 with violation of the Neutrality Act. The first case ended in nolle prosequi and the second trial in acquittal.

Although O'Sullivan's reputation was tarnished, he was appointed by the Pierce administration as the U.S. Minister to Portugal, serving from 1854 to 1858. When the American Civil War broke out, O'Sullivan moved to Europe and became an active supporter of the Confederate States of America. He wrote a number of pamphlets promoting the Confederate cause, arguing that the presidency had become too powerful and that states' rights needed to be protected against encroachment by the central government. He even tried to obtain ironclads from Sweden for the Confederate Navy, and applied for Confederate citizenship. Although he had earlier supported the "free soil" movement, he now defended the institution of slavery, writing that blacks and whites could not live together in harmony without it. His activities greatly damaged his reputation and brought an end to his political life. After the war, O'Sullivan spent several more years in self-imposed exile in Europe. He returned to New York in 1879, where he lived obscurely until his death. He suffered a stroke in 1889 and died in obscurity from influenza in a residential hotel in New York City in 1895.

The following text was an early attempt in 1839 by O'Sullivan to emphasize the

American exceptionalism, as he said "we may confidently assume that our country is destined to be the great nation of futurity", which prepared his coinage of the term "Manifest Destiny" in 1845.

 Text 1

The Great Nation of Futurity
John Louis O'Sullivan, 1839

1   The American people having derived their origin from many other nations, and the Declaration of National Independence① being entirely based on the great principle of human equality, these facts demonstrate at once our disconnected position as regards any other nation; that we have, in reality, but little connection with the past history of any of them, and still less with all antiquity, its glories, or its crimes. On the contrary, our national birth was the beginning of a new history, the formation and progress of an untried political system, which separates us from the past and connects us with the future only; and so far as regards the entire development of the natural rights of man, in moral, political, and national life, we may confidently assume that our country is destined to be the great nation of futurity.

2   It is so destined, because the principle upon which a nation is organized fixes its destiny, and that of equality is perfect, is universal. It presides in all the operations of the physical world, and it is also the conscious law of the soul — the self-evident dictate of morality, which accurately defines the duty of man to man, and consequently man's rights as man. Besides, the truthful annals of any nation furnish abundant evidence, that its happiness, its greatness, its duration, were always proportionate to the democratic equality in its system of government.

3   How many nations have had their decline and fall, because the equal rights of the minority were trampled on by the despotism of the majority; or the interests of the many sacrificed to the aristocracy of the few; or the rights and interests of all given up to the monarchy of one? These three kinds of government have figured so frequently and so largely in the ages that have passed away, that their history, through all time to come, can only furnish a resemblance. Like causes produce like effects, and the true philosopher of history will easily discern the principle of equality, or of privilege, working out its inevitable result. The first is regenerative, because it is natural and right; the latter is destructive to society, because it is unnatural and wrong.

4   What friend of human liberty, civilization, and refinement, can cast his view over the past history of the monarchies and aristocracies of antiquity, and not deplore that they ever existed? What philanthropist can contemplate the oppressions, the cruelties, and injustice inflicted by

---

① 指美国的《独立宣言》（the *Declaration of Independence*）。

them on the masses of mankind, and not turn with moral horror from the retrospect?

5   America is destined for better deeds. It is our unparalleled glory that we have no reminiscences of battle fields, but in defense of humanity, of the oppressed of all nations, of the rights of conscience, the rights of personal enfranchisement. Our annals describe no scenes of horrid carnage, where men were led on by hundreds of thousands to slay one another, dupes and victims to emperors, kings, nobles, demons in the human form called heroes. We have had patriots to defend our homes, our liberties, but no aspirants to crowns or thrones; nor have the American people ever suffered themselves to be led on by wicked ambition to depopulate the land, to spread desolation far and wide, that a human being might be placed on a seat of supremacy.

6   We have no interest in the scenes of antiquity, only as lessons of avoidance of nearly all their examples. The expansive future is our arena, and for our history. We are entering on its untrodden space, with the truths of God in our minds, beneficent objects in our hearts, and with a clear conscience unsullied by the past. We are the nation of human progress, and who will, what can, set limits to our onward march? Providence is with us, and no earthly power can. We point to the everlasting truth on the first page of our national declaration, and we proclaim to the millions of other lands, that "the gates of hell" — the powers of aristocracy and monarchy — "shall not prevail against it."

7   The far-reaching, the boundless future will be the era of American greatness. In its magnificent domain of space and time, the nation of many nations is destined to manifest① to mankind the excellence of divine principles; to establish on earth the noblest temple ever dedicated to the worship of the Most High — the Sacred and the True. Its floor shall be a hemisphere — its roof the firmament of the star-studded heavens, and its congregation a Union of many Republics, comprising hundreds of happy millions, calling, owning no man master, but governed by God's natural and moral law of equality, the law of brotherhood — of "peace and good will amongst men."

8   But although the mighty constituent truth upon which our social and political system is founded will assuredly work out the glorious destiny herein shadowed forth, yet there are many untoward circumstances to retard our progress, to procrastinate the entire fruition of the greatest good to the human race. There is a tendency to imitativeness, prevailing amongst our professional and literary men, subversive of originality of thought, and wholly unfavorable to progress. Being in early life devoted to the study of the laws, institutions, and antiquities of other nations, they are far behind the mind and movement of the age in which they live; so much so, that the spirit of improvement, as well as of enfranchisement, exists chiefly in the great masses — the agricultural and mechanical population.

9   This propensity to imitate foreign nations is absurd and injurious. It is absurd, for we have never yet drawn on our mental resources that we have not found them ample and of unsurpassed excellence; witness our constitutions of government, where we had no foreign

---

① 奥沙利文虽然没有在这里正式提出"天定命运论"的概念，但已有了概念的雏形。

ones to imitate. It is injurious, for never have we followed foreign examples in legislation; witness our laws, our charters of monopoly, that we did not inflict evil on ourselves, subverting common right, in violation of common sense and common justice. The halls of legislation and the courts of law in a Republic are necessarily the public schools of the adult population. If, in these institutions, foreign precedents are legislated, and foreign decisions adjudged over again, is it to be wondered at that an imitative propensity predominates amongst professional and business men. Taught to look abroad for the highest standards of law, judicial wisdom, and literary excellence, the native sense is subjugated to a most obsequious idolatry of the tastes, sentiments, and prejudices of Europe. Hence our legislation, jurisprudence, literature, are more reflective of foreign aristocracy than of American democracy.

10 European governments have plunged themselves in debt, designating burthens on the people "national blessings." Our State legislatures, humbly imitating their pernicious example, have pawned, bonded the property, labor, and credit of their constituents to the subjects of monarchy. It is by our own labor, and with our own materials, that our internal improvements are constructed, but our British-law-trained legislators have enacted that we shall be in debt for them, paying interest, but never to become owners. With various climates, soils, natural resources, and products, beyond any other country, and producing more real capital annually than any other sixteen millions of people on earth, we are, nevertheless, borrowers, paying tribute to the money powers of Europe.

11 Our businessmen have also conned the lesson of example, and devoted themselves body and mind to the promotion of foreign interests. If States can steep themselves in debt, with any propriety in times of peace, why may not merchants import merchandise on credit? If the one can bond the labor and property of generations yet unborn, why may not the other contract debts against the yearly crops and daily labor of their contemporary fellow citizens?

12 And our literature! — Oh, when will it breathe the spirit of our republican institutions? When will it be imbued with the God-like aspiration of intellectual freedom — the elevating principle of equality? When will it assert its national independence, and speak the soul — the heart of the American people? Why cannot our literati comprehend the matchless sublimity of our position amongst the nations of the world — our high destiny — and cease bending the knee to foreign idolatry, false tastes, false doctrines, false principles? When will they be inspired by the magnificent scenery of our own world, imbibe the fresh enthusiasm of a new heaven and a new earth, and soar upon the expanded wings of truth and liberty? Is not nature as original — her truths as captivating — her aspects as various, as lovely, as grand — her Promethean fire as glowing in this, our Western hemisphere, as in that of the East? And above all, is not our private life as morally beautiful and good — is not our public life as politically right, as indicative of the brightest prospects of humanity, and therefore as inspiring of the highest conceptions? Why, then, do our authors aim at no higher degree of merit, than a successful imitation of English writers of celebrity?

13   But with all the retrograde tendencies of our laws, our judicature, our colleges, our literature, still they are compelled to follow the mighty impulse of the age; they are carried onward by the increasing tide of progress; and though they cast many a longing look behind, they cannot stay the glorious movement of the masses, nor induce them to venerate the rubbish, the prejudices, the superstitions of other times and other lands, the theocracy of priests, the divine right of kings, the aristocracy of blood, the metaphysics of colleges, the irrational stuff of law libraries. Already the brightest hopes of philanthropy, the most enlarged speculations of true philosophy, are inspired by the indications perceptible amongst the mechanical and agricultural population. There, with predominating influence, beats the vigorous national heart of America, propelling the onward march of the multitude, propagating and extending, through the present and the future, the powerful purpose of soul, which, in the seventeenth century, sought a refuge among savages, and reared in the wilderness the sacred altars of intellectual freedom. This was the seed that produced individual equality, and political liberty, as its natural fruit; and this is our true nationality. American patriotism is not of soil; we are not aborigines, nor of ancestry, for we are of all nations; but it is essentially personal enfranchisement, for "where liberty dwells," said Franklin, the sage of the Revolution, "there is my country."

14   Such is our distinguishing characteristic, our popular instinct, and never yet has any public functionary stood forth for the rights of conscience against any, or all, sects desirous of predominating over such right, that he was not sustained by the people. And when a venerated patriot of the Revolution appealed to his fellow-citizens against the overshadowing power of a monarch institution, they came in their strength, and the moneyed despot was brought low. Corporate powers and privileges shrink to nothing when brought in conflict against the rights of individuals. Hence it is that our professional, literary, or commercial aristocracy, have no faith in the virtue, intelligence or capability of the people. The latter have never responded to their exotic sentiments nor promoted their views of a strong government irresponsible to the popular majority, to the will of the masses.

15   Yes, we are the nation of progress, of individual freedom, of universal enfranchisement. Equality of rights is the cynosure of our union of States, the grand exemplar of the correlative equality of individuals; and while truth sheds its effulgence, we cannot retrograde, without dissolving the one and subverting the other. We must onward to the fulfillment of our mission — to the entire development of the principle of our organization — freedom of conscience, freedom of person, freedom of trade and business pursuits, universality of freedom and equality. This is our high destiny, and in nature's eternal, inevitable decree of cause and effect we must accomplish it. All this will be our future history, to establish on earth the moral dignity and salvation of man — the immutable truth and beneficence of God. For this blessed mission to the nations of the world, which are shut out from the life-giving light of truth, has America been chosen; and her high example shall smite unto death the tyranny of kings, hierarchs, and oligarchs, and carry the glad tidings of peace and good will where myriads now endure an existence scarcely more enviable than that of beasts of the field. Who, then, can doubt that our country is destined to be the great nation of futurity?①

Vocabulary

antiquity (para. 1)	*n.* the quality of being old or ancient
annals (para. 2)	*n.* a narrative of events written year by year
despotism (para. 3)	*n.* absolute power or control
enfranchisement (para. 5)	*n.* admission to political rights
carnage (para. 5)	*n.* massive slaughter, massacre
depopulate (para. 5)	*v.* to reduce sharply the population of
firmament (para. 7)	*n.* the sky or heavens
procrastinate (para. 8)	*v.* to defer or delay
propensity (para. 9)	*n.* tendency, inclination
adjudge (para. 9)	*v.* to settle, determine, or decide judicially
obsequious (para. 9)	*adj.* unduly or servilely compliant
burthen (para. 10)	*n.* burden
literati (para. 12)	*n.* men of letters; the learned class as a whole
imbibe (para. 12)	*v.* absorb
retrograde (para. 13)	*adj.* moving backward
cynosure (para. 15)	*n.* something that serves for guidance or direction
effulgence (para. 15)	*n.* brilliant radiance
hierarch (para. 15)	*n.* a senior clergyman and dignitary
myriad (para. 15)	*n.* innumerable people

Questions for discussion

1. According to O'Sullivan, in what ways was the United States exceptional?
2. According to O'Sullivan, what made the United States destined to be a great nation of futurity?
3. According to O'Sullivan, what was the greatest obstacle to the progress of the United States?
4. How did O'Sullivan depict the United States, its relationship with God and its role in the world?

---

① "那么，谁能质疑我们国家未来注定会成为一个伟大的国家？"这一反问，清晰提出了"天定命运论"的思想，虽还未明确提出这一概念。这个思想和殖民地时期提出的"山巅之城"期许一脉相承。

Text 2

Annexation
John Louis O'Sullivan, 1845

1 It is now time for the opposition to the Annexation of Texas① to cease, all further agitation of the waters of bitterness and strife, at least in connexion with this question, — even though it may perhaps be required of us as a necessary condition of the freedom of our institutions, that we must live on forever in a state of unpausing struggle and excitement upon some subject of party division or other. But, in regard to Texas, enough has now been given to party. It is time for the common duty of Patriotism to the Country to succeed; — or if this claim will not be recognized, it is at least time for common sense to acquiesce with decent grace in the inevitable and the irrevocable.

2 Texas is now ours. Already, before these words are written, her Convention has undoubtedly ratified the acceptance, by her Congress, of our proffered invitation into the Union; and made the requisite changes in her already republican form of constitution to adapt it to its future federal relations. Her star and her stripe may already be said to have taken their place in the glorious blazon of our common nationality; and the sweep of our eagle's wing already includes within its circuit the wide extent of her fair and fertile land. She is no longer to us a mere geographical space — a certain combination of coast, plain, mountain, valley, forest and stream. She is no longer to us a mere country on the map. She comes within the dear and sacred designation of Our Country; no longer a "*pays*②", she is a part of "*la patrie*③"; and that which is at once a sentiment and a virtue, Patriotism, already begins to thrill for her too within the national heart. It is time then that all should cease to treat her as alien, and even adverse — cease to denounce and vilify all and everything connected with her accession — cease to thwart and oppose the remaining steps for its consummation; or where such efforts are felt to be unavailing, at least to embitter the hour of reception by all the most ungracious frowns of aversion and words of unwelcome. There has been enough of all this. It has had its fitting day during the period when, in common with every other possible question of practical policy that can arise, it unfortunately became one of the leading topics of party division, of presidential electioneering. But that period has passed, and with it let its prejudices and its passions, its discords and its denunciations, pass away too. The next session of Congress will see the representatives of the new young State in their places in both our halls of national legislation, side by side with those of the old Thirteen. Let their reception into "the family" be frank, kindly, and cheerful, as befits such an occasion, as comports not less with our own self-

---

① 得克萨斯原属墨西哥，1836 年脱离墨西哥独立，自立为得克萨斯共和国，1845 年并入美国，成为美国第 28 个州。
② the French equivalent for "state".
③ the French equivalent for "home" or "native country".

respect than patriotic duty towards them. Ill betide those foul birds that delight to file their own nest, and disgust the ear with perpetual discord of ill-omened croak.

3 Why, were other reasoning wanting, in favor of now elevating this question of the reception of Texas into the Union, out of the lower region of our past party dissensions, up to its proper level of a high and broad nationality, it surely is to be found, found abundantly, in the manner in which other nations have undertaken to intrude themselves into it, between us and the proper parties to the case, in a spirit of hostile interference against us, for the avowed object of thwarting our policy and hampering our power, limiting our greatness and checking the fulfillment of our manifest destiny① to overspread the continent allotted by Providence for the free development of our yearly multiplying millions. This we have seen done by England, our old rival and enemy; and by France, strangely coupled with her against us, under the influence of the Anglicism strongly tinging the policy of her present prime minister, Guizot②. The zealous activity with which this effort to defeat us was pushed by the representatives of those governments, together with the character of intrigue accompanying it, fully constituted that case of foreign interference, which Mr. Clay③ himself declared should, and would unite us all in maintaining the common cause of our country against foreigner and the foe. We are only astonished that this effect has not been more fully and strongly produced, and that the burst of indignation against this unauthorized, insolent and hostile interference against us, has not been more general even among the party before opposed to Annexation, and has not rallied the national spirit and national pride unanimously upon that policy. We are very sure that if Mr. Clay himself were now to add another letter to his former Texas correspondence, he would express this sentiment, and carry out the idea already strongly stated in one of them, in a manner which would tax all the powers of blushing belonging to some of his party adherents.

4 It is wholly untrue, and unjust to ourselves, the pretence that the Annexation has been a measure of spoliation, unrightful and unrighteous — of military conquest under forms of peace and law — of territorial aggrandizement at the expense of justice, and justice due by a double sanctity to the weak. This view of the question is wholly unfounded, and has been before so amply refuted in these pages, as well as in a thousand other modes, that we shall not again dwell upon it. The independence of Texas was complete and absolute. It was an independence, not only in fact, but of right. No obligation of duty towards Mexico tended in

---

① 这是奥沙利文第一次正式提出"天定命运论"的概念。

② François Guizot (1787—1874), French historian, orator, and statesman, was a dominant figure in French politics prior to the Revolution of 1848, holding offices such as Minister of Education (1832—1836), Foreign Minister (1840—1847), and finally Prime Minister of France (1847—1848). His works include *General History of Civilization in Europe* and *The History of France from the Earliest Times to the Year 1789*.

③ Henry Clay (1777—1852) was a leading American politician and leader of the Whig Party. He ran and lost three times for president (1824, 1832, 1844), and is best known for brokering compromises between the North and the South that held the Union together. Clay opposed immediate annexation of Texas, arguing that gradual development of occupied land was preferential to a policy that could lead to war with Mexico.

the least degree to restrain our right to effect the desired recovery of the fair province once our own — whatever motives of policy might have prompted a more deferential consideration of her feelings and her pride, as involved in the question. If Texas became peopled with an American population; it was by no contrivance① of our government, but on the express invitation of that of Mexico herself; accompanied with such guaranties of State independence, and the maintenance of a federal system analogous to our own, as constituted a compact fully justifying the strongest measures of redress on the part of those afterwards deceived in this guaranty, and sought to be enslaved under the yoke imposed by its violation. She was released, rightfully and absolutely released, from all Mexican allegiance, or duty of cohesion to the Mexican political body, by the acts and fault of Mexico herself, and Mexico alone. There never was a clearer case. It was not revolution; it was resistance to revolution: and resistance under such circumstances as left independence the necessary resulting state, caused by the abandonment of those with whom her former federal association had existed. What then can be more preposterous than all this clamor by Mexico and the Mexican interest, against Annexation, as a violation of any rights of hers, any duties of ours?

5   We would not be understood as approving in all its features the expediency or propriety of the mode in which the measure, rightful and wise as it is in itself, has been carried into effect. Its history has been a sad tissue of diplomatic blundering. How much better it might have been managed — how much more smoothly, satisfactorily, and successfully! Instead of our present relations with Mexico — instead of the serious risks which have been run, and those plausibilities of opprobrium which we have had to combat, not without great difficulty, nor with entire success — instead of the difficulties which now throng the path to a satisfactory settlement of all our unsettled questions with Mexico — Texas might, by a more judicious and conciliatory diplomacy, have been as securely in the Union as she is now — her boundaries defined — California probably ours — and Mexico and ourselves united by closer ties than ever; of mutual friendship and mutual support in resistance to the intrusion of European interference in the affairs of the American republics. All this might have been, we little doubt, already secured, had counsels less violent, less rude, less one-sided, less eager in precipitation from motives widely foreign to the national question, presided over the earlier stages of its history. We cannot too deeply regret the mismanagement which has disfigured the history of this question; and especially the neglect of the means which would have been so easy of satisfying even the unreasonable pretensions and the excited pride and passion of Mexico. The singular result has been produced, that while our neighbor has, in truth, no real right to blame or complain — when all the wrong is on her side, and there has been on ours a degree of delay and forbearance, in deference to her pretensions, which is to be paralleled by few precedents in the history of other nations — we have yet laid ourselves open to a great deal of denunciation hard to repel, and impossible to silence; and all history will carry it down as a certain fact, that Mexico would have declared war against us, and would have waged it

---

① by no contrivance: by no invention.

seriously, if she had not been prevented by that very weakness which should have constituted her best defence.

6 We plead guilty to a degree of sensitive annoyance — for the sake of the honor of our country, and its estimation in the public opinion of the world — which does not find even in satisfied conscience full consolation for the very necessity of seeking consolation there. And it is for this state of things that we hold responsible that gratuitous mismanagement — wholly apart from the main substantial rights and merits of the question, to which alone it is to be ascribed; and which had its origin in its earlier stages, before the accession of Mr. Calhoun[①] to the department of State.

7 California will, probably, next fall away from the loose adhesion which, in such a country as Mexico, holds a remote province in a slight equivocal kind of dependence on the metropolis. Imbecile and distracted, Mexico never can exert any real governmental authority over such a country. The impotence of the one and the distance of the other, must make the relation one of virtual independence; unless, by stunting the province of all natural growth, and forbidding that immigration which can alone develop its capabilities and fulfill the purposes of its creation, tyranny may retain a military dominion, which is no government in the legitimate sense of the term. In the case of California this is now impossible. The Anglo-Saxon foot is already on its borders. Already the advance guard of the irresistible army of Anglo-Saxon emigration has begun to pour down upon it, armed with the plough and the rifle, and marking its trail with schools and colleges, courts and representative halls, mills and meeting-houses. A population will soon be in actual occupation of California, over which it will be idle for Mexico to dream of dominion. They will necessarily become independent. All this without agency of our government, without responsibility of our people — in the natural flow of events, the spontaneous working of principles, and the adaptation of the tendencies and wants of the human race to the elemental circumstances in the midst of which they find themselves placed. And they will have a right to independence — to self-government — to the possession of the homes conquered from the wilderness by their own labors and dangers, sufferings and sacrifices — a better and a truer right than the artificial tide of sovereignty in Mexico, a thousand miles distant, inheriting from Spain a title good only against those who have none better. Their right to independence will be the natural right of self-government belonging to any community strong enough to maintain it — distinct in position, origin and character, and free from any mutual obligations of membership of a common political body, binding it to others by the duty of loyalty and compact of public faith. This will be their title to independence; and by this title, there can be no doubt that the population now fast streaming down upon California will both assert and maintain that independence. Whether they will then attach themselves to our Union or not, is not to be predicted with any certainty. Unless

---

① John Caldwell Calhoun (1782—1850), the 7th Vice President of the United States, and Secretary of State (April 1, 1844—March 10, 1845) in the Cabinet of President John Tyler, was a leading Southern politician from South Carolina during the first half of the 19th century, who championed states' rights and slavery and was a symbol of the Old South.

the projected railroad across the continent to the Pacific be carried into effect, perhaps they may not; though even in that case, the day is not distant when the Empires of the Atlantic and Pacific would again flow together into one, as soon as their inland border should approach each other. But that great work, colossal as appears the plan on its first suggestion, cannot remain long unbuilt. Its necessity for this very purpose of binding and holding together in its iron clasp our fast-settling Pacific region with that of the Mississippi valley — the natural facility of the route — the ease with which any amount of labor for the construction can be drawn in from the overcrowded populations of Europe, to be paid in the lands made valuable by the progress of the work itself — and its immense utility to the commerce of the world with the whole eastern Asia, alone almost sufficient for the support of such a road — these considerations give assurance that the day cannot be distant which shall witness the conveyance of the representatives from Oregon and California to Washington within less time than a few years ago was devoted to a similar journey by those from Ohio; while the magnetic telegraph will enable the editors of the "San Francisco Union," the "Astoria Evening Post," or the "Nootka Morning News," to set up in type the first half of the President's Inaugural before the echoes of the latter half shall have died away beneath the lofty porch of the Capitol, as spoken from his lips.

8 Away, then, with all idle French talk of *balances of power* on the American Continent. There is no growth in Spanish America! Whatever progress of population there may be in the British Canadas, is only for their own early severance of their present colonial relation to the little island three thousand miles across the Atlantic; soon to be followed by Annexation, and destined to swell the still accumulating momentum of our progress. And whosoever may hold the balance, though they should cast into the opposite scale all the bayonets and cannon, not only of France and England, but of Europe entire, how would it kick the beam against the simple, solid weight of the two hundred and fifty, or three hundred millions — and American millions — destined to gather beneath the flutter of the stripes and stars, in the fast hastening year of the Lord 1845!

Vocabulary

annexation (para. 1)   *n.* incorporation
connexion (para. 1)   *n.* connection
proffer (para. 2)   *v.* to offer for acceptance
blazon (para. 2)   *n.* display
consummation (para. 2)   *n.* fulfillment
comport (para. 2)   *v.* to agree, correspond, or harmonize
betide (para. 2)   *v.* to happen to, to befall
allot (para. 3)   *v.* to assign

guaranty (para. 4)	*n.* guarantee, warrant
preposterous (para. 4)	*adj.* absurd
opprobrium (para. 5)	*n.* infamy
precipitation (para. 5)	*n.* abrupt haste, sudden movement
gratuitous (para. 6)	*adj.* unnecessary
distracted (para. 7)	*adj.* torn or disordered by dissension or the like
stunt (para. 7)	*v.* to check the growth or development of
momentum (para. 8)	*n.* impetus gained by movement

Questions for discussion

1. Did the document propose a war with Mexico? Did it suggest that Mexico might go to war to prevent the annexation of Texas?
2. How did O'Sullivan suggest that California would become separated from Mexico?
3. What sorts of terms did O'Sullivan use to describe Mexico? What racial or ethnic language did he associate with the United States? Would you describe the document as racist?
4. What impacts might O'Sullivan's words have had on the American decision to annex Texas and later to go to war with Mexico?

About the author

Albert Beveridge (1862—1927), U.S. Senator and historian, is known as one of the great American imperialists, who successfully captured the spirit of American nationalism at the start of the 20th century. Beveridge adhered to a strongly nationalistic faith that embraced both liberal social reforms and aggressive foreign policy. He was remembered by his contemporaries for his intense energy and self-confidence, especially at the start of his political career.

Beveridge was born in the midst of civil warfare and grew up under harsh conditions. Determined to rise above his poor beginnings, he studied the classical works of Plutarch and Caesar, winning him financial sponsorship to Indiana's Ashbury College. While still an undergraduate, Beveridge won local renown as a political orator for his fervent nationalism and support for a strong Federal government. Beveridge earned a law degree in 1887. That same year, he moved to Indianapolis, got married, and quickly became a leading member of the Indiana bar. Beveridge started to rise in Republican Party circles, speaking widely during the 1892 and 1896 presidential campaigns. His well-reasoned orations emphasized short, incisive phrases and contrasted with the more ornate speechmaking styles of the era. By age 30, he was considered one of the leading political orators in the United States, delivering speeches supporting territorial expansion by the U.S. and increasing the power of the federal government.

In 1898, Beveridge gained national fame as a fervent exponent of U.S. colonial expansion following the Spanish-American War. In his famous 1898 "March of the Flag" speech, Beveridge appealed to his country's sense of destiny to advocate imperialism overseas. This speech helped to advance his political career. He was subsequently elected as a Republican to the United States Senate on January 17, 1899. His election at age 36 made him one of the youngest senators in American history. In the Senate, Beveridge quickly became an important voice in American foreign policy. His eloquence in urging America to accept its place as a world power took on a messianic tone. "We will not renounce our part in the mission of our race, trustee, under God, of the civilization of the world," he told his fellow senators in a speech on January 9, 1900. Valued as a firm supporter of conservative economic policy and overseas expansion, Beveridge was predicted by many for great things, including the presidency.

However, following his re-election as Senator in 1905, Beveridge gradually moved away from his uncritical support of American big business. He began to seek to check the excessive influence of big business in politics. By 1907, he had become a leading figure in the emerging Progressive movement, working to enact reformist legislation of pure food, child labor, and tariff reform. This change of political platforms inevitably caused Beveridge's clashes with and alienation from the more conservative Republicans and finally led to his defeat for re-election in 1911.

For the next decade, Beveridge's political career was gloomy. After a futile attempt to run for the U.S. Senate in Indiana once again, he turned away from active politics and devoted himself almost exclusively to writing history for the remainder of his life. As a historian, his fame rested mainly upon his four-volume *The Life of John Marshall*, which won him a Pulitzer Prize. He died of a heart attack at his Indianapolis home on April 27, 1927 when he was in the process of writing a biography of Abraham Lincoln.

 Text 3

The March of the Flag
Albert Beveridge, September 16, 1898

1   It is a noble land that God has given us; a land that can feed and clothe the world; a land whose coastlines would enclose half the countries of Europe; a land set like a sentinel between the two imperial oceans of the globe, a greater England with a nobler destiny.

2   It is a mighty people that He has planted on this soil; a people sprung from the most masterful blood of history; a people perpetually revitalized by the virile, man-producing working-folk of all the earth; a people imperial by virtue of their power, by right of their institutions, by authority of their Heaven-directed purposes — the propagandists and not the misers of liberty.

3 It is a glorious history our God has bestowed upon His chosen people; a history heroic with faith in our mission and our future; a history of statesmen who flung the boundaries of the Republic out into unexplored lands and savage wilderness; a history of soldiers who carried the flag across blazing deserts and through the ranks of hostile mountains, even to the gates of sunset; a history of a multiplying people who overran a continent in half a century; a history of prophets who saw the consequences of evils inherited from the past and of martyrs who died to save us from them; a history divinely logical, in the process of whose tremendous reasoning we find ourselves today.

4 Therefore, in this campaign, the question is larger than a party question. It is an American question. It is a world question. Shall the American people continue their march toward the commercial supremacy of the world? Shall free institutions broaden their blessed reign as the children of liberty wax in strength, until the empire of our principles is established over the hearts of all mankind?

5 Have we no mission to perform, no duty to discharge to our fellow man? Has God endowed us with gifts beyond our deserts and marked us as the people of His peculiar favor, merely to rot in our own selfishness, as men and nations must, who take cowardice for their companion and self for their Deity — as India has, as Egypt has?

6 Shall we be as the man who had one talent and hid it, or as he who had ten talents and used them until they grew to riches? And shall we reap the reward that waits on our discharge of our high duty; shall we occupy new markets for what our farmers raise, our factories make, our merchants sell — aye, and please God, new markets for what our ships shall carry?

7 Hawaii is ours; Porto Rico is to be ours; at the prayer of her people Cuba finally will be ours; in the islands of the East, even to the gates of Asia, coaling stations are to be ours at the very least; the flag of a liberal government is to float over the Philippines, and may it be the banner that Taylor[①] unfurled in Texas and Fremont[②] carried to the coast. And the burning question of this campaign is, whether the American people will accept the gifts of events; whether they will rise as lifts their soaring destiny; whether they will proceed upon the lines of national development surveyed by the statesmen of our past; or whether, for the first time, the American people doubt their mission, question fate, prove apostate to the spirit of their race, and halt the ceaseless march of free institutions.

---

① Zachary Taylor (1784—1850), commander of U.S. forces during the first phase of the Mexican War and later the 12th President of the U.S. (1849—1850), who died of illness during his term of office.
② John Charles Fremont (1813—1890), nicknamed "The Pathfinder", was one of most famous explorers of the American West. In the Mexican War, he was appointed major and helped conquer California.

8   The Opposition tells us that we ought not to govern a people without their consent.① I answer: The rule of liberty that all just government derives its authority from the consent of the governed, applies only to those who are capable of self-government. We govern the Indians without their consent, we govern our territories without their consent, we govern our children without their consent. How do you assume that our government would be without their consent? Would not the people of the Philippines prefer the just, humane, civilizing government of this Republic to the savage, bloody rule of pillage and extortion from which we have rescued them?

9   And, regardless of this formula of words made only for enlightened, self-governing people, do we owe no duty to the world? Shall we turn these peoples back to the reeking hands from which we have taken them? Shall we abandon them to their fate, with the wolves of conquest all about them — with Germany, Russia, France, even Japan, hungering for them? Shall we save them from those nations, to give them a self-rule of tragedy?

10   They ask us how we shall govern these new possessions.② I answer: Out of local conditions and the necessities of the case methods of government will grow. If England can govern foreign lands, so can America. If Germany can govern foreign lands, so can America. If they can supervise protectorates, so can America. Why is it more difficult to administer Hawaii than New Mexico or California? Both had a savage and an alien population; both were more remote from the seat of government when they came under our dominion than Hawaii is today.

11   Will you say by your vote that American ability to govern has decayed, that a century's experience in self-rule has failed of a result? Will you affirm by your vote that you are an infidel to American power and practical sense? Or will you say that ours is the blood of government; ours the heart of dominion; ours the brain and genius of administration? Will you remember that we do but what our fathers did — we but pitch the tents of liberty farther westward, farther southward — we only continue the march of the flag?

12   The march of the flag! In 1789 the flag of the Republic waved over 4,000,000 souls in thirteen states, and their savage territory which stretched to the Mississippi, to Canada, to the Floridas. The timid minds of that day said that no new territory was needed, and, for the hour, they were right. But Jefferson, through whose intellect the centuries marched; Jefferson, who dreamed of Cuba as an American state; Jefferson, the first Imperialist of the Republic — Jefferson acquired that imperial territory which swept from the Mississippi to the mountains, from Texas to the British possessions, and the march of the flag began!

13   The infidels to the gospel of liberty raved, but the flag swept on! The title to that noble land out of which Oregon, Washington, Idaho and Montana have been carved was uncertain; Jefferson, strict constructionist of constitutional power though he was, obeyed the Anglo-

---

① 贝弗里奇是典型的实用主义者、种族主义者、扩张主义者。美国的政治传统认为，统治必须建立在被统治人同意基础之上。贝弗里奇认为，这一原则只适用于有能力自治的民族。显然，这样的论调极其荒谬。
② 贝弗里奇在寻找各种借口和理由，试图突破宪法对美国所管辖范围和领土的限制。

Saxon impulse within him, whose watchword is, "Forward"; another empire was added to the Republic, and the march of the flag went on!

14 Those who deny the power of free institutions to expand urged every argument, and more, that we hear, today; but the people's judgment approved the command of their blood, and the march of the flag went on!

15 A screen of land from New Orleans to Florida shut us from the Gulf, and over this and the Everglade Peninsula① waved the saffron flag of Spain; Andrew Jackson seized both, the American people stood at his back, and, under Monroe, the Floridas came under the dominion of the Republic, and the march of the flag went on! The Cassandras prophesied every prophecy of despair we hear, today, but the march of the flag went on!

16 Then Texas responded to the bugle calls of liberty, and the march of the flag went on! And, at last, we waged war with Mexico, and the flag swept over the southwest, over peerless California, past the Gate of Gold to Oregon on the north, and from ocean to ocean its folds of glory blazed.

17 And, now, obeying the same voice that Jefferson heard and obeyed, that Jackson heard and obeyed, that Monroe heard and obeyed, that Seward heard and obeyed, that Grant heard and obeyed, that Harrison heard and obeyed, our President② today plants the flag over the islands of the seas, outposts of commerce, citadels of national security, and the march of the flag goes on!

18 Distance and oceans are no arguments. The fact that all the territory our fathers bought and seized is contiguous, is no argument. In 1819 Florida was farther from New York than Porto Rico is from Chicago today; Texas, farther from Washington in 1845 than Hawaii is from Boston in 1898; California, more inaccessible in 1847 than the Philippines are now. Gibraltar③ is farther from London than Havana is from Washington; Melbourne is farther from Liverpool than Manila is from San Francisco.

19 The ocean does not separate us from lands of our duty and desire — the oceans join us, rivers never to be dredged, a canal never to be repaired. Steam joins us; electricity joins us — the very elements are in league with④ our destiny. Cuba not contiguous! Porto Rico not contiguous! Hawaii and the Philippines not contiguous! The oceans make them contiguous. And our navy will make them contiguous.

20 But the Opposition is right — there is a difference. We did not need the western

---

① 佛罗里达半岛。

② Here it refers to President William McKinley (25th president, 1897—1901). Other statesmen mentioned include Thomas Jefferson (3rd president, 1801—1809), Andrew Jackson (7th president, 1829—1837), James Monroe (5th president, 1817—1825), William Henry Seward (Secretary of State, 1861—1869, most famous for his successful acquisition of Alaska from Russia), Ulysses S. Grant (18th president, 1869—1877) and Benjamin Harrison (23rd president, 1889—1893).

③ Gibraltar Strait, a British colony at the northwest end of the Rock of Gibraltar, connecting the Mediterranean Sea and the Atlantic Ocean between Spain and northern Africa. 直布罗陀海峡。

④ in league with: 与……密切配合；与……联盟。

Mississippi Valley when we acquired it, nor Florida, nor Texas, nor California, nor the royal provinces of the far northwest. We had no emigrants to people this imperial wilderness, no money to develop it, even no highways to cover it. No trade awaited us in its savage fastnesses. Our productions were not greater than our trade. There was not one reason for the landlust of our statesmen from Jefferson to Grant, other than the prophet and the Saxon within them. But, today, we are raising more than we can consume, making more than we can use. Therefore we must find new markets for our produce.①

21   And so, while we did not need the territory taken during the past century at the time it was acquired, we do need what we have taken in 1898 and we need it now. The resource and the commerce of the immensely rich dominions will be increased as much as American energy is greater than Spanish sloth.

22   In Cuba, alone, there are 15,000,000 acres of forest unacquainted with the ax, exhaustless mines of iron, priceless deposits of manganese, millions of dollars' worth of which we must buy, today, from the Black Sea districts. There are millions of acres yet unexplored.

23   The resources of Porto Rico have only been trifled with. The riches of the Philippines have hardly been touched by the fingertips of modern methods. And they produce what we consume, and consume what we produce — the very predestination of reciprocity — a reciprocity "not made with hands, eternal in the heavens." They sell hemp, sugar, cocoanuts, fruits of the tropics, timber of price like mahogany; they buy flour, clothing, tools, implements, machinery and all that we can raise and make. Their trade will be ours in time. Do you indorse that policy with your vote?

24   Cuba is as large as Pennsylvania, and is the richest spot on the globe. Hawaii is as large as New Jersey; Porto Rico half as large as Hawaii; the Philippines larger than all New England, New York, New Jersey and Delaware combined. Together they are larger than the British Isles, larger than France, larger than Germany, larger than Japan.

25   If any man tells you that trade depends on cheapness and not on government influence, ask him why England does not abandon South Africa, Egypt, India?

26   Our trade with Porto Rico, Hawaii and the Philippines must be as free as between the states of the Union, because they are American territory, while every other nation on earth must pay our tariff before they can compete with us. Until Cuba shall ask for annexation, our trade with her will, at the very least, be like the preferential trade of Canada with England. That, and the excellence of our goods and products; that, and the convenience of traffic; that, and the kinship of interests and destiny, will give the monopoly of these markets to the American people.

27   The commercial supremacy of the Republic means that this Nation is to be the sovereign

---

① "因此，我们必须为我们的产品找到新的市场。"当时，美国作为新兴资本主义国家，开拓市场是真正的国家利益。其他借口或理由归根到底都是为发展美国的资本主义服务。

factor in the peace of the world.① For the conflicts of the future are to be conflicts of trade — struggles for markets — commercial wars for existence. And the golden rule of peace is impregnability of position and invincibility of preparedness. So, we see England, the greatest strategist of history, plant her flag and her cannon on Gibraltar, at Quebec, in the Bermudas, at Vancouver, everywhere.

28 So Hawaii furnishes us a naval base in the heart of the Pacific; the Ladrones② another, a voyage further on; Manila another, at the gates of Asia — Asia, to the trade of whose hundreds of millions American merchants, manufacturers, farmers, have as good right as those of Germany or France or Russia or England; Asia, whose commerce with the United Kingdom alone amounts to hundreds of millions of dollars every year; Asia, to whom Germany looks to take her surplus products; Asia, whose doors must not be shut against American trade. Within five decades the bulk of Oriental commerce will be ours.

29 In the light of that golden future our chain of new-won stations rise like ocean sentinels from the night of waters — Porto Rico, a nobler Gibraltar; the Isthmian canal③, a greater Suez; Hawaii, the Ladrones, the Philippines, commanding the Pacific! Ah! As our commerce spreads, the flag of liberty will circle the globe and the highways of the ocean-carrying trade of all mankind be guarded by the guns of the Republic. Shall this future of the race be left with those who, under God, began this career of sacred duty and immortal glory; or, shall we risk it to those who would build a dam in the current of destiny's large designs. We are enlisted in the cause of American supremacy, which will never end until American commerce has made the conquest of the world; until American citizenship has become the lord of civilization, and the stars and stripes the flag of flags throughout the world.

….

30 There are so many real things to be done — canals to be dug, railways to be laid, forests to be felled, cities to be built, fields to be tilled, markets to be won, ships to be launched, peoples to be saved, civilization to be proclaimed and the flag of liberty flung to the eager air of every sea. Is this an hour to waste upon triflers with Nature's laws? Is this a season to give our destiny over to word mongers and prosperity wreckers? It is an hour to remember your duty to the home. It is a moment to realize the opportunities Fate has opened to this favored people and to you. It is a time to bethink you of the conquering march of the flag. It is a time to bethink you of your Nation and its sovereignty of the seas. It is a time to remember that the God of our fathers is our God and that the gifts and the duties He gave to them, enriched and multiplied, He renews to us, their children. It is a time to sustain that devoted man, servant of the people and of the most high God, who is guiding the Republic out into the ocean of infinite

---

① 美国在19世纪末已是全球第一经济大国，它的政治野心初现端倪。贝弗里奇希望凭借美国强大的商业力量在"世界和平"事业中发挥美国至高无上的作用。贝弗里奇大胆预测未来世界的争端主要是贸易战。
② the Ladrones：马里亚纳群岛。
③ the Isthmian canal：巴拿马运河。

possibility. It is a time to cheer the beloved President of God's chosen people①, till the whole world is vocal with American loyalty to the American government of William McKinley, its head and chief.

31 Fellow-Americans, we are God's chosen people. Yonder at Bunker Hill and Yorktown His providence was above us. At New Orleans and on ensanguined seas His hand sustained us. Abraham Lincoln was his minister; and his was the altar of freedom, the boys in blue set on a hundred smoking battlefields. His power directed Dewey in the East, and He delivered the Spanish fleet into our hands on the eve of Liberty's natal day as He delivered the elder Armada into the hands of our English sires two centuries ago. His great purposes are revealed in the progress of the flag, which surpasses the intentions of Congresses and Cabinets, and leads us, like a holier pillar of cloud by day and pillar of fire by night, into situations unforeseen by finite wisdom and duties unexpected by the unprophetic heart of selfishness. The American people cannot use a dishonest medium of exchange; it is ours to set the world its example of right and honor. We cannot fly from our world duties; it is ours to execute the purpose of a fate that has driven us to be greater than our small intentions. We cannot retreat from any soil where Providence has unfurled our banner; it is ours to save that soil for liberty and civilization. For liberty and civilization and God's promises fulfilled, the flag must henceforth be the symbol and the sign to all mankind.

Vocabulary

sentinel (para. 1)	*n.* a sentry; one that keeps guard
virile (para. 2)	*adj.* masculine
apostate (para. 7)	*adj.* unfaithful, renegade
protectorate (para. 10)	*n.* a state or territory placed or taken under the protection of a superior power
infidel (para. 11)	*n.* one who doubts or rejects a particular doctrine, system, or principle
rave (para. 13)	*v.* to speak wildly, irrationally, or incoherently
Cassandra (para. 15)	*n.* people who utter unheeded prophecies
peerless (para. 16)	*adj.* without peer, unequalled, or matchless
citadel (para. 17)	*n.* a strong fortress, a stronghold
contiguous (para. 18)	*adj.* neighboring
sloth (para. 21)	*n.* laziness
reciprocity (para. 23)	*n.* a state or relationship in which there is mutual action, influence, giving and taking, correspondence, etc., between two parties or things
impregnability (para. 27)	*n.* having the strength to withstand attack

---

① God's chosen people: 上帝的选民。这是"天定命运论"的思想，典型的盎格鲁—撒克逊人的种族上论。

vocal (para. 30)   *adj.* full of voice, resounding
ensanguined (para. 31) *adj.* blood-stained, bloody

Questions for discussion

1. How did Beveridge characterize the purposes and goals of the U.S.?
2. How did Beveridge justify the subjugation of the Cubans, Puerto Ricans, and Filipinos by the U.S.?
3. Why did Beveridge believe that the U.S. needed an overseas empire?

 Text 4

America's Destiny
Albert Beveridge, January 9, 1900

1 Mr. President①, the times call for candor. The Philippines are ours forever, "territory belonging to the United States," as the Constitution calls them. And just beyond the Philippines are China's illimitable markets. We will not retreat from either. We will not repudiate our duty in the archipelago. We will not abandon our opportunity in the Orient. We will not renounce our part in the mission of our race, trustee, under God, of the civilization of the world.② And we will move forward to our work, not howling out regrets like slaves whipped to their burdens, but with gratitude for a task worthy of our strength, and thanksgiving to Almighty God that He has marked us as His chosen people, henceforth to lead in the regeneration of the world.③

2 This island empire is the last land left in all the oceans. If it should prove a mistake to abandon it, the blunder once made would be irretrievable. If it proves a mistake to hold it, the error can be corrected when we will. Every other progressive nation stands ready to relieve us.④

3 But to hold it will be no mistake. Our largest trade henceforth must be with Asia. The Pacific is our ocean. More and more Europe will manufacture the most it needs, secure

---

① 参议院主席，美国参议院主席由副总统担任。
② "我们不会从其中任何一一撤退。我们不会推卸在菲律宾群岛的责任。我们不会放弃在东方的良机。我们不会否认自己在上帝赋予我们种族的使命中发挥的作用，担任世界文明的托管人。"
③ "我们将勇往直前，完成任务，不是像受鞭打负起重担的奴隶那样哀号后悔，而是对这项值得为之努力的任务心怀感激，感激全能的上帝选择我们作为他的子民，领导世界的重建。"
④ "其他任何一个进步的民族都时刻准备取代我们。"意指美国必须尽快采取行动。

from its colonies the most it consumes.① Where shall we turn for consumers of our surplus? Geography answers the question. China is our natural customer. She is nearer to us than to England, Germany, or Russia, the commercial powers of the present and the future. They have moved nearer to China by securing permanent bases on her borders. The Philippines give us a base at the door of all the East.

4 Lines of navigation from our ports to the Orient and Australia; from the Isthmian Canal to Asia; from all Oriental ports to Australia, converge at and separate from the Philippines. They are a self supporting, dividend-paying fleet, permanently anchored at a spot selected by the strategy of Providence, commanding the Pacific. And the Pacific is the ocean of the commerce of the future. Most future wars will be conflicts for commerce. The power that rules the Pacific, therefore, is the power that rules the world. And, with the Philippines, that power is and will forever be the American Republic....

5 Nothing is so natural as trade with one's neighbors. The Philippines make us the nearest neighbors of all the East. Nothing is more natural than to trade with those you know. This is the philosophy of all advertising.② The Philippines bring us permanently face to face with the most sought-for customers of the world. National prestige, national propinquity, these and commercial activity are the elements of commercial success. The Philippines give the first; the character of the American people supply the last. It is a providential conjunction of all the elements of trade, of duty, and of power. If we are willing to go to war rather than let England have a few feet of frozen Alaska, which affords no market and commands none, what should we not do rather than let England, Germany, Russia, or Japan have all the Philippines? And no man on the spot can fail to see that this would be their fate if we retired....

6 Here, then, Senators, is the situation. Two years ago③ there was no land in all the world which we could occupy for any purpose. Our commerce was daily turning toward the Orient, and geography and trade developments made necessary our commercial empire over the Pacific. And in that ocean we had no commercial, naval, or military base. Today we have one of the three great ocean possessions of the globe, located at the most commanding commercial, naval, and military points in the eastern seas, within hail of India, shoulder to shoulder with China, richer in its own resources than any equal body of land on the entire globe, and peopled by a race which civilization demands shall be improved. Shall we abandon it? That man little knows the common people of the Republic, little understands the instincts of our race, who thinks we will not hold it fast and hold it forever, administering just government by simplest methods.④ We may trick up devices to shift our burden and lessen our opportunity; they will

---

① "欧洲将越来越多地在殖民地制造它最需要的产品,从那里获得它消耗最多的资源。"意指殖民地的重要作用。美国曾是一个殖民地国家,当它自己面临是否要拥有殖民地的时候,这是一个历史性的抉择。
② "没有什么比与你认识的人做交易更自然了……这是一切广告的原理。"
③ 指 1898 年,这一年爆发了美西战争。
④ "如果有谁认为我们不会迅速并永久地占领它,通过最简单的方法管理正义的政府,那他就对共和国的普通民众一无所知,对我们民族的天性一无所知。"

avail us nothing but delay. We may tangle conditions by applying academic arrangements of self-government to a crude situation; their failure will drive us to our duty in the end....

7   But, Senators, it would be better to abandon this combined garden and Gibraltar of the Pacific, and count our blood and treasure already spent a profitable loss, than to apply any academic arrangement of self-government to these children. They are not capable of self-government. How could they be? They are not of a self-governing race. They are Orientals, Malays①, instructed by Spaniards in the latter's worst estate.

8   They know nothing of practical government except as they have witnessed the weak, corrupt, cruel, and capricious rule of Spain. What magic will anyone employ to dissolve in their minds and characters those impressions of governors and governed which three centuries of misrule have created? What alchemy will change the oriental quality of their blood and set the self-governing currents of the American pouring through their Malay veins? How shall they, in the twinkling of an eye, be exalted to the heights of self-governing peoples which required a thousand years for us to reach, Anglo-Saxon though we are...?②

9   The Declaration of Independence does not forbid us to do our part in the regeneration of the world. If it did, the Declaration would be wrong, just as the Articles of Confederation③, drafted by the very same men who signed the Declaration, was found to be wrong. The Declaration has no application to the present situation. It was written by self-governing men for self-governing men....

10   Senators in opposition are stopped from denying our constitutional power to govern the Philippines as circumstances may demand, for such power is admitted in the case of Florida, Louisiana, Alaska. How, then, is it denied in the Philippines? Is there a geographical interpretation to the Constitution? Do degrees of longitude fix constitutional limitations? Does a thousand miles of ocean diminish constitutional power more than a thousand miles of land...?

11   No; the oceans are not limitations of the power which the Constitution expressly gives Congress to govern all territory the nation may acquire. The Constitution declares that "Congress shall have power to dispose of and make all needful rules and regulations respecting the territory belonging to the United States."

....

12   Mr. President, this question is deeper than any question of party politics; deeper than any question of the isolated policy of our country even; deeper even than any question of constitutional power. It is elemental. It is racial. God has not been preparing the English-speaking and Teutonic peoples④ for a thousand years for nothing but vain and idle self-

---

① Malays: 马来人（主要居住在马来半岛及马来群岛一带）。
② "他们如何能在一眨眼的功夫，就跻身自治民族之列？即使对身为盎格鲁—撒克逊人的我们来说，这也需要一千年的时间。" 这里充分表现了贝弗里奇的种族优越感和强烈的种族主义色彩。
③ the Articles of Confederation:《邦联条例》，是13个独立的州筹建统一政府的第一个正式文件，1777年由第二届大陆会议提出。
④ 指盎格鲁—撒克逊人和日耳曼人，他们是美国早期移民的主要来源。

contemplation and self-admiration. No! He has made us the master organizers of the world to establish system where chaos reigns. He has given us the spirit of progress to overwhelm the forces of reaction throughout the earth. He has made us adepts in government that we may administer government among savage and senile peoples. Were it not for such a force as this the world would relapse into barbarism and night. And of all our race He has marked the American people as His chosen nation to finally lead in the regeneration of the world. This is the divine mission of America, and it holds for us all the profit, all the glory, all the happiness possible to man. We are trustees of the world's progress, guardians of its righteous peace.① The judgment of the Master is upon us: "Ye have been faithful over a few things; I will make you ruler over many things."

13 What shall history say of us? Shall it say that we renounced that holy trust, left the savage to his base condition, the wilderness to the reign of waste, deserted duty, abandoned glory, forgot our sordid profit even, because we feared our strength and read the charter of our powers with the doubter's eye and the quibbler's mind? Shall it say that, called by events to captain and command the proudest, ablest, purest race of history in history's noblest work, we declined that great commission? Our fathers would not have had it so. No! They founded no paralytic government, incapable of the simplest acts of administration. They planted no sluggard people, passive while the world's work calls them. They established no reactionary nation. They unfurled no retreating flag....

14 Mr. President and Senators, adopt the resolution offered, that peace may quickly come and that we may begin our saving, regenerating, and uplifting work.... Reject it, and the world, history, and the American people will know where to forever fix the awful responsibility for the consequences that will surely follow such failure to do our manifest duty....

Vocabulary

repudiate (para. 1)	*v.* to reject the validity or authority of
archipelago (para. 1)	*n.* a large group of islands
blunder (para. 2)	*n.* a usually serious mistake typically caused by ignorance or confusion
navigation (para. 4)	*n.* the theory and practice of navigating, especially the charting of a course for a ship or an aircraft
converge (para. 4)	*v.* to tend toward or approach an intersecting point
Providence (para. 4)	*n.* God
propinquity (para. 5)	*n.* proximity; nearness
possessions (para. 6)	*n.* the act or fact of possessing tangle
capricious (para. 8)	*adj.* characterized by or subject to whim; impulsive and unpredictable

① "我们是世界进步的委托人,是正义和平的护卫者。"这番陈词是19世纪上半叶"天定命运论"的新发展。

expressly (para. 11)	*adj.* explicitly
adept (para. 12)	*n.* a highly skilled person; an expert
senile (para. 12)	*adj.* relating to, characteristic of, or resulting from old age
relapse (para. 12)	*v.* to fall or slide back into a former state
Ye (para. 12)	*n.* [古] 汝，尔等
quibbler (para. 13)	*n.* a person who likes arguing about small or unimportant matters
sluggard (para. 13)	*n.* a slothful person; an idler
unfurl (para. 13)	*v.* to spread or open sth. out or become spread or opened out

Questions for discussion

1. On what grounds did Beveridge make enormous claims for the strategic importance of the Philippines?
2. In the speech, Beveridge mentioned God many times. Why did he do that?
3. No doubt, Beveridge was a racist. Can you find evidence from the speech?
4. To what extent was the concept of *Manifest Destiny* reflected in the speech? Was it very attractive at that time?

Background

Origin of the Term *Manifest Destiny*

The phrase Manifest Destiny is used to express the belief that it was the fate of the United States to expand across the American continent. The idea of Manifest Destiny was not new to America in the 1840s. However, the term itself did not appear until John O'Sullivan used it to describe his dream of America's future. Many people credit O'Sullivan with coining the term when it first appeared in an essay called "Annexation" in the July-August 1845 issue *The United States Magazine and Democratic Review*. The term symbolized the ideology and desire for the United States to expand. In the essay, O'Sullivan voiced support for the American acquisition of Texas. According to O'Sullivan, it was the "fulfillment of our manifest destiny to overspread the continent allotted by Providence for the free development of our yearly multiplying millions."

O'Sullivan's first use of the term Manifest Destiny went virtually unnoticed. Later that year, in the December 27 issue of the *New York Morning News*, O'Sullivan again used the term Manifest Destiny to explain his view about the dispute about the Oregon territory. O'Sullivan maintained that the United States had rights to all of Oregon. O'Sullivan then declared that this "claim is by the right of our manifest destiny to overspread and possess the whole of the continent which Providence has given us for the development of the great experiment of liberty and federated self-government entrusted to us." In short, O'Sullivan argued that Providence had ordained the United States to extend its unique and relatively new form of government, the so-called "great experiment of liberty and federated self-government." O'Sullivan felt that America's Manifest Destiny embodied a higher law — God's law — and so held the moral high ground over Britain's claims to Oregon.

The term Manifest Destiny was almost immediately picked up and adopted by others after O'Sullivan applied it to justify the US claim to Oregon. Promoters of expansion used the term, which clearly stated their view of America's spreading out. To such people, American expansion and entitlement to western lands was obvious, or manifest. Because such expansion was sure to happen, it was America's destiny. The term Manifest Destiny came to embody all the hopes and expectations of expansionists in nineteenth-century America.

Meaning of Manifest Destiny

At the least, Manifest Destiny "meant expansion, prearranged by Heaven, over an area not clearly defined." Other points of view saw Manifest Destiny as the right for the United States to gain land all the way to the Pacific Ocean. Still others enlarged the view to include all of North America, or even the entire Western Hemisphere. Regardless of the interpretation, the concept of Manifest Destiny spurred a political movement in the 1840s. The ideals of expansionism captured the nation, resulting in war with Mexico and an American Indian policy that virtually destroyed the culture of the continent's original inhabitants.

Although the United States did not adopt Manifest Destiny as a policy, the concept of Manifest Destiny influenced U.S. policy, especially in the last six decades of the nineteenth century. The term encompassed several beliefs. These were expansionism, nationalism, American exceptionalism, and, in some cases, the idea of racial superiority. Historian Ernest Lee Tuveson summarized the assortment of views this way: "A vast complex of ideas, policies, and actions is comprehended under the phrase 'Manifest Destiny.' They are not, as we should expect, all compatible, nor do they come from any one source." Despite these complexities, the idea of Manifest Destiny generally meant that Americans and their government were certain to gain ownership of and establish political control over much of North America, and that their country would stretch from the Atlantic Ocean to the Pacific.

To its proponents, the idea of Manifest Destiny contained three identifiable themes: "the special virtues of the American people and their institutions; their mission to redeem and remake the world in the image of America; and the American destiny under God to accomplish this sublime task." Expansionists of the 1840s and 1850s believed in the rightness of the American way of life. They recognized the unique place and time in which they lived — a time and place that allowed them to expand the United States. They were also convinced of the certainty of their success. These beliefs make up the fundamental spirit of Manifest Destiny.

Supporters usually included three key concepts in their arguments for Manifest Destiny: virtue, mission, and destiny. First, American society and citizens were virtuous. Because of their virtue, they were justified in expanding. Second, it was the mission of Americans to extend their society. In doing this, Americans would influence the rest of the world. Finally, it was the destiny of America to undertake the task of accomplishing these things. Manifest Destiny implied not simply territorial growth, but sanctified ideology and institutions.

Roots of Manifest Destiny

The ideals contained within the concept of Manifest Destiny were certainly not novel. Indeed, in 1630, an early Puritan leader named John Winthrop described the Massachusetts Bay Colony "as a city upon a hill." This city on a hill was to serve as an example for all humankind, for all time. To this end, many of the early Massachusetts settlers believed that the institutions they established, the society they designed, and the lives they led laid the foundation for this city on a hill. Later, when the American War of Independence broke out, it was seen to be the opportunity for Americans to influence the future of the world. For example, the famous Political philosopher Thomas Paine wrote in *Common Sense*, "We have it in our power to begin the world over again."

Coupled with this mission-like idea of shaping the future of the world, early American leaders believed in the inevitable westward expansion of the young republic. The 1783 Treaty of Paris extended the western boundary of the new-born country to the Mississippi River, thus doubling the territory of the early 13 states. Then the Louisiana Purchase of 1803 extended the western limits of the United States to reach the Rocky Mountains. This early growth fed and fanned the desire to expand the new nation's territorial holdings across the continent. John Quincy Adams envisaged an expanded American nation in 1811, claiming that North America appeared to be destined by Divine Providence to be associated in one federal Union, peopled by one nation, speaking one language, professing one general system of religious and political principles, and accustomed to one general tenor of social usages and customs. Another contributing factor to the success of America's Manifest Destiny of the 1840s was the formulation, in the 1820s, of a cornerstone of American foreign policy. That cornerstone was the Monroe Doctrine, which helped to pave the way for the acquisition of vast territories.

As the United States charted its course of westward expansion, booming with territorial gains and an ever-increasing appetite for more territory, the full-bodied ideal of Manifest Destiny took hold in the 1840s when the United States snatched more than half of Mexico's territory. The concept of Manifest Destiny was seized on by the expansionists to explain and justify expansionism both to Europeans, who viewed American aggrandizement with alarm, and to the American people themselves, who needed reassurance that the course was righteous. Then, as the 19th century came to its closing decade, the United States found that it could no longer move westward as it had reached the shores of the Pacific. As the American historian Frederick Jackson Turner sighed in 1893, America's moving frontier now "has gone, and with its going has closed the first period of American history." The history of continental expansion did end for the United States, yet its history of overseas expansion was just to unfold, and when that moment came, the concept of Manifest Destiny would be revitalized.

Chapter 3 Manifest Destiny & Imperialism（天定命运论与帝国主义）

Later Use of Manifest Destiny

The power and success of Manifest Destiny as a way to convey American ideals and Americans' desire to expand their territorial holdings led to the concept's use in later years. In the 1890s, the term Manifest Destiny resurfaced. This time, however, Manifest Destiny was used to defend American expansion outside North America. Specifically, some people wanted to establish the United States as a world power by gaining colonies. In 1898, the Spanish-American War provided such an opportunity.

Few Americans in the 20th century continued to use Manifest Destiny to describe their policy goals. Other terms emerged, however, and several of these carried some of the same ideas. Specifically, the concept that America needed to lead the free world as part of its mission contained many of the ideals of Manifest Destiny. Expressions such as "Big Stick," "Dollar Diplomacy," and "Good Neighbor" were, to some extent, manifestations of Manifest Destiny. Regardless of the name, each of these foreign policies contained elements of Manifest Destiny. One of these elements was the idea that an infusion of American values and institutions can bring benefits to other nations. Consistent with Manifest Destiny, these later ideals tied policy initiatives and aims to national pride and to the role of America as a world power.

The ideals of Manifest Destiny continued to influence the United States in sometimes surprising, sometimes subtle ways. When the United States entered World War I in 1917, it did so under the banner of making the world safe for democracy. Such idealism was a realization of America's perceived destiny. The idea that the United States had an important role to play in protecting and promoting democracy around the world and vision of American leadership and involvement in world affairs dominated later American foreign policies. Although the term of Manifest Destiny was no longer cited as justification for US foreign policy approaches, the idea that America had role and place as a world leader in the defense of freedom and democracy was heartily embraced.

Today, America's role as a superpower embodies many of these same elements of Manifest Destiny, including the desire to encourage the establishment of democratic governments around the world. John O'Sullivan and other nineteenth century expansionists might not recognize much of their world in modern-day America. They might, however, recognize the fruits of their labors and dreams to fulfill the Manifest Destiny of the United States.

American Imperialism

At the end of the 19th century, America had finished its industrialization. The vast economic development made external expansion necessary. The economic crisis in 1893 led foreign markets more attractive and important. The victory of the Spanish-American War in 1898 gave America great opportunities to take over many formal Spanish colonies. However, some American people were fairly cautious and suspicious of this new emerging imperialism, and were divided in the issue. Within the Congress, a hot debate was under way. In *America's Destiny*, fervent Senator Albert Beveridge emotionally laid out the basic arguments supporting

American imperialism in the 20th century.

"天定命运论"是一种扩张主义理论。1845年7月和8月间,《美国杂志和民主评论》(一般简称为《民主评论》)创始人、主编约翰·奥沙利文在该杂志发表一篇关于得克萨斯问题的社论,首次提出这一概念。当年12月27日,经纽约《早晨新闻》关于俄勒冈争端的一篇社论宣传后,"天定命运论"成为19世纪40年代美国领土扩张的专门用语。1846年1月3日,在关于俄勒冈问题的辩论中,马萨诸塞州共和党参议员罗伯特·C.温斯罗普又在国会首先使用这一词汇。

"天定命运论"宣扬如下观点:一指美利坚合众国建立的必然性。"在北美大陆范围内建立一个自由、联合、自治的共和国——这就是天定命运,它是基于各州联合的共和主义。"二指美国领土扩张的合法性。"它意味着上天预先安排的向尚未明白确定的地区扩张。在一些人的心目中,向北美大陆扩张;在其他一些人的心目中,则是向西半球扩张。"三指美国传播民主制度的神圣性。"民主制度是如此尽善尽美,以致不会受到任何国界的限制……扩张是上天安排的启发邻近国家遭到暴君蹂躏的人民大众的一种手段,它不是帝国主义,而是强行的拯救!"实际上,"天定命运论"的思想可追溯到殖民地时期。当时这一思想被一些政治家用来维护英国在北美的扩张。曾负责组织英国殖民地弗吉尼亚的地理学家理查德·黑克路易特断言,盎格鲁—撒克逊人命中注定要占领、拓殖和发展新大陆。世上没有一个民族可以承担如此重大的任务。

美国独立之后,这一思想开始与领土扩张联系起来。在众多鼓吹者中,以约翰·昆西·亚当斯最甚。早在1787年,他就公开宣称,新共和国"命中注定"要"扩张到全球四分之一的北部(北美洲)"。1811年,他在给父亲的信中写道:"上帝似乎已经预定整个北美大陆要由一个国家的国民定居,他们说同一种语言,信奉同样的宗教和政治原则,习惯于相同的社会习俗。"在1819年的一次内阁会议上,他又指出,美国对整个大陆的控制如同密西西比河要流向海洋一样,完全是自然法则。

1839年,约翰·奥沙利文在《民主评论》杂志上发表题为《未来的伟大国家》一文。该文表现的扩张意图十分明显,其中写道:"遥远无限的未来,将是美国的伟大时代。在其富丽堂皇的时空领域中,这个多民族的国家,注定将向人类显示出神意的完美,在大地上将建立起前所未有的极其高贵的殿堂。"到40年代中期,"天定命运论"的概念正式推出,并且在美国各地迅速扩散,说明扩张主义者迫不及待地要将"遥远无限的未来"完成的"伟大业绩"立即付诸实现。

"天定命运论"能够甚嚣尘上,首先是因为经济危机的打击。1837年的经济萧条持续到1845年才有明显好转。急于寻求新市场成为扩张的驱动力之一。其次,随着美国国内资本主义的发展,南北矛盾、劳资矛盾等日益凸显。扩张主义舆论和行动可起到转移视线的作用,而扩张主义的成果也有助于缓解国内矛盾,因此可以最大限度将国内各种政治力量汇集在它的旗帜之下,暂时缓解各阶级、各派别在内部问题上的纷争。再次,人口迅速增加的巨大压力也是扩张主义言行盛行的原因之一。"天定命运论"的出现,正逢其时,适应扩张主义者的需要,为其提供了合理性的理论基础。

除上述因素外,"天定命运论"中还有一种影响十分深刻的种族主义思想,以种族优越论为美国的扩张作鼓吹和辩护。

自17世纪开始,"选民"思想就已在清教徒中流行。早期殖民地的生根发展,之后又打败强大的英国,成功实现革命,再后来又经历令世界瞠目的飞速发展和扩张,这一切都被解读成上帝恩宠的表现。同时,作为来自英国的殖民者,美国人自认为继承了盎格鲁—萨克逊人的传统,身体中流淌着爱好自由民主的血液,这种优越感使他们成功建立起殖民地进而在独立战争后建立联邦政府,这一点一再被津津乐道。不过此时的种族观念尚不具有显见的种族主义优劣之分的危害。建国早期的美国人仍对革命中建立起来的民主共和制度保有热情,对盎格鲁—萨克逊传统的追溯更多的是一种民族自豪感的表现。

18世纪后期开始,受浪漫主义运动影响,有关语言、民族、种族的寻根努力在欧洲流行开来,进一步加强了既有的种族观念。盎格鲁—萨克逊的源头不断被追溯到条顿人或雅利安人,后者又进一步被追溯到中亚的原始部落高加索人,进而演绎出一幅壮观的西进文明之旅的神话来。这些原始部落追随太阳的轨迹向西扩散,将文明传播到欧洲,进而到英格兰,重现了昔日罗马帝国的光荣,再后来,又向西跨过大西洋,将文明带到美洲。在这个文明西进神话的背景下,美国向西扩张至太平洋乃至最终进入亚洲被解读成优等种族势不可挡的文明西进运动的一部分或最新显现。美国因为其历史发展的具体情况,尤其狂热地拥抱这种特殊种族使命的观念。拓殖的成功、革命的胜利、物质的繁荣、领土的激增、"落后"种族如黑人和印第安人之作为反证,这一切都使美国人更加倾心于接受种族主义思想。在19世纪上半叶,许多美国人急于证明,奴役黑人有理,排斥乃至灭绝印第安人有理。在当时的时代,报纸、杂志乃至政客热衷于找寻科学依据,证明种族差异,证明美国的优越,证明美国在世界秩序中的地位。于是美国知识界关于人种优劣对比的所谓科学研究理论应运而生。

到19世纪中叶,"天定命运论"中的种族主义思想已然成型。早期的清教殖民者、独立战争时期的爱国者、北美大陆荒野的征服者、巨大物质财富的创造者,这一连串的成功形象加之所谓的科学证明为当时的美国人提供了足够的证据,使他们相信,作为盎格鲁—萨克逊人、雅利安人乃至最早期高加索人的后裔,美国人继承了善于民主政治的天分,有着优于其他种族的血液,继承了追随太阳西进、传布文明的使命。美国人作为盎格鲁—萨克逊人的后裔,是与众不同、天生高人一等的优等民族,而劣等民族注定要臣服或被消灭。这样的观念成为为扩张辩护的重点。"天定命运论"中的种族主义思想开始甚嚣尘上。

在刺耳的种族主义喧嚣中,美国被描绘成一个天定命运的优等民族,注定要改造世界许多地方的命运,而美国制度之妙又是那些劣等民族所无法消受的,于是劣等民族注定要在美国向外扩张的过程中臣服或消亡,于是,离美国太近、离上帝太远的墨西哥自然成为牺牲品。种族主义加上天定命运,使"天定命运论"的表达更为露骨和肆无忌惮,也使美国的扩张活动更具野心、好战性和侵略性。

1898年,通过美西战争,美国又从西班牙手中夺取了古巴、菲律宾群岛、波多黎各、西印度群岛以及马里亚纳群岛中的关岛。"天定命运论"发挥得淋漓尽致。贝弗里奇的文献《美国的命运》更是从美国在亚洲的利益出发,打着履行"上帝所赋使命"的旗号,着重指出了菲律宾群岛对美国在太平洋地区利益的巨大重要性及将其变成稳固的美国殖民地的重要意义。文中言语间充斥着盎格鲁—萨克逊种族的优越感和对东方民族的歧视。"天定命运论"逐渐演变为美国的帝国主义政策。

Further reading

Beveridge, Albert J., *The Meaning of the Times, and Other Speeches*, Indianapolis: Bobbs-Merrill, 1908.

Bowers, Claude, *Beveridge and the Progressive Era*, Boston: Houghton-Mifflin Company, 1932.

Braeman, John, *Albert J. Beveridge: American Nationalist*, Chicago: University of Chicago Press, 1971.

Haynes, Sam W. and Christopher Morris (ed.), *Manifest Destiny and Empire: American Antebellum Expansionism*, College Station: The University of Texas, 1997.

Horsman, Reginald, *Race and Manifest Destiny: The Origins of American Racial Anglo-Saxonism*, Cambridge, Massachusetts: Harvard University Press, 1981.

Miller, Robert J., *Native America, Discovered and Conquered: Thomas Jefferson, Lewis & Clark, and Manifest Destiny*, Westport, Connecticut: Praeger Publishers, 2006.

Mountjoy, Shane, *Manifest Destiny: Westward Expansion*, New York: Infobase Publishing, 2009.

Sampson, Robert D., *John L. O'Sullivan and His Times*, Kent, Ohio: Kent State University Press, 2003.

丁则民主编：《美国通史（第三卷）：美国内战与镀金时代 1861—19世纪末》，北京：人民出版社，2002年。

李庆余：《美西战争》，北京：商务印书馆，1984年。

李庆余：《美西战争的研究成果概述》，《国外社会科学情况》1987年第3期。

杨生茂等编：《美西战争资料选辑》，上海：上海人民出版社，1981年。

张江河：《美西战争与美国向东南亚地缘政治扩张的历史脉络》，《东南亚研究》2013年第5期。

张友伦主编：《美国通史（第二卷）：美国的独立和初步繁荣 1775—1860》，北京：人民出版社，2002年。

Chapter 4

Open Door Policy

（门户开放）

Pre-reading questions

1. What was the motivation of the United States in formulating the Open Door Policy?
2. What was the impact of the Open Door Policy?

About the author

John Hay (1838—1905), American statesman and writer, Secretary of State during the expansion of United States international activity under Presidents William McKinley and Theodore Roosevelt, and an important biographer of President Abraham Lincoln.

John Hay was born on October 8, 1838, in Salem, Indiana, and educated at Brown University in Providence, Rhode Island. Hay joined his uncle's law office in Springfield, Illinois, in 1858. In 1861—1865, during the American Civil War, he was assistant to his friend John Nicolay, private secretary to Lincoln. During this period, he and Nicolay collected the material for the two monumental works on which they later collaborated: *Abraham Lincoln: A History* (10 volumes, 1890), a critical biography still highly regarded today; and *Abraham Lincoln: Collected Works* (2 volumes, 1894).

Hay held minor diplomatic posts in Europe in 1865—1870 and then, except for serving as Assistant Secretary of State in 1879—1880, devoted himself to writing until 1897. Besides serving on the editorial board of the *New York Tribune* he published sketches of his experiences in Spain, *Castilian Days* (1871), a collection of poems in Illinois frontier dialect, *Pike County Ballads* (1871), and the two Lincoln works. Hay was Ambassador to Britain in 1897—1898 and then served until his death as Secretary of State to McKinley and Roosevelt. As Secretary he directed peace negotiations after the Spanish-American War (1898), secured U.S. influence in the Pacific by annexing the Philippines, and in China initiated (1899) the Open Door Policy, which guaranteed equal trade opportunities for all countries.

In 1900, following the outbreak of the Boxer Uprising, Hay defined U.S. policy even more emphatically, declaring that the U.S. would uphold both the territorial and administrative integrity of China and the policy of free trade. In 1901 he negotiated the Hay-Pauncefote

Treaty, which opened the way for U.S. construction of the Panama Canal.

Hay died on July 1, 1905, in Newbury, New Hampshire.

 Text 1

The First Open Door Note①
John Hay, 1899

Germany

Mr. Hay to Mr. White②

Department of State, Washington, September 6, 1899.

1   Sir: At the time when the Government of the United States was informed by that of Germany that it had leased from His Majesty the Emperor of China the port of Kiao-chao③ and the adjacent territory in the province of Shantung, assurances were given to the ambassador of the United States at Berlin by the Imperial German minister for foreign affairs that the rights and privileges insured by treaties with China to citizens of the United States would not thereby suffer or be in anywise impaired within the area over which Germany had thus obtained control.

2   More recently, however, the British Government recognized by a formal agreement with Germany the exclusive right of the latter country to enjoy in said leased area and the contiguous "sphere of influence or interest" certain privileges, more especially those relating to railroads and mining enterprises; but, as the exact nature and extent of the rights thus recognized have not been clearly defined, it is possible that serious conflicts of interest may at any time arise, not only between British and German subjects within said area, but that the interests of our citizens may also be jeopardized thereby.

3   Earnestly desirous to remove any cause of irritation and to insure at the same time to the commerce of all nations in China the undoubted benefits which should accrue from a formal recognition by the various powers claiming "spheres of interest"④ that they shall enjoy perfect equality of treatment for their commerce and navigation within such "spheres," the Government of the United States would be pleased to see His German Majesty's Government

---

① Secretary of State John Hay first articulated the concept of "the Open Door" in China in a series of notes in 1899—1900. These Open Door Notes aimed to secure international agreement to the U.S. policy of promoting equal opportunity for international trade and commerce in China, and respect for China's administrative and territorial integrity. In response to concerns both in the United States and in Great Britain about the integrity of China, although this policy was not endorsed by other nations, their silence was taken by Hay as concurrence, and the policy became accepted doctrine in the U.S. if not elsewhere.

② Andrew D. White (1832—1918), the first U.S. Ambassador to Germany (1879—1881).

③ Kiao-chao: 胶州。

④ spheres of interest: 利益范围。

give formal assurances and lend its cooperation in securing like assurances from the other interested powers that each within its respective spheres of whatever influence.

4   First. Will in no way interfere with any treaty port or any vested interest within any so-called "sphere of interest" or leased territory it may have in China.

5   Second. That the Chinese treaty tariff of the time being shall apply to all merchandise landed or shipped to all such ports as are within said "sphere of interest" (unless they be "free ports"), no matter to what nationality it may belong, and that duties so leviable shall be collected by the Chinese Government.

6   Third. That it will levy no higher harbor dues on vessels of another nationality frequenting any port in such "sphere" than shall be levied on vessels of its own nationality, and no higher railroad charges over lines built, controlled, or operated within its "sphere" on merchandise belonging to citizens or subjects of other nationalities transported through such "sphere" than shall be levied on similar merchandise belonging to its own nationals transported over equal distances.

7   The liberal policy pursued by His Imperial German Majesty in declaring Kiao-chao a free port and in aiding the Chinese Government in the establishment there of a custom-house are so clearly in line with the proposition which this Government is anxious to see recognized that it entertains the strongest hope that Germany will give its acceptance and hearty support.

8   The recent ukase of His Majesty the Emperor of Russia declaring the port of Ta-lien-wan[①] open during the whole of the lease under which it is held from China, to the merchant ships of all nations, coupled with the categorical assurances made to this Government by His Imperial Majesty's representative at this capital at the time, and since repeated to me by the present Russian ambassador, seem to insure the support of the Emperor to the proposed measure. Our ambassador at the Court of St. Petersburg has, in consequence, been instructed to submit it to the Russian Government and to request their early consideration of it. A copy of my instruction on the subject to Mr. Tower[②] is herewith enclosed for your confidential information.

9   The commercial interests of Great Britain and Japan will be so clearly served by the desired declaration of intentions, and the views of the Governments of these countries as to the desirability of the adoption of measures insuring the benefits of equality of treatment of all foreign trade throughout China are so similar to those entertained by the United States, that their acceptance of the propositions herein outlined and their cooperation in advocating their adoption by the other powers can be confidently expected. I inclose herewith copy of the instruction which I have sent to Mr. Choate[③] on the subject.

---

① Ta-lien-wan: 大连湾。

② Charlemagne Tower, Jr. (1848—1923), American businessman, scholar, and diplomat. He served as Ambassador to Germany from 1902 to 1908 under President Theodore Roosevelt.

③ Joseph Hodges Choate (1832—1917), American lawyer and diplomat. He was appointed by President McKinley, U.S. Ambassador to the United Kingdom to succeed John Hay in 1899.

10 In view of the present favorable conditions, you are instructed to submit the above considerations to His Imperial German Majesty's minister for foreign affairs, and to request his early consideration of the subject.

11 Copy of this instruction is sent to our ambassadors at London and at St. Petersburg for their information.

I have, etc.,

John Hay

Vocabulary

adjacent (para. 1)	*adj.* close to, next to
anywise (para. 1)	*adv.* in any case
impair (para. 1)	*v.* to cause to diminish, as in strength, value, or quality; injure
contiguous (para. 2)	*adj.* connected in time; uninterrupted
subject (para. 2)	*n.* one who is under the rule of another or others, especially one who owes allegiance to a government or ruler
accrue (para. 3)	*v.* to increase, accumulate, or come about as a result of growth
like (para. 3)	*adj.* similar
vested (para. 4)	*adj.* settled, fixed, or absolute; being without contingency
ukase (para. 8)	*n.* an authoritative order or decree; an edict
categorical (para. 8)	*adj.* being without exception or qualification; absolute

Questions for discussion

1. What were the internal and external factors that made the United States declare the Open Door Note in September 1899?
2. Why did the United States prefer economic gains to actual territorial domination?
3. Do you agree that the Note was nothing but a statement of the United States' China policy? Why?
4. Do you agree that the Open Door Policy was a strange mixture of American anti-colonialism and economic imperialism? Why?

About the author

Joseph H. Choate (1832—1917), an American lawyer and diplomat, was born in Salem, Massachusetts, and educated at Harvard University. Among the many legal cases in his long career were the Tweed Ring prosecution, the Bering Sea controversy over fur seal rookeries, and income tax disputes in which he persuaded the U.S. Supreme Court that the income tax of 1894 was unconstitutional. From 1899 to 1905, as Ambassador to Britain, Choate worked to annul the Clayton-Bulwer Treaty, thus facilitating construction of the Panama Canal. He also helped secure Britain's agreement to the Open Door Policy toward China. In 1907 he headed the U.S. delegation to the Second International Peace Conference.

Joseph H. Choate

Lord Salisbury

Lord Salisbury (full name was Robert Arthur Talbot Gascoyne-Cecil, 1830—1903), British statesman, noted for his achievements in foreign affairs, especially for the expansion of British power in Africa. Born at Hatfield, his family estate in Hertfordshire, on February 3, 1830, Robert Arthur Talbot Gascoyne-Cecil, 3rd Marquess of Salisbury, was educated at the University of Oxford. He entered the House of Commons as a Conservative in 1853 and soon became noted as a foreign policy expert. He was Secretary of State for India in 1866—1867 and became Marquess of Salisbury when his father died in 1868. He was Indian Secretary again from 1874 to 1878. As Foreign Secretary (1878—1880) under Benjamin Disraeli, he prevented Russia from achieving hegemony over Ottoman Turkey and acquired Cyprus for Britain. Salisbury became Prime Minister in 1885 and — except for a brief period in 1886 — held that post until 1892, becoming his own foreign secretary in 1887. In domestic affairs his ministry was responsible for the Local Government Act of 1888 and for the establishment of free public education (1891). In 1889 he secured British possession of what later became the colonies of Northern and Southern Rhodesia (now Zambia and Zimbabwe), and the following year he negotiated an agreement with Germany that divided East Africa into British and German spheres of influence. Returning to office as Prime Minister and Foreign Secretary in 1895, he won French agreement to Anglo-Egyptian control of the Sudan in 1899 and in the same year involved his country in the Boer War, which led to British control over all of South Africa. Just before leaving office in 1902 he concluded the Anglo-Japanese Alliance, which remained in effect until after World War I. Salisbury died at Hatfield on August 22, 1903.

Text 2

Communications Between Mr. Choate and Lord Salisbury
Joseph H. Choate & Lord Salisbury, 1899

A.

Mr. Choate to Lord Salisbury
Embassy of the United States
London, September 22, 1899

1 MY LORD: I am instructed by the Secretary of State to present to your lordship a matter which the President regards as of great and equal importance to Great Britain and the United States — in the maintenance of trade and commerce in the East, in which the interest of the two nations differs, not in character, but in degree only[①] — and to ask for action on the part of Her Majesty's Government which the President conceives to be in exact accord with its uniformly declared policy and traditions, and which will greatly promote the welfare of commerce.

2 He understands it to be the settled policy and purpose of Great Britain not to use any privileges which may be granted to it in China as a means of excluding any commercial rivals, and that freedom of trade for it in that Empire means freedom of trade for all the world alike. Her Majesty's Government, while conceding by formal agreements with Germany and Russia the possession of "spheres of influence or interest" in China, in which they are to enjoy especial rights and privileges, particularly in respect to railroads and mining enterprises, has at the same time sought to maintain what is commonly called the "open-door" policy, to secure to the commerce and navigation of all nations equality of treatment within such "spheres." The maintenance of this policy is alike urgently demanded by the commercial communities of our two nations, as it is justly held by them to be the only one which will improve existing conditions, enable them to maintain their positions in the markets of China, and extend their future operations.

3 While the Government of the United States will in no way commit itself to any recognition of the exclusive rights of any power within or control over any portion of the Chinese Empire, under such agreements as have been recently made, it cannot conceal its apprehensions that there is danger of complications arising between the treaty powers which may imperil the rights insured to the United States by its treaties with China.

4 It is the sincere desire of my Government that the interests of its citizens may not be prejudiced through exclusive treatment by any of the controlling powers within their respective "spheres of interests" in China, and it hopes to retain there an open market for all the world's commerce, remove dangerous sources of international irritation, and thereby

---

① 这里充分说明，美、英两国利益一致，只是利益大小不同而已。

hasten united action of the powers at Peking to promote administrative reforms so greatly needed for strengthening the Imperial Government and maintaining the integrity of China, in which it believes the whole Western world is alike concerned. It believes that such a result may be greatly aided and advanced by declarations by the various powers claiming "spheres of interest" in China as to their intentions in regard to the treatment of foreign trade and commerce therein, and that the present is a very favorable moment for informing Her Majesty's Government of the desire of the United States to have it make on its own part and to lend its powerful support in the effort to obtain from each of the various powers claiming "spheres of interest" in China a declaration substantially to the following effect:

(1) That it will in no wise① interfere with any treaty port or any vested interest within any so-called "sphere of interest" or leased territory it may have in China.

(2) That the Chinese treaty tariff of the time being shall apply to all merchandise landed or shipped to all such ports as are within such "spheres of interest" (unless they be "free ports"), no matter to what nationality it may belong, and that duties so leviable shall be collected by the Chinese Government.

(3) That it will levy no higher harbor dues on vessels of another nationality frequenting any port in such "sphere" than shall be levied on vessels of its own nationality, and no higher railroad charges over lines built, controlled, or operated within its "sphere" on merchandise belonging to citizens or subjects of other nationalities transported through such "sphere" than shall be levied on similar merchandise belonging to its own nationals transported over equal distances.

5   The President has strong reason to believe that the Governments of both Russia and Germany will cooperate in such an understanding as is here proposed. The recent ukase of His Majesty the Emperor of Russia declaring the port of Ta-lien-wan open to the merchant ships of all nations during the whole term of the lease under which it is to beheld by Russia removes all uncertainty as to the liberal and conciliatory policy of that power, and justifies the expectation that His Majesty would accede to the similar request of the United States now being presented to him and make the desired declaration.

6   The recent action of Germany in declaring the port of Kiao-chao a "Freeport" and the aid which its Government has given China in establishing there a Chinese custom-house, coupled with oral assurances given the United States by Germany that the interests of the United States and its citizens within its "sphere" would in no wise be affected by its occupation of this portion of the province of Shantung, encourage the belief that little opposition is to be anticipated to the President's request for a similar declaration from that power.

7   It is needless also to add that Japan, the power next most largely interested in the trade of China, must be in entire sympathy with the views here expressed, and that its interests will be largely served by the proposed arrangement; and the declarations of its statesmen within the last year are so entirely in line with it that the cooperation of that power is confidently relied

---

① in no wise: 绝不，根本不会。

upon.

8 It is therefore with the greatest pleasure that I present this matter to your lordship's attention and urge its prompt consideration by Her Majesty's Government, believing that the action is in entire harmony with its consistent theory and purpose, and that it will greatly redound to the benefit and advantage of all commercial nations alike. The prompt and sympathetic cooperation of Her Majesty's Government with the United States in this important matter will be very potent in promoting its adoption by all the powers concerned.

I have, etc.,

Joseph H. Choate

B.

Lord Salisbury to Mr. Choate
Foreign Office
London, September 29, 1899.

1 YOUR EXCELLENCY: I have read with great interest the communication which you handed me on the 23rd instant, in which you inform me of the desire of the United States Government to obtain from the various powers claiming spheres of interest in China declarations as to their intentions in regard to the treatment of foreign trade and commerce therein.

2 I have the honor to inform your excellency that I will lose no time in consulting my colleagues in regard to a declaration by Her Majesty's Government and on the proposal that they should cooperate with the Government of the United States in obtaining similar declarations by the other powers concerned.

3 In the meantime, I may assure your excellency that the policy consistently advocated by this country is one of securing equal opportunity for the subjects and citizens of all nations in regard to commercial enterprise in China, and from this policy Her Majesty's Government have no intention or desire to depart.

I have, etc.,

Salisbury

Vocabulary

apprehension (para. 3, A) *n.* fearful or uneasy anticipation of the future
complication (para. 3, A) *n.* a factor, a condition, or an element that complicates
leviable (para. 4, A)   *adj.* liable to be taxed
redound (para. 8, A)   *v.* to return

Questions for discussion

1. Do you think Mr. Choate satisfactorily stated in his letter to Lord Salisbury John Hay's Open Door policy? Why?
2. How did Mr. Choate try to convince Lord Salisbury that both Russia and Germany would cooperate in the understanding of the Open Door policy?
3. What was the British government's response to Mr. Choate suggestion?

Text 3

The Second Open Door Note
John Hay, 1900

Department of State, Washington
July 3, 1900

1 In this critical posture of affairs in China it is deemed appropriate to define the attitude of the United States as far as present circumstances permit this to be done. We adhere to the policy initiated by us in 1857, of peace with the Chinese nation, of furtherance of lawful commerce, and of protection of lives and property of our citizens by all means guaranteed under extraterritorial treaty rights and by the law of nations. If wrong be done to our citizens we propose to hold the responsible authors to the uttermost accountability. We regard the condition at Peking as one of virtual anarchy, whereby power and responsibility are practically devolved upon the local provincial authorities. So long as they are not in overt collusion with rebellion and use their power to protect foreign life and property we regard them as representing the Chinese people, with whom we seek to remain in peace and friendship. The purpose of the President is, as it has been heretofore, to act concurrently with the other powers, first, in opening up communication with Peking and rescuing the American officials, missionaries, and other Americans who are in danger; secondly, in affording all possible protection everywhere in China to American life and property; thirdly, in guarding and protecting all legitimate American interests; and fourthly, in aiding to prevent a spread of the disorders to the other provinces of the Empire and a recurrence of such disasters. It is, of course, too early to forecast the means of attaining this last result; but the policy of the government of the United States is to seek a solution which may bring about permanent safety and peace to China, preserve Chinese territorial and administrative entity, protect all rights guaranteed to friendly powers by treaty and international law, and safeguard for the world the principle of equal and impartial trade with all parts of the Chinese Empire.

2 You will communicate the purport of this instruction to the minister for foreign affairs.

Hay

Vocabulary

posture (para.1)   *n.* a stance or disposition with regard to something
concurrently (para. 1)   *adv.* happening at the same time as something else
purport (para. 2)   *n.* intention; purpose

Questions for discussion

1. Why did John Hay decide to circulate another message to foreign powers involved in China?
2. Do you agree that internal affairs in China threatened the Open Door policy? Why?
3. What do you know about the anti-foreign movement known as the Boxer Rebellion then in China?
4. Why did John Hay at that time note the importance of respecting the principles of territorial and administrative integrity? Do you agree that his goal was to prevent the powers from using the Boxer Rebellion as an excuse to carve China into their own colonies? Why?

Background

Open Door policy is the statement of principles initiated by the United States (1899, 1900) for the protection of equal privileges among countries trading with China and in support of Chinese territorial and administrative integrity. The statement was issued in the form of circular notes dispatched by U.S. Secretary of State John Hay to Great Britain, Germany, France, Italy, Japan, and Russia. The Open Door policy was received with almost universal approval in the United States, and for more than 40 years it was a cornerstone of American foreign policy.

The principle that all nations should have equal access to any of the ports open to trade in China had been stipulated in the Anglo-Chinese treaties of Nanjing (Nanking, 1842) and Wangxia (Wangxia, 1844). Great Britain had greater interests in China than any other power and successfully maintained the policy of the open door until the late 19th century. After the first Sino-Japanese War (1894—1895), however, a scramble for "spheres of influence" in various parts of coastal China — primarily by Russia, France, Germany, and Great Britain — began. Within each of these spheres the controlling major power claimed exclusive privileges of investment, and it was feared that each would likewise seek to monopolize the trade. Moreover, it was generally feared that the breakup of China into economic segments dominated by various great powers would lead to complete subjection and the division of the country into colonies.

Chapter 4 Open Door Policy（门户开放）

The crisis in China coincided with several major developments in the United States. A new interest in foreign markets had emerged there following the economic depression of the 1890s. The United States also had just gained the Philippines, Guam, and Hawaii as a result of the Spanish-American War and was becoming increasingly interested in China, where American textile manufacturers had found markets for cheap cotton goods.

The 1899 Open Door notes provided that (1) each great power should maintain free access to a treaty port or to any other vested interest within its sphere, (2) only the Chinese government should collect taxes on trade, and (3) no great power having a sphere should be granted exemptions from paying harbour dues or railroad charges. The replies from the various nations were evasive, but Hay interpreted them as acceptances.

In reaction to the presence of European armies in North China to suppress the Boxer Rebellion, Hay's second circular of 1900 stressed the importance of preserving China's territorial and administrative integrity. Hay did not ask for replies, but all the powers except Japan expressed agreement with those principles.

Japan violated the Open Door principle with its presentation of Twenty-one Demands to China (1915). The Nine-Power Treaty after the Washington Conference (1921—1922) reaffirmed the principle, however. The Manchurian crisis of 1931 and the war between China and Japan that broke out in 1937 led the United States to adopt a rigid stand in favor of the Open Door policy, including the cutting off of supplies to Japan. Japan's defeat in World War II (1945) and the the founding of People's Republic of China (1949), which ended all special privileges to foreigners, made the Open Door policy meaningless.

　　门户开放政策在美国历史上具有极为重要和特殊的地位，它是近代美国远东政策的重要组成部分，为美国资本主义的发展立下了汗马功劳。独立战争之后直到19世纪80年代，由于国力限制，美国对华政策主要是追随英国等列强，作为其侵华帮凶，以便在侵略分赃中确保自己的利益。

　　19世纪90年代，美国成为实力雄厚的地区性大国之后，以单方面声明的方式提出了极有远见的门户开放政策，这标志着美国对华政策开始走上自主独立的道路。从1899年到20世纪40年代，美国对门户开放政策尽管时冷时热，但始终没有放弃。因为它一直对美国利益有利，符合美国的战略需要。

　　1899年9月6日至12月9日，美国国务卿海约翰向列强提出第一次门户开放政策照会。次年7月3日，海约翰又向列强发出第二次门户开放政策照会。美国门户开放政策主要包含两方面的原则：经济方面，各侵略国一律"机会均等""利益均沾"；政治方面，宜保持被侵略国形式上的"完整"或"独立"，以免因别国的瓜分或独占而损害这一政策倡导国的利益。其中经济原则是门户开放政策的核心。海约翰两次门户开放政策照会的提出，标志着列强对华门户开放政策的最终形成。

　　起初，迫于实力不足及当时远东的均势，美国只求在列强的在华利益中"分取杯羹"。接着，为了便于其在华侵略扩张，美国抛出了门户开放政策。当然美国的目的是在华获得利益越多越好，最好是独占中国。随着形势的发展和美国实力的增强，美国以门户开放之名，行扩展其在华利益、图谋独霸中国之实。由于这一政策的欺骗性，出于自身利益考虑，美国国内及其他列强都予以承认、接受，使其很有生命力，直到中国第三次国内革命战争结束它才退出历史舞台。所以，从1899年到1949年，尽管国际形势纵横捭阖，复杂多变，但是即便在形势危机时刻美国也未曾以武力方式推行其门户开放政策。虽然美国因全局或其他利益考虑对这一政策表现出时冷时热的态度，但美国历届政府从未放弃在华推行这一政策，而且在门户开放政策的旗号下，得"利益均沾"之利，又不负侵犯中国主权领土完整之责，进而以"门户开放"排挤其他列强，扩展美国利益，企图独霸中国。这正是美国门户开放政策的实质所在。

因此，门户开放政策首先是一种帝国主义侵略政策。它的内容虽有发展演变，但都是从美国的切身利益及战略需要出发。几十年间，它使美国大获其利，使中国备受其害，是美国在远东扩张、同列强争夺控制中国的政策。当然，这一政策在历史上客观地起到过阻止俄国独占中国东北、抑制日本独占中国的作用。但这仅仅是美国维护其在中国及远东利益时所带来的"副产品"。如果联系到美国反对别国扩大其在华利益、反对别国独占中国恰恰是为了自己达到这样的目的，则美国门户开放政策对其他列强在华扩张的制衡作用也就不足称道了。

Further reading

Bickerton, Ian James, *Bankers, Businessmen, and the Open Door Policy, 1899—1911*, Ann Arbor, Mich.: UMI, 1975.

Campbell, Charles. S., *Special Business Interests and the Open Door Policy*, New Haven: Archon Books, 1951.

Dulles, Foster Rhea, *The Old China Trade,* Boston and New York: Houghton Mifflin Company, 1930.

Griswold, A.W., *The Far Eastern Policy of the United States*, New Haven: Yale University Press, 1962.

Koo, V. K. Wellington, *The Open Door Policy and World Peace*, London, New York, Toronto: Oxford University Press, 1939.

Moore, Gregory, *Defining and Defending the Open Door Policy: Theodore Roosevelt and China, 1901—1909*, Lanham, Maryland: Lexington Books, 2015.

Yen, En Tsung, *The Open Door Policy*, Boston, Mass., The Stratford Co.,1923.

阿伦·米利特、彼得·马斯洛斯金：《美国军事史》，军事科学院外国军事研究部译，北京：军事科学出版社，1989年。

B. 阿瓦林：《帝国主义在满洲》，北京对外贸易学院俄语教研室译，北京：商务印书馆，1980年。

保罗·S. 芮恩施：《一个美国外交官使华记》，李抱宏等译，游燮庭校，北京：商务印书馆，1982年。

邓蜀生：《伍德罗·威尔逊》，上海：上海人民出版社，1982年。

董小川：《关于美国对华门户开放政策的几个问题》，《美国研究》1998年第4期。
费正清：《美国与中国》（第四版），北京：世界知识出版社，1999年。
福森科：《瓜分中国的斗争和美国的门户开放政策（1895—1900）》，杨诗浩译，北京：读书·生活·新知三联书店，1958年。
洪育沂：《1931—1939年国际关系简史》，北京：读书·生活·新知三联书店，1980年。
黄安年：《二十世纪美国史》，石家庄：河北人民出版社，1989年。
加尔文·D.林顿编著：《美国两百年大事记》，谢延光等译，上海：上海译文出版社，1984年。
贾士毅：《华会见闻录》，台北：文海出版社，1975年影印版。
蒋相泽、吴机鹏主编：《简明中美关系史》，广州：中山大学出版社，1989年。
金卫星：《从"门户开放"到世界贸易组织：20世纪美国全球扩张战略的历史轨迹》，苏州：苏州大学出版社，2001年。
王雁：《"山东问题"与美国的门户开放政策（1914—1922）》，济南：山东人民出版社，2016年。

Chapter 5

Wilsonism

(威尔逊主义)

Pre-reading questions

1. What influenced Wilson in his foreign policy making and what was the essence of Wilsonism?
2. What do you think might be the relationship between the American foreign policy tradition and Wilsonism?

About the author

Thomas Woodrow Wilson (1856—1924), 28th President of the United States, led the country into World War I and was a primary architect of the League of Nations. Wilson attended Davison University in North Carolina for a brief time but graduated from Princeton in 1879. In his senior year he published an important essay in the *International Review*, revealing his early interest in American government. He pursued graduate studies at Johns Hopkins University, receiving his doctorate in 1886. In his doctoral thesis Wilson analyzed the American political system, pointing to the fracturing of power that flowed from the committee system in Congress.

From 1886 to 1910 Wilson was in academic life — as a professor of political science at Bryn Mawr, Wesleyan, and Princeton and, after 1902, president of Princeton. In 1910, the Democratic Party in New Jersey offered him the nomination for governor. He was elected by a large plurality. As governor, Wilson demonstrated masterly leadership, pushing through the legislature a direct primary law, a corrupt-practices act, an employers' liability act, and a law regulating the public utilities. His success made him a prominent candidate for the presidency in 1912. Once elected, Wilson proceeded to put into practice his theory of presidential leadership.

In August 1914 World War I broke out in Europe. The basis of Wilson's policy was the preservation of neutrality. But there can be little doubt that in his heart he sympathized with France and Great Britain and feared the victory of imperial Germany. The warring powers soon began interfering with American trade. The British more and more restricted American commerce, but the Germans proclaimed a new kind of warfare, submarine warfare, with the prospect of American ships being sunk and their passengers and crew being lost. For a time thereafter Wilson took no action. But on May 7, 1915, the liner Lusitania was sunk, with over a hundred American lives lost. The President addressed a stiff note to Germany but clung to the hope that the war might be ended by the good offices of the United States. He engaged in a debate with Berlin and, after other painful submarine episodes, got Germany to abandon the U-boat war in 1916.

In the meantime the presidential campaign of 1916 was approaching. He was re-nominated virtually by acclamation; the Democratic platform praised him for keeping the country out of war. He won in a very close campaign. Though the Democratic politicians made the most of the slogan "He kept us out of war," Wilson promised nothing for the future.

When the German government cast the die for unlimited warfare on the sea, Wilson severed diplomatic relations with Berlin but continued to hope that a direct challenge could be avoided. No president has ever taken more seriously the immense responsibility of leading the American people into war. But on April 2, 1917, Wilson demanded a declaration of war against Germany from Congress, and Congress responded by overwhelming majorities.

Wilson was a great war president. He appealed to American idealism in a striking way. Though he believed that the defeat of Germany was necessary, he held out hope that at the end of the war a League of Nations might be established which would make impossible the recurrence of another bloody struggle. Throughout the war Wilson insisted on two things: the defeat of German militarism and the establishment of peace resting on just principles. In January 1918 he gave his speech of the Fourteen Points. In the negotiations that autumn he made the acceptance of these points the primary condition on the part of his European associates and of the Germans as well. Wilson was at the apogee of his career in November 1918, when the armistice was signed. No American president had ever attained so high a position in world esteem, and millions looked to him as the prophet of a new order.

But difficulties loomed. The 1918 elections returned a Republican majority to Congress. Though he selected able men for his delegation to the forthcoming peace conference at Paris, he did not think of conciliating the Republican opposition. By insisting on going to Paris in person and remaining there until the treaty was finished, he cut himself off from American opinion.

At the peace conference Wilson strove to realize his ideals. But the Treaty of Versailles was not to stand the test of time. In detaching substantial territories from Germany and in fixing Germany with responsibility for the war, it furnished the basis for that German nationalism which was to come to full flower with Adolf Hitler.

Wilson returned to the United States with a political battle ahead. There was much partisanship in the opposition to him but also a genuine dislike of the Treaty of Versailles and honest opposition to "entanglement" in world politics. The Senate in November rejected unconditional ratification but adopted the treaty with reservations which the President refused to accept. The 1920 presidential campaign resulted in an overwhelming Republican victory and the election of Warren G. Harding as president. The new chief executive never sought to bring the Treaty of Versailles to the Senate or to bring the United States into the League, which was by now actually in existence.

Despite his failure to secure American adherence to the League, the long-run judgment on the President must be that Wilson was one of the few great presidents of the United States. His idealism and his vision receive their due praise from posterity. Wilson was twice married. His first wife bore him three daughters. She died in the White House shortly after the outbreak of World War I. In 1916 he married Edith Bolling Galt, who survived him by many years. He died on Feb. 3, 1924.

 Text 1

The World Must Be Made Safe for Democracy
Thomas Woodrow Wilson, April 2, 1917

Gentlemen of the Congress:

1   I have called the Congress into extraordinary session because there are serious, very serious, choices of policy to be made, and made immediately, which it was neither right nor constitutionally permissible that I should assume the responsibility of making.①

2   On the 3rd of February last I officially laid before you the extraordinary announcement of the Imperial German Government that on and after the 1st day of February it was its purpose to put aside all restraints of law or of humanity and use its submarines to sink every vessel that sought to approach either the ports of Great Britain and Ireland or the western coasts of Europe or any of the ports controlled by the enemies of Germany within the Mediterranean. That had seemed to be the object of the German submarine warfare② earlier in the war, but since April of last year the Imperial Government had somewhat restrained the commanders of its undersea craft③ in conformity with its promise then given to us that passenger boats④ should not be sunk and that due warning would be given to all other vessels which its submarines might seek to destroy, when no resistance was offered or escape attempted, and care taken that their crews were given at least a fair chance to save their lives in their open boats. The precautions taken were meagre and haphazard enough, as was proved in distressing

---

① 威尔逊总统意指他没有宣战权，国会才是政策的制定者。作为总统，他的责任是告知国会实际情况，由国会做决定。
② 德国在第一次世界大战中实行的潜艇战。
③ 这里指潜艇。
④ 普通客轮。

instance after instance in the progress of the cruel and unmanly business, but a certain degree of restraint was observed. The new policy has swept every restriction aside. Vessels of every kind, whatever their flag, their character, their cargo, their destination, their errand, have been ruthlessly sent to the bottom without warning and without thought of help or mercy for those on board, the vessels of friendly neutrals along with those of belligerents. Even hospital ships and ships carrying relief to the sorely bereaved and stricken people of Belgium, though the latter were provided with safe-conduct through the proscribed areas by the German Government itself and were distinguished by unmistakable marks of identity, have been sunk with the same reckless lack of compassion or of principle.

3   I was for a little while unable to believe that such things would in fact be done by any government that had hitherto subscribed to the humane practices of civilized nations. International law had its origin in the attempt to set up some law which would be respected and observed upon the seas, where no nation had right of dominion and where lay the free highways of the world. By painful stage after stage has that law been built up, with meagre enough results, indeed, after all was accomplished that could be accomplished, but always with a clear view, at least, of what the heart and conscience of mankind demanded. This minimum of right the German Government has swept aside under the plea of retaliation and necessity and because it had no weapons which it could use at sea except these which it is impossible to employ as it is employing them without throwing to the winds all scruples of humanity or of respect for the understandings that were supposed to underlie the intercourse of the world. I am not now thinking of the loss of property involved, immense and serious as that is, but only of the wanton and wholesale destruction of the lives of noncombatants, men, women, and children, engaged in pursuits which have always, even in the darkest periods of modern history, been deemed innocent and legitimate. Property can be paid for; the lives of peaceful and innocent people cannot be. The present German submarine warfare against commerce is a warfare against mankind.

4   It is a war against all nations. American ships have been sunk, American lives taken, in ways which it has stirred us very deeply to learn of, but the ships and people of other neutral and friendly nations have been sunk and overwhelmed in the waters in the same way. There has been no discrimination. The challenge is to all mankind. Each nation must decide for itself how it will meet it. The choice we make for ourselves must be made with a moderation of counsel and a temperateness of judgment befitting our character and our motives as a nation. We must put excited feeling away.① Our motive will not be revenge or the victorious assertion of the physical might of the nation, but only the vindication of right, of human right, of which we are only a single champion.②

5   When I addressed the Congress on the 26th of February last, I thought that it would suffice to assert our neutral rights with arms, our right to use the seas against unlawful

---

① 即便事态紧急，威尔逊还是强调必须冷静应对并决策，宣战对于他和美国来说，是无比巨大的决定。
② 虽是宣战，但是这篇演讲处处折射出威尔逊的道义原则，理想主义色彩浓厚。

interference, our right to keep our people safe against unlawful violence. But armed neutrality, it now appears, is impracticable. Because submarines are in effect outlaws when used as the German submarines have been used against merchant shipping, it is impossible to defend ships against their attacks as the law of nations has assumed that merchantmen would defend themselves against privateers or cruisers, visible craft giving chase upon the open sea. It is common prudence in such circumstances, grim necessity indeed, to endeavour to destroy them before they have shown their own intention. They must be dealt with upon sight, if dealt with at all. The German Government denies the right of neutrals to use arms at all within the areas of the sea which it has proscribed, even in the defense of rights which no modern publicist has ever before questioned their right to defend. The intimation is conveyed that the armed guards which we have placed on our merchant ships will be treated as beyond the pale of law and subject to be dealt with as pirates would be. Armed neutrality is ineffectual enough at best; in such circumstances and in the face of such pretensions it is worse than ineffectual; it is likely only to produce what it was meant to prevent; it is practically certain to draw us into the war without either the rights or the effectiveness of belligerents. There is one choice we cannot make, we are incapable of making: we will not choose the path of submission and suffer the most sacred rights of our nation and our people to be ignored or violated. The wrongs against which we now array ourselves are no common wrongs; they cut to the very roots of human life.

6 With a profound sense of the solemn and even tragical character of the step I am taking and of the grave responsibilities which it involves, but in unhesitating obedience to what I deem my constitutional duty, I advise that the Congress declare the recent course of the Imperial German Government to be in fact nothing less than war against the Government and people of the United States; that it formally accept the status of belligerent which has thus been thrust upon it, and that it take immediate steps not only to put the country in a more thorough state of defense but also to exert all its power and employ all its resources to bring the Government of the German Empire to terms and end the war.①

7 What this will involve is clear. It will involve the utmost practicable cooperation in counsel and action with the governments now at war with Germany, and, as incident to that, the extension to those governments of the most liberal financial credits, in order that our resources may so far as possible be added to theirs. It will involve the organization and mobilization of all the material resources of the country to supply the materials of war and serve the incidental needs of the nation in the most abundant and yet the most economical and efficient way possible. It will involve the immediate full equipment of the Navy in all respects but particularly in supplying it with the best means of dealing with the enemy's submarines. It will involve the immediate addition to the armed forces of the United States already provided for by law in case of war at least 500,000 men, who should, in my opinion, be chosen upon the principle of universal liability to service, and also the authorization of subsequent additional

---

① 这里可以看出威尔逊总统对战争准备的重视和对战争的看法。

increments of equal force so soon as they may be needed and can be handled in training. It will involve also, of course, the granting of adequate credits to the Government, sustained, I hope, so far as they can equitably be sustained by the present generation, by well conceived taxation....

8 While we do these things, these deeply momentous things, let us be very clear, and make very clear to all the world what our motives and our objects are. My own thought has not been driven from its habitual and normal course by the unhappy events of the last two months, and I do not believe that the thought of the nation has been altered or clouded by them I have exactly the same things in mind now that I had in mind when I addressed the Senate on the 22nd of January last; the same that I had in mind when I addressed the Congress on the 3rd of February and on the 26th of February. Our object now, as then, is to vindicate the principles of peace and justice in the life of the world as against selfish and autocratic power and to set up amongst the really free and self-governed peoples of the world such a concert of purpose and of action as will henceforth ensure the observance of those principles.① Neutrality is no longer feasible or desirable where the peace of the world is involved and the freedom of its peoples, and the menace to that peace and freedom lies in the existence of autocratic governments backed by organized force which is controlled wholly by their will, not by the will of their people.② We have seen the last of neutrality in such circumstances. We are at the beginning of an age in which it will be insisted that the same standards of conduct and of responsibility for wrong done shall be observed among nations and their governments that are observed among the individual citizens of civilized states.

9 We have no quarrel with the German people. We have no feeling towards them but one of sympathy and friendship. It was not upon their impulse that their Government acted in entering this war. It was not with their previous knowledge or approval. It was a war determined upon as wars used to be determined upon in the old, unhappy days when peoples were nowhere consulted by their rulers and wars were provoked and waged in the interest of dynasties or of little groups of ambitious men who were accustomed to use their fellow men as pawns and tools. Self-governed nations do not fill their neighbour states with spies or set the course of intrigue to bring about some critical posture of affairs which will give them an opportunity to strike and make conquest. Such designs can be successfully worked out only under cover and where no one has the right to ask questions. Cunningly contrived plans of deception or aggression, carried, it may be, from generation to generation, can be worked out and kept from the light only within the privacy of courts or behind the carefully guarded confidences of a narrow and privileged class. They are happily impossible where public opinion commands and insists upon full information concerning all the nation's affairs.

10 A steadfast concert for peace can never be maintained except by a partnership of

---

① 威尔逊总统提出了战争的目标。
② 华盛顿时代就遵循的中立政策不再适用，这个决定对于美国来说是巨大的，孤立主义的影响依旧。所以，威尔逊总统必须清晰地指出事态的严重性，表明自己的立场和态度。

democratic nations. No autocratic government could be trusted to keep faith within it or observe its covenants. It must be a league of honour, a partnership of opinion. Intrigue would eat its vitals away; the plottings of inner circles who could plan what they would and render account to no one would be a corruption seated at its very heart. Only free peoples can hold their purpose and their honour steady to a common end and prefer the interests of mankind to any narrow interest of their own.

11 Does not every American feel that assurance has been added to our hope for the future peace of the world by the wonderful and heartening things that have been happening within the last few weeks in Russia? Russia was known by those who knew it best to have been always in fact democratic at heart, in all the vital habits of her thought, in all the intimate relationships of her people that spoke their natural instinct, their habitual attitude towards life. The autocracy that crowned the summit of her political structure, long as it had stood and terrible as was the reality of its power, was not in fact Russian in origin, character, or purpose; and now it has been shaken off and the great, generous Russian people have been added in all their naive majesty and might to the forces that are fighting for freedom in the world, for justice, and for peace. Here is a fit partner for a league of honour.

12 One of the things that has served to convince us that the Prussian autocracy was not and could never be our friend is that from the very outset of the present war it has filled our unsuspecting communities and even our offices of government with spies and set criminal intrigues everywhere afoot against our national unity of counsel, our peace within and without our industries and our commerce. Indeed it is now evident that its spies were here even before the war began; and it is unhappily not a matter of conjecture but a fact proved in our courts of justice that the intrigues which have more than once come perilously near to disturbing the peace and dislocating the industries of the country have been carried on at the instigation, with the support, and even under the personal direction of official agents of the Imperial Government accredited to the Government of the United States. Even in checking these things and trying to extirpate them we have sought to put the most generous interpretation possible upon them because we knew that their source lay, not in any hostile feeling or purpose of the German people towards us (who were, no doubt, as ignorant of them as we ourselves were), but only in the selfish designs of a Government that did what it pleased and told its people nothing. But they have played their part in serving to convince us at last that that Government entertains no real friendship for us and means to act against our peace and security at its convenience. That it means to stir up enemies against us at our very doors the intercepted note to the German Minister at Mexico City is eloquent evidence.

13 We are accepting this challenge of hostile purpose because we know that in such a government, following such methods, we can never have a friend; and that in the presence of its organized power, always lying in wait to accomplish we know not what purpose, there can be no assured security for the democratic governments of the world. We are now about to accept gage of battle with this natural foe to liberty and shall, if necessary, spend the whole force of the nation to check and nullify its pretensions and its power. We are glad, now that we see the facts with no veil of false pretence about them, to fight thus for the ultimate peace of the world and for the liberation of its peoples, the German peoples included: for the rights of nations great and small and the privilege of men everywhere to choose their way of life and of obedience. The world must be made safe for democracy.① Its peace must be planted upon the tested foundations of political liberty. We have no selfish ends to serve. We desire no conquest, no dominion. We seek no indemnities for ourselves, no material compensation for the sacrifices we shall freely make. We are but one of the champions of the rights of mankind. We shall be satisfied when those rights have been made as secure as the faith and the freedom of nations can make them.

14 Just because we fight without rancour and without selfish object, seeking nothing for ourselves but what we shall wish to share with all free peoples, we shall, I feel confident, conduct our operations as belligerents without passion and ourselves observe with proud punctilio the principles of right and of fair play we profess to be fighting for.

15 I have said nothing of the governments allied with the Imperial Government of Germany because they have not made war upon us or challenged us to defend our right and our honour. The Austro-Hungarian Government has, indeed, avowed its unqualified endorsement and acceptance of the reckless and lawless submarine warfare adopted now without disguise by the Imperial German Government, and it has therefore not been possible for this Government to receive Count Tarnowski, the Ambassador recently accredited to this Government by the Imperial and Royal Government of Austria-Hungary; but that Government has not actually engaged in warfare against citizens of the United States on the seas, and I take the liberty, for the present at least, of postponing a discussion of our relations with the authorities at Vienna. We enter this war only where we are clearly forced into it because there are no other means of defending our rights.

16 It will be all the easier for us to conduct ourselves as belligerents in a high spirit of right and fairness because we act without animus, not in enmity towards a people or with the desire to bring any injury or disadvantage upon them, but only in armed opposition to an irresponsible government which has thrown aside all considerations of humanity and of right and is running amuck. We are, let me say again, the sincere friends of the German people, and shall desire nothing so much as the early reestablishment of intimate relations of mutual advantage between us — however hard it may be for them, for the time being, to believe that this is spoken from our hearts. We have borne with their present government through all these bitter months because of that friendship — exercising a patience and forbearance which would otherwise have been impossible. We shall, happily, still have an opportunity to prove that friendship in our daily attitude and actions towards the millions of men and women of German birth and native sympathy, who live amongst us and share our life, and we shall be proud to prove it towards all who are in fact loyal to their neighbours and to the Government

---

① "为了民主,世界必须和平。"这里既体现了威尔逊总统的理想主义外交色彩,也预示着美国希望在世界上发挥更大的作用。所以,这一外交政策也是现实主义的,展示了美国对未来的野心。

in the hour of test. They are, most of them, as true and loyal Americans as if they had never known any other fealty or allegiance. They will be prompt to stand with us in rebuking and restraining the few who may be of a different mind and purpose. If there should be disloyalty, it will be dealt with with a firm hand of stern repression; but, if it lifts its head at all, it will lift it only here and there and without countenance except from a lawless and malignant few.

17 It is a distressing and oppressive duty, gentlemen of the Congress, which I have performed in thus addressing you. There are, it may be, many months of fiery trial and sacrifice ahead of us.① It is a fearful thing to lead this great peaceful people into war, into the most terrible and disastrous of all wars, civilization itself seeming to be in the balance. But the right is more precious than peace, and we shall fight for the things which we have always carried nearest our hearts — for democracy, for the right of those who submit to authority to have a voice in their own governments, for the rights and liberties of small nations, for a universal dominion of right by such a concert of free peoples as shall bring peace and safety to all nations and make the world itself at last free. To such a task we can dedicate our lives and our fortunes, everything that we are and everything that we have, with the pride of those who know that the day has come when America is privileged to spend her blood and her might for the principles that gave her birth and happiness and the peace which she has treasured. God helping her, she can do no other.

Vocabulary

submarine (para. 2)	*n.* a ship, especially a military one, that can stay under water
due (para. 2)	*adj.* [only before noun] (*formal*) proper or suitable
meagre (para. 2)	*adj.* too small and much less than you need
haphazard (para. 2)	*adj.* happening or done in a way that is not planned or organized
errand (para. 2)	*n.* a short journey in order to do something for someone, for example delivering or collecting something for them
sorely (para. 2)	*adv.* very much or very seriously
bereaved (para. 2)	*adj.* having lost a close friend or relative because they have recently died
reckless (para. 2)	*adj.* not caring or worrying about the possible bad or dangerous results of your actions
hitherto (para. 3)	*adv.* (*formal*) up to this time
retaliation (para. 3)	*n.* action against someone who has done something bad to you
scruple (para. 3)	*n.* a belief about what is right and wrong that prevents you from doing bad things

---

① 威尔逊总统意识到战争既是残酷的，也经常是长期的，他希望美国人民做好准备，毕竟卷入欧洲的战争对于美国人来说，是一个无比巨大的决心。

wanton (para. 3)	adj. deliberately harming someone or damaging something for no reason
noncombatant (para. 3)	n. someone who is in the army, navy, etc. during a war but who does not actually fight, for example an army doctor
temperate (para. 4)	adj. (formal) not extreme in behavior; calm and sensible
vindication (para. 4)	n. to prove that someone or something is right or true [= justify]
privateer (para. 5)	n. an armed ship in the past that was not in the navy but attacked and robbed enemy ships carrying goods
endeavour (para. 5)	v. (formal) to try very hard
pirate (para. 5)	n. someone who sails on the seas, attacking other boats and stealing things from them
array (para. 5)	v. to put soldiers in position ready to fight
increment (para. 7)	n. the amount by which a number, value, or amount increases
autocrat (para. 8)	n. someone who makes decisions and gives orders to people without asking them for their opinion
menace (para. 8)	n. something or someone that is dangerous [= threat]
intrigue (para. 9)	n. the making of secret plans to harm someone or make them lose their position of power, or a plan of this kind
contrived (para. 9)	adj. seeming false and not natural
covenant (para. 10)	n. a legal agreement in which someone promises to pay a person or organization an amount of money regularly
conjecture (para. 12)	n. an opinion or idea that is not based on definite knowledge and is formed by guessing
perilously (para. 12)	adv. in a way that is dangerous and likely to result in something bad soon [= dangerously]
at the instigation (para. 12)	(formal) because of someone's suggestion, request, or demand
nullify (para. 13)	v. (formal) to make something lose its effect or value
indemnity (para. 13)	n. protection against loss or damage, especially in the form of a promise to pay for any losses or damage
rancour (para. 14)	n. (formal) a feeling of hatred and anger towards someone you cannot forgive because they harmed you in the past
avow (para. 15)	v. (formal) to make a public statement about something you believe in
animus (para. 16)	n. (formal) a feeling of strong dislike or hatred [= animosity, hostility]
fealty (para. 16)	n. old-fashioned loyalty to a king, queen, etc.
countenance (para. 16)	n. (literary) your face or your expression
malignant (para. 16)	adj. (formal) showing that you hate someone

Questions for discussion

1. How much do you know about the German submarine warfare in the war?
2. Why did Wilson make the decision to enter into World War I?
3. Did Wilson go too far away from the tradition of American foreign policy since the founding of the nation?
4. What was the real purpose or target of Wilson's foreign policy?
5. What were the essential features of Wilson's idealism?
6. What might be the origin of idealism in American foreign policy?

 Text 2

Fourteen Points
Thomas Woodrow Wilson, January 8, 1918

Gentlemen of the Congress:

1 Once more, as repeatedly before, the spokesmen of the Central Empires① have indicated their desire to discuss the objects of the war and the possible basis of a general peace. Parleys have been in progress at Brest-Litovsk② between Russian representatives and representatives of the Central Powers to which the attention of all the belligerents have been invited for the purpose of ascertaining whether it may be possible to extend these parleys into a general conference with regard to terms of peace and settlement.

2 The Russian representatives presented not only a perfectly definite statement of the principles upon which they would be willing to conclude peace but also an equally definite program of the concrete application of those principles. The representatives of the Central Powers, on their part, presented an outline of settlement which, if much less definite, seemed susceptible of liberal interpretation until their specific program of practical terms was added. That program proposed no concessions at all either to the sovereignty of Russia or to the preferences of the populations with whose fortunes it dealt, but meant, in a word, that the Central Empires were to keep every foot of territory their armed forces had occupied — every province, every city, every point of vantage — as a permanent addition to their territories and their power.

3 It is a reasonable conjecture that the general principles of settlement which they at first suggested originated with the more liberal statesmen of Germany and Austria, the men who

---

① Central Empires: name of military alliance of Germany and Austro-Hungarian Monarchy in World War I.
② Treaty of Brest-Litovsk:《布列斯特—立陶夫斯克条约》。It was a peace treaty signed on March 3, 1918, at Brest-Litovsk (now Brest, Belarus) between the Russian SFSR (Soviet Federative Socialist Republic) and the Central Powers, marking Russia's exit from World War I.

have begun to feel the force of their own people's thought and purpose, while the concrete terms of actual settlement came from the military leaders who have no thought but to keep what they have got. The negotiations have been broken off. The Russian representatives were sincere and in earnest. They cannot entertain① such proposals of conquest and domination.

4   The whole incident is full of significances. It is also full of perplexity. With whom are the Russian representatives dealing? For whom are the representatives of the Central Empires speaking? Are they speaking for the majorities of their respective parliaments or for the minority parties, that military and imperialistic minority which has so far dominated their whole policy and controlled the affairs of Turkey and of the Balkan states which have felt obliged to become their associates in this war?

5   The Russian representatives have insisted, very justly, very wisely, and in the true spirit of modern democracy, that the conferences they have been holding with the Teutonic and Turkish statesmen should be held within open, not closed, doors, and all the world has been audience, as was desired. To whom have we been listening, then? To those who speak the spirit and intention of the resolutions of the German Reichstag② of the 9th of July last, the spirit and intention of the Liberal leaders and parties of Germany, or to those who resist and defy that spirit and intention and insist upon conquest and subjugation? Or are we listening, in fact, to both, unreconciled and in open and hopeless contradiction? These are very serious and pregnant questions. Upon the answer to them depends the peace of the world.

6   But, whatever the results of the parleys at Brest-Litovsk, whatever the confusions of counsel and of purpose in the utterances of the spokesmen of the Central Empires, they have again attempted to acquaint the world with their objects in the war and have again challenged their adversaries to say what their objects are and what sort of settlement they would deem just and satisfactory. There is no good reason why that challenge should not be responded to, and responded to with the utmost candor. We did not wait for it. Not once, but again and again, we have laid our whole thought and purpose before the world, not in general terms only, but each time with sufficient definition to make it clear what sort of definite terms of settlement must necessarily spring out of them. Within the last week Mr. Lloyd George has spoken with admirable candor and in admirable spirit for the people and Government of Great Britain.

7   There is no confusion of counsel among the adversaries of the Central Powers, no uncertainty of principle, no vagueness of detail. The only secrecy of counsel, the only lack of fearless frankness, the only failure to make definite statement of the objects of the war, lies with Germany and her allies. The issues of life and death hang upon these definitions. No statesman who has the least conception of his responsibility ought for a moment to permit himself to continue this tragic and appalling outpouring of blood and treasure unless he is sure

---

① entertain: here it means admit or accept.
② Reichstag: 帝国议会。The Reichstag (German for "Imperial Diet") was the parliament of the Holy Roman Empire, the North German Confederation, and of Germany until 1945. The main chamber of the German parliament is now called Bundestag ("Federal Diet"), but the building in which it meets is still called "Reichstag."

beyond a peradventure that the objects of the vital sacrifice are part and parcel of the very life of Society and that the people for whom he speaks think them right and imperative as he does.

8   There is, moreover, a voice calling for these definitions of principle and of purpose which is, it seems to me, more thrilling and more compelling than any of the many moving voices with which the troubled air of the world is filled. It is the voice of the Russian people. They are prostrate and all but hopeless, it would seem, before the grim power of Germany, which has hitherto known no relenting and no pity. Their power, apparently, is shattered. And yet their soul is not subservient. They will not yield either in principle or in action. Their conception of what is right, of what is humane and honorable for them to accept, has been stated with a frankness, a largeness of view, a generosity of spirit, and a universal human sympathy which must challenge the admiration of every friend of mankind; and they have refused to compound their ideals or desert others that they themselves may be safe.

9   They call to us to say what it is that we desire, in what, if in anything, our purpose and our spirit differ from theirs; and I believe that the people of the United States would wish me to respond, with utter simplicity and frankness. Whether their present leaders believe it or not, it is our heartfelt desire and hope that some way may be opened whereby we may be privileged to assist the people of Russia to attain their utmost hope of liberty and ordered peace.

10   It will be our wish and purpose that the processes of peace, when they are begun, shall be absolutely open and that they shall involve and permit henceforth no secret understandings of any kind. The day of conquest and aggrandizement is gone by; so is also the day of secret covenants entered into in the interest of particular governments and likely at some unlooked-for moment to upset the peace of the world. It is this happy fact, now clear to the view of every public man whose thoughts do not still linger in an age that is dead and gone, which makes it possible for every nation whose purposes are consistent with justice and the peace of the world to avow now or at any other time the objects it has in view[①].

11   We entered this war because violations of right had occurred which touched us to the quick[②] and made the life of our own people impossible unless they were corrected and the world secure once for all against their recurrence. What we demand in this war, therefore, is nothing peculiar to ourselves. It is that the world be made fit and safe to live in; and particularly that it be made safe for every peace-loving nation which, like our own, wishes to live its own life, determine its own institutions, be assured of justice and fair dealing by the other peoples of the world as against force and selfish aggression. All the peoples of the world are in effect partners in this interest, and for our own part we see very clearly that unless justice be done to others it will not be done to us. The program of the world's peace, therefore, is our program; and that program, the only possible program, as we see it, is this:

---

① "目前，公众的思维并不仅仅停留在一个已经消亡逝去的时代，他们对于以上这一可喜的事实了然于心。于是，每一个坚持以维护正义和世界和平为宗旨的国家，今后便可以在任何时候把它的目标，公开地陈述出来。"

② to the quick: 触及要害或痛处。

I Open covenants of peace, openly arrived at, after which there shall be no private international understandings of any kind but diplomacy shall proceed always frankly and in the public view.

II Absolute freedom of navigation upon the seas, outside territorial waters, alike in peace and in war, except as the seas may be closed in whole or in part by international action for the enforcement of international covenants.

III The removal, so far as possible, of all economic barriers and the establishment of an equality of trade conditions among all the nations consenting to the peace and associating themselves for its maintenance.

IV Adequate guarantees given and taken that national armaments will be reduced to the lowest point consistent with domestic safety.

V A free, open-minded, and absolutely impartial adjustment of all colonial claims, based upon a strict observance of the principle that in determining all such questions of sovereignty the interests of the populations concerned must have equal weight with the equitable claims of the government whose title is to be determined①.

VI The evacuation of all Russian territory and such a settlement of all questions affecting Russia as will secure the best and freest cooperation of the other nations of the world in obtaining for her an unhampered and unembarrassed opportunity for the independent determination of her own political development and national policy and assure her of a sincere welcome into the society of free nations under institutions of her own choosing②; and, more than a welcome, assistance also of every kind that she may need and may herself desire. The treatment accorded Russia by her sister nations in the months to come will be the acid test of their good will, of their comprehension of her needs as distinguished from their own interests, and of their intelligent and unselfish sympathy.

VII Belgium, the whole world will agree, must be evacuated and restored, without any attempt to limit the sovereignty which she enjoys in common with all other free nations. No other single act will serve as this will serve to restore confidence among the nations in the laws which they have themselves set and determined for the government of their relations with one another. Without this healing act the whole structure and validity of international law is forever impaired.

VIII All French territory should be freed and the invaded portions restored, and the wrong done to France by Prussia in 1871 in the matter of Alsace-Lorraine③, which has unsettled the peace of the world for nearly fifty years, should be righted, in order that peace may once more

---

① "我们应当针对各殖民地的主张进行自由、开明和大公无私的调整。在调整时，所有关于主权的问题都应遵循以下原则，即当地居民的利益，应当与尚未完全决定管辖权的政府所提出的合理要求获得同等的重视。"
② "撤出现在在俄国领土上的所有军队。要解决目前所有关于俄国的问题，解决的原则应该是：由世界上其他的国家，以最合理最自由的合作，使俄国获得毫无阻挠与毫无困扰的机会，以独立决定它本身的政治发展和国家政策，并且保证它在自己决定的制度之下，可获得自由国家组成的国际社会的诚挚欢迎。"
③ Alsace-Lorraine: 阿尔萨斯—洛林（法国东部地区）。

be made secure in the interest of all.

IX A readjustment of the frontiers of Italy should be effected along clearly recognizable lines of nationality.

X The peoples of Austria-Hungary, whose place among the nations we wish to see safeguarded and assured, should be accorded the freest opportunity to autonomous development.

XI Rumania, Serbia, and Montenegro① should be evacuated; occupied territories restored; Serbia accorded free and secure access to the sea; and the relations of the several Balkan states to one another determined by friendly counsel along historically established lines of allegiance and nationality②; and international guarantees of the political and economic independence and territorial integrity of the several Balkan states should be entered into.

XII The Turkish portion of the present Ottoman Empire should be assured a secure sovereignty, but the other nationalities which are now under Turkish rule should be assured an undoubted security of life and an absolutely unmolested opportunity of autonomous development③, and the Dardanelles④ should be permanently opened as a free passage to the ships and commerce of all nations under international guarantees.

XIII An independent Polish state should be erected which should include the territories inhabited by indisputably Polish populations, which should be assured a free and secure access to the sea, and whose political and economic independence and territorial integrity should be guaranteed by international covenant.

XIV A general association of nations must be formed under specific covenants for the purpose of affording mutual guarantees of political independence and territorial integrity to great and small states alike.

12   In regard to these essential rectifications of wrong and assertions of right we feel ourselves to be intimate partners of all the governments and peoples associated together against the Imperialists. We cannot be separated in interest or divided in purpose. We stand together until the end. For such arrangements and covenants we are willing to fight and to continue to fight until they are achieved; but only because we wish the right to prevail and desire a just and stable peace such as can be secured only by removing the chief provocations to war, which this program does remove. We have no jealousy of German greatness, and there is nothing in this program that impairs it. We grudge her no achievement or distinction of learning or of pacific enterprise such as have made her record very bright and very enviable⑤. We do not wish to injure her or to block in any way her legitimate influence or power. We do

---

① Montenegro: 黑山。

② historically established lines of allegiance and nationality: 历史上因为效忠和民族关系建立的边界线。allegiance: 忠诚，效忠。

③ absolutely unmolested opportunity autonomous development：绝对不受干涉的自主发展机会。unmolested: not disturbed or attacked by sb; not prevented from doing sth. 不受干涉的。

④ Dardanelles: 达达尼尔海峡，连接爱琴海和马尔马拉海的海峡。

⑤ "我们不嫉妒曾使德国的历史非常光辉可羡的那些在学术或和平事业上的成就或荣誉。"

not wish to fight her either with arms or with hostile arrangements of trade if she is willing to associate herself with us and the other peace-loving nations of the world in covenants of justice and law and fair dealing. We wish her only to accept a place of equality among the peoples of the world — the new world in which we now live — instead of a place of mastery.

13   Neither do we presume to suggest to her any alteration or modification of her institutions. But it is necessary, we must frankly say, and necessary as a preliminary to any intelligent dealings with her on our part, that we should know whom her spokesmen speak for when they speak to us, whether for the Reichstag majority or for the military party and the men whose creed is imperial domination.

14   We have spoken now, surely, in terms too concrete to admit of any further doubt or question. An evident principle runs through the whole program I have outlined. It is the principle of justice① to all peoples and nationalities, and their right to live on equal terms of liberty and safety with one another, whether they be strong or weak.

15   Unless this principle be made its foundation no part of the structure of international justice can stand. The people of the United States could act upon no other principle; and to the vindication of this principle they are ready to devote their lives, their honor, and everything they possess. The moral climax of this the culminating and final war for human liberty has come, and they are ready to put their own strength, their own highest purpose, their own integrity and devotion to the test.

Vocabulary

parley (para. 1)	*n.* a discussion between enemies or people who disagree, in order to try and find a way of solving a problem
belligerent (para. 1)	*n.* a country or group that is fighting a war
ascertain (para. 1)	*v.* to find out the true or correct information about something
perplexity (para. 4)	*n.* the state of feeling confused and anxious because you do not understand something
pregnant (para. 5)	*adj.* significant
prostrate (para. 8)	*adj.* having lost all strength, courage, and ability to act 被制服的
subservient (para. 8)	*adj.* too willing to obey other people
aggrandizement (para. 10)	*n.* increase in size, power, or rank, esp. when intentionally planned
provocation (para. 12)	*n.* the act of doing or saying something deliberately in order to make somebody angry or upset

---

① 威尔逊总统在这里提出了国际关系中的公正原则。

Questions for discussion

1. How much do you know about the historical context of the Fourteen Points?
2. What intentions did Wilson have in his Fourteen Points? Did Wilson achieve his goals?
3. According to Wilson, what was the evident principle that "runs through the whole program" he had outlined?
4. What was the practical significance of the Fourteen Points? How did the Fourteen Points influence the war situation then and the international relations afterwards?
5. Do you think Wilson was a realist or an idealist? And why?

Text 3

In Favour of the League of Nations
Thomas Woodrow Wilson, September 25, 1919

Mr. Chairman and fellow countrymen:

1   It is with a great deal of genuine pleasure that I find myself in Pueblo①, and I feel it a compliment in this beautiful hall. One of the advantages of this hall, as I look about, is that you are not too far away from me, because there is nothing so reassuring to men who are trying to express the public sentiment as getting into real personal contact with their fellow citizens.

2   I have gained a renewed impression as I have crossed the continent this time of the homogeneity of this great people to whom we belong. They come from many stocks, but they are all of one kind. They come from many origins, but they are all shot through with the same principles and desire the same righteous and honest things. I have received a more inspiring impression this time of the public opinion of the United States than it was ever my privilege to receive before.

3   The chief pleasure of my trip has been that it has nothing to do with my personal fortunes, that it has nothing to do with my personal reputation, that it has nothing to do with anything except great principles uttered by Americans of all sorts and of all parties which we are now trying to realize at this crisis of the affairs of the world.

4   But there have been unpleasant impressions as well as pleasant impressions, my fellow citizens, as I have crossed the continent. I have perceived more and more that men have been busy creating an absolutely false impression of what the treaty of peace and the Covenant of

---

① 普韦布洛，美国科罗拉多州中部一城市。

the League of Nations① contain and mean.

5 I find, moreover, that there is an organized propaganda against the League of Nations and against the treaty proceeding from exactly the same sources that the organized propaganda proceeded from which threatened this country here and there with disloyalty, and I want to say — I cannot say too often — any man who carries a hyphen about with him carries a dagger that he is ready to plunge into the vitals of this Republic whenever he gets ready.

6 If I can catch any man with a hyphen in this great contest I will know that I have got an enemy of the Republic. My fellow citizens, it is only certain bodies of foreign sympathies, certain bodies of sympathy with foreign nations that are organized against this great document which the American representatives have brought back from Paris.

7 Therefore, in order to clear away the mists, in order to remove the impressions, in order to check the falsehoods that have clustered around this great subject, I want to tell you a few very simple things about the treaty and the covenant.

8 Do not think of this treaty of peace as merely a settlement with Germany. It is that. It is a very severe settlement with Germany, but there is not anything in it that she did not earn. Indeed, she earned more than she can ever be able to pay for, and the punishment exacted of her is not a punishment greater than she can bear, and it is absolutely necessary in order that no other nation may ever plot such a thing against humanity and civilization.

9 But the treaty is so much more than that. It is not merely a settlement with Germany; it is a readjustment of those great injustices which underlie the whole structure of European and Asiatic society. This is only the first of several treaties. They are all constructed upon the same plan. The Austrian treaty follows the same lines. The treaty with Hungary follows the same lines.

10 The treaty with Bulgaria follows the same lines. The treaty with Turkey, when it is formulated, will follow the same lines. What are those lines? They are based upon the purpose to see that every government dealt with in this great settlement is put in the hands of the people and taken out of the hands of coteries and of sovereigns who had no right to rule over the people.

11 It is a people's treaty, that accomplishes by a great sweep of practical justice the liberation of men who never could have liberated themselves, and the power of the most powerful nations has been devoted not to their aggrandizement but to the liberation of people whom they could have put under their control if they had chosen to do so.

12 Not one foot of territory is demanded by the conquerors, not one single item of submission to their authority is demanded by them. The men who sat around that table in

---

① The League of Nations (LON) was an inter-governmental organization founded as a result of the Treaty of Versailles in 1919—1920, and the precursor to the United Nations. The League's primary goals, as stated in its Covenant, included preventing war through collective security, disarmament, and settling international disputes through negotiation and arbitration. Other goals in this and related treaties included labor conditions, just treatment of native inhabitants, trafficking in persons and drugs, arms trade, global health, prisoners of war, and protection of minorities in Europe.

Paris knew that the time had come when the people were no longer going to consent to live under masters, but were going to live the lives that they chose themselves, to live under such governments as they chose themselves to erect. That is the fundamental principle of this great settlement.

13   And we did not stop with that. We added a great international charter for the rights of labour. Reject this treaty, impair it, and this is the consequence of the labouring end of the world, that there is no international tribunal which can bring the moral judgments of the world to bear upon the great labour questions of the day.

14   What we need to do with regard to the labour questions of the day, my fellow countrymen, is tilt them into the light, is to lift them out of the haze and distraction of passion, of hostility, out into the calm spaces where men look at things without passion. The more men you get into a great discussion is the more you exclude passion.

15   Just as soon as the calm judgment of the world is directed upon the question of justice to labour, labour is going to have to forum such as it never was supplied with before, and men everywhere are going to see that the problem of labour is nothing more or less than the problem of the elevation of humanity.

16   We must see that all the questions which have disturbed the world, all the questions which have eaten into the confidence of men toward their governments, all the questions which have disturbed the processes of industry, shall be brought out where men of all points of view, men of all attitudes of mind, men of all kinds of experience, may contribute their part of the settlement of the great questions which we must settle and cannot ignore.

17   At the front of this great treaty is put the Covenant of the League of Nations. It will also be at the front of the Austrian, treaty and the Hungarian treaty and the Bulgarian treaty and the treaty with Turkey. Every one of them will contain the Covenant of the League of Nations, because you cannot work any of them without the Covenant of the League of Nations.

18   Unless you get the united, concerted purpose and power of the great Governments of the world behind this settlement, it will fall down like a house of cards①. There is only one power to put behind the liberation of mankind, and that is the power of mankind. It is the power of the united moral forces of the world, and in the Covenant of the League of Nations the moral forces of the world are mobilized.② For what purpose?

19   Reflect, my fellow citizens, that the membership of this great League is going to include all the great fighting nations of the world, as well as the weak ones. It is not for the present going to include Germany, but for the time being Germany is not a great fighting country. All the nations that have power that can be mobilized are going to be members of this League, including the United States.

20   And what do they unite for? They enter into a solemn promise to one another that

---

① 用纸牌搭房子，比喻不可靠。
② 威尔逊总统期望用道义的力量来建立联合国，展现了他的理想主义。不过在当时各国利益矛盾交织冲突的情况下，根本无法实现。

they will never use their power against one another for aggression; that they never will impair the territorial integrity of a neighbour; that they never will interfere with the political independence of a neighbour; that they will abide by the principle that great populations are entitled to determine their own destiny and that they will not interfere with that destiny; and that no matter what differences arise amongst them they will never resort to war without first having done one or other of two things — either submitted the matter of controversy to arbitration, in which case they agree to abide by the result without question, or submitted it to the consideration of the council of the League of Nations, laying before that council all the documents, all the facts, agreeing that the council can publish the documents and the facts to the whole world, agreeing that there shall be six months allowed for the mature consideration of those facts by the council, and agreeing that at the expiration of the six months, even if they are not then ready to accept the advice of the council with regard to the settlement of the dispute, they will still not go to war for another three months.

21   In other words, they consent, no matter what happens, to submit every matter of difference between them to the judgment of mankind, and just so certainly as they do that, my fellow citizens, war will be in the far background, war will be pushed out of that foreground of terror in which it has kept the world for generation after generation, and men will know that there will be a calm time of deliberate counsel.

22   The most dangerous thing for a bad cause is to expose it to the opinion of the world. The most certain way that you can prove that a man is mistaken is by letting all his neighbours know what he thinks, by letting all his neighbours discuss what he thinks, and if he is in the wrong you will notice that he will stay at home, he will not walk on the street.

23   He will be afraid of the eyes of his neighbours. He will be afraid of their judgment of his character. He will know that his cause is lost unless he can sustain it by the arguments of right and of justice. The same law that applies to individuals applies to nations.

24   But, you say, "We have heard that we might be at a disadvantage in the League of Nations." Well, whoever told you that either was deliberately falsifying or he had not read the Covenant of the League of Nations. I leave him the choice. I want to give you a very simple account of the organization of the League of Nations and let you judge for yourselves.

25   It is a very simple organization. The power of the League, or rather the activities of the league, lie in two bodies. There is the council, which consists of one representative from each of the principal allied and associated powers — that is to say, the United States, Great Britain, France, Italy, and Japan, along with four other representatives of smaller powers chosen out of the general body of the membership of the League.

26   The council is the source of every active policy of the League, and no active policy of the League can be adopted without a unanimous vote of the council. That is explicitly stated in the Covenant itself. Does it not evidently follow that the League of Nations can adopt no policy whatever without the consent of the United States?

27   The affirmative vote of the representative of the United States is necessary in every

case. Now, you have heard of six votes belonging to the British Empire. Those six votes are not in the council. They are in the assembly, and the interesting thing is that the assembly does not vote. I must qualify that statement a little, but essentially it is absolutely true.

28   In every matter in which the assembly is given a voice, and there are only four or five, its vote does not count unless concurred in by the representatives of all the nations represented on the council, so that there is no validity to any vote of the assembly unless in that vote also the representative of the United States concurs.

29   That one vote of the United States is as big as the six votes of the British Empire. I am not jealous for advantage, my fellow citizens, but I think that is a perfectly safe situation. There is no validity in a vote, either by the council or the assembly, in which we do not concur. So much for the statements about the six votes of the British Empire.

30   Look at it in another aspect. The assembly is the talking body. The assembly was created in order that anybody that purposed anything wrong should be subjected to the awkward circumstance that everybody could talk about it.

31   This is the great assembly in which all the things that are likely to disturb the peace of the world or the good understanding between nations are to be exposed to the general view, and I want to ask you if you think it was unjust, unjust to the United States, that speaking parts should be assigned to the several portions of the British Empire? Do you think it unjust that there should be some spokesman in debate for that fine little stout Republic down in the Pacific, New Zealand?

32   Do you think it was unjust that Australia should be allowed to stand up and take part in the debate—Australia, from which we have learned some of the most useful progressive policies of modern time, a little nation only five million in a great continent, but counting for several times five in its activities and in its interest in liberal reform?

33   Do you think it unjust that that little Republic down in South Africa whose gallant resistance to being subjected to any outside authority at all we admired for so many months and whose fortunes we followed with such interest, should have a speaking part?

34   Great Britain obliged South Africa to submit to her sovereignty, but she immediately after that felt that it was convenient and right to hand the whole self government of that colony over to the very men whom she had beaten.

35   The representatives of South Africa in Paris were two of the most distinguished generals of the Boer[①] Army, two of the realest men I ever met, two men that could talk sober counsel and wise advice, along with the best statesmen in Europe. To exclude Gen. Botha and Jan. Smuts from the right to stand up in the parliament of the world and say something concerning the affairs of mankind would be absurd.

36   And what about Canada? Is not Canada a good neighbour? I ask you, is not Canada more likely to agree with the United States than with Great Britain? Canada has a speaking part. And then, for the first time in the history of the world, that great voiceless multitude that

---

① Boer：布尔人，南非荷兰移民的后裔。第二次布尔战争：1899—1902 年间英国人与布尔人的战争。

throng hundreds of millions strong in India, has a voice, and I want to testify that some of the wisest and most dignified figures in the peace conference at Paris came from India, men who seemed to carry in their minds an older wisdom than the rest of us had, whose traditions ran back into so many of the unhappy fortunes of mankind that they seemed very useful counselors as to how some ray of hope and some prospect of happiness could be opened to its people.

37　I for my part have no jealousy whatever of those five speaking parts in the assembly. Those speaking parts cannot translate themselves into five votes that can in any matter override the voice and purpose of the United States.

38　Let us sweep aside all this language of jealousy. Let us be big enough to know the facts and to welcome the facts, because the facts are based upon the principle that America has always fought for, namely, the equality of self-governing peoples, whether they were big or little — not counting men, but counting rights, not counting representation, but counting the purpose of that representation.①

39　When you hear an opinion quoted you do not count the number of persons who hold it; you ask, "Who said that?" You weigh opinions, you do not count them, and the beauty of all democracies is that every voice can be heard, every voice can have its effect, every voice can contribute to the general judgment that is finally arrived at. That is the object of democracy.

40　Let us accept what America has always fought for, and accept it with pride that America showed the way and made the proposal. I do not mean that America made the proposal in this particular instance; I mean that the principle was an American principle, proposed by America.

41　Well you come to the heart of the Covenant, my fellow citizens, you will end it in article ten, and I am very much interested to know that the other things have been blown away like bubbles. There is nothing in the other contentions with regard to the League of Nations, but there is something in article ten that you ought to realize and ought to accept or reject.

42　Article ten is the heart of the whole matter. What is article ten? I never am certain that I can from memory give a literal repetition of its language, but I am sure that I can give an exact interpretation of its meaning. Article ten provides that every member of the league covenants to respect and preserve the territorial integrity and existing political independence of every other member of the league as against external aggression.

43　Not against internal disturbance. There was not a man at that table who did not admit the sacredness of the right of self determination, the sacredness of the right of any body of people to say that they would not continue to live under the Government they were then living under, and under article eleven of the Covenant they are given a place to say whether they will live under it or not.

44　For following article ten is article eleven, which makes it the right of any member of the League at any time to call attention to anything, anywhere, that is likely to disturb the peace of the world or the good understanding between nations upon which the peace of the world

---

① 威尔逊总统希望抛弃成见，抛弃形式，更看重目的。显然，他过于理想主义了，更何况涉及国家利益。

depends. I want to give you an illustration of what that would mean.

45   You have heard a great deal — something that was true and a great deal that was false—about that provision of the treaty which hands over to Japan the rights which Germany enjoyed in the Province of Shantung in China. In the first place, Germany did not enjoy any rights there that other nations had not already claimed.

46   For my part, my judgment, my moral judgment, is against the whole set of concessions. They were all of them unjust to China, they ought never to have been exacted, they were all exacted by duress, from a great body of thoughtful and ancient and helpless people.

47   There never was it any right in any of them. Thank God, America never asked for any, never dreamed of asking for any. But when Germany got this concession in 1898, the Government of the United States made no protest whatever.

48   That was not because the Government of the United States was not in the hands of high-minded and conscientious men. It was. William McKinley was President and John Hay was Secretary of State — as safe hands to leave the honour of the United States in as any that you can cite.

49   They made no protest because the state of international law at that time was that it was none of their business unless they could show that the interests of the United States were affected, and the only thing that they could show with regard to the interests of the United States was that Germany might close the doors of Shantung Province against the trade of the United States.

50   They, therefore, demanded and obtained promises that we could continue to sell merchandise in Shantung. Immediately following that concession to Germany there was a concession to Russia of the same sort, of Port Arthur① and Port Arthur was handed over subsequently to Japan on the very territory of the United States.

51   Don't you remember that when Russia and Japan got into war with one another the war was brought to a conclusion by a treaty written at Portsmouth, N. H., and in that treaty without the slightest intimation from any authoritative sources in America that the Government of the United States had any objection, Port Arthur, Chinese territory, was turned over to Japan?

52   I want you distinctly to understand that there is no thought of criticism in my mind. I am expounding to you a state of international law. Now, read articles ten and eleven. You will see that international law is revolutionized by putting morals into it. Article ten says that no member of the League, and that includes all these nations that have demanded these things unjustly of China, shall impair the territorial integrity or the political independence of any other member of the League.

53   China is going to be a member of the League. Article eleven says that any member of the League can call attention to anything that is likely to disturb the peace of the world or the good understanding between nations, and China is for the first time in the history of mankind

---

① Port Arthur: 旅顺港的旧称。

afforded a standing before the jury of the world.

54 I, for my part, have a profound sympathy for China, and I am proud to have taken part in an arrangement which promises the protection of the world to the rights of China. The whole atmosphere of the world is changed by a thing like that, my fellow citizens. The whole international practice of the world is revolutionized.

55 But you will say, "What is the second sentence of article ten? That is what gives very disturbing thoughts." The second sentence is that the council of the League shall advise what steps, if any, are necessary to carry out the guaranty of the first sentence, namely, that the members will respect and preserve the territorial integrity and political independence of the other members.

56 I do not know any other meaning for the word "advise" except "advise." The council advises, and it cannot advise without the vote of the United States. Why gentlemen should fear that the Congress of the United States would be advised to do something that it did not want to do I frankly cannot imagine, because they cannot even be advised to do anything unless their own representative has participated in the advice.

57 It may be that that will impair somewhat the vigour of the League, but, nevertheless, the fact is so, that we are not obliged to take any advice except our own, which to any man who wants to go his own course is a very satisfactory state of affairs. Every man regards his own advice as best, and I dare say every man mixes his own advice with some thought of his own interest.

58 Whether we use it wisely or unwisely, we can use the vote of the United States to make impossible drawing the United States into any enterprise that she does not care to be drawn into.

59 Yet article ten strikes at the taproot of① war. Article ten is a statement that the very things that have always been sought in imperialistic wars are henceforth foregone by every ambitious nation in the world. I would have felt very much disturbed if, sitting at the peace table in Paris, I had supposed that I was expounding my own ideas.

60 Whether you believe it or not, I know the relative size of my own ideas; I know how they stand related in bulk and proportion to the moral judgments of my fellow countrymen, and I proposed nothing whatever at the peace table at Paris that I had not sufficiently certain knowledge embodied the moral judgment of the citizens of the United States.

61 I had gone over there with, so to say, explicit instructions. Don't you remember that we laid down fourteen points which should contain the principles of the settlement? They were not my points. In every one of them I was conscientiously trying to read the thought of the people of the United States, and after I uttered those points I had every assurance that could be given me that they did speak the moral judgment of the United States and not my single judgment.

62 Then when it came to that critical period just a little less than a year ago, when it was

---

① at the taproot of: 在根基层面。taproot: （植物的）主根。

evident that the war was coming to its critical end, all the nations engaged in the war accepted those fourteen principles explicitly as the basis of the armistice and the basis of the peace. In those circumstances I crossed the ocean under bond to my own people and to the other governments with which I was dealing.

63   The whole specification of the method of settlement was written down and accepted before hand, and we were architects building on those specifications. It reassures me and fortifies my position to find how before I went over men whose judgment the United States has often trusted were of exactly the same opinion that I went abroad to express. Here is something I want to read from Theodore Roosevelt:

64   "The one effective move for obtaining peace is by an agreement among all the great powers in which each should pledge itself not only to abide by the decisions of a common tribunal but to back its decisions by force. The great civilized nations should combine by solemn agreement in a great world league for the peace of righteousness; a court should be established. A changed and amplified Hague court would meet the requirements, composed of representatives from each nation, whose representatives are sworn to act as judges in each case and not in a representative capacity." Now there is article ten.

65   He goes on and says this: "The nations should agree on certain rights that should not be questioned, such as territorial integrity, their right to deal with their domestic affairs, and with such matters as whom they should admit to citizenship. All such guarantee each of their number in possession of these rights."

66   Now, the other specification is in the Covenant. The Covenant in another portion guarantees to the members the independent control of their domestic questions. There is not a leg for these gentlemen to stand on when they say that the interests of the United States are not safeguarded in the very points where we are most sensitive.

67   You do not need to be told again that the Covenant expressly says that nothing in this covenant shall be construed as affecting the validity of the Monroe doctrine①, for example. You could not be more explicit than that. And every point of interest is covered, partly for one very interesting reason.

68   This is not the first time that the Foreign Relations Committee of the Senate of the United States has read and considered this covenant. I brought it to this country in March last in a tentative, provisional form, in practically the form that it now has, with the exception of certain additions which I shall mention immediately.

69   I asked the Foreign Relations Committees of both Houses to come to the White House and we spent a long evening in the frankest discussion of every portion that they wished to discuss.② They made certain specific suggestions as to what should be contained in this document when it was to be revised.

70   I carried those suggestions to Paris, and every one of them was adopted. What more

---

① 门罗主义。
② 由此可见,威尔逊总统要说服国会批准协议异常艰难。归根到底,孤立主义传统依然影响巨大。

could I have done? What more could have been obtained?

71 The very matters upon which these gentlemen were most concerned were, the right of withdrawal, which is now expressly stated; the safeguarding of the Monroe doctrine, which is now accomplished; the exclusion from action by the League of domestic questions, which is now accomplished. All along the line, every suggestion of the United States was adopted after the Covenant had been drawn up in its first form and had been published for the criticism of the world. There is a very true sense in which I can say this is a tested American document.

72 I am dwelling upon these points, my fellow citizens, in spite of the fact that I dare say to most of you they are perfectly well known, because in order to meet the present situation we have got to know what we are dealing with.

73 We are not dealing with the kind of document which this is represented by some gentlemen to be; and inasmuch as we are dealing with a document simon-pure in respect of the very principles we have professed and lived up to, we have got to do one or other of two things—we have got to adopt it or reject it. There is no middle course.

74 You cannot go in on a special-privilege basis of your own. I take it that you are too proud to ask to be exempted from responsibilities which the other members of the League will carry. We go in upon equal terms or we do not go in at all; and if we do not go in, my fellow citizens, think of the tragedy of that result — the only sufficient guaranty to the peace of the world withheld!

75 Ourselves drawn apart with that dangerous pride which means that we shall be ready to take care of ourselves, and that means that we shall maintain great standing armies and an irresistible navy; that means we shall have the organization of a military nation; that means we shall have a general staff, with the kind of power that the general staff of Germany had; to mobilize this great manhood of the Nation when it pleases, all the energy of our young men drawn into the thought and preparation for war.

76 What of our pledges to the men that lie dead in France? We said that they went over there not to prove the prowess of America or her readiness for another war but to see to it that there never was such a war again. It always seems to make it difficult for me to say anything, my fellow citizens, when I think of my clients in this case.

77 My clients are the children; my clients are the next generation. They do not know what promises and bonds I undertook when I ordered the armies of the United States to the soil of France, but I know, and I intend to redecm my pledges to the children; they shall not be sent upon a similar errand.

78 Again and again, my fellow citizens, mothers who lost their sons in France have come to me and, taking my hand, have shed tears upon it not only, but they have added, "God bless you, Mr. President!" Why, my fellow citizens, should they pray God to bless me?

79 I advised the Congress of the United States to create the situation that led to the death of their sons. I ordered their sons overseas. I consented to their sons being put in the most difficult parts of the battle line, where death was certain, as in the impenetrable difficulties of the forest of Argonne.

80 Why should they weep upon my hand and call down the blessings of God upon me? Because they believe that their boys died for something that vastly transcends any of the immediate and palpable objects of the war. They believe and they rightly believe, that their sons saved the liberty of the world.

81 They believe that wrapped up with the liberty of the world is the continuous protection of that liberty by the concerted powers of all civilized people. They believe that this sacrifice was made in order that other sons should not be called upon for a similar gift — the gift of life, the gift of all that died — and if we did not see this thing through, if we fulfilled the dearest present wish of Germany and now dissociated ourselves from those alongside whom we fought in the world, would not something of the halo go away from the gun over the mantelpiece, or the sword? Would not the old uniform lose something of its significance?

82 These men were crusaders.① They were not going forth to prove the might of the United States. They were going forth to prove the might of justice and right, and all the world accepted them as crusaders, and their transcendent achievement② has made all the world believe in America as it believes in no other nation organized in the modern world.

83 There seem to me to stand between us and the rejection or qualification of this treaty the serried ranks of those boys in khaki, not only these boys who came home, but those dear ghosts that still deploy upon the fields of France.

84 My friends, on last Decoration day I went to a beautiful hillside near Paris, where was located the cemetery of Suresnes③, a cemetery given over to the burial of the American dead. Behind me all the slopes was rank upon rank of living American soldiers, and lying before me upon the levels of the plain was rank upon rank of departed American soldiers.

85 Right by the side of the stand where I spoke there was a little group of French women who had adopted those graves, had made themselves mothers of those dear ghosts by putting flowers every day upon those graves, taking them as their own sons, their own beloved, because they had died in the same cause — France was free and the world was free because America had come!

86 I wish some men in public life who are now opposing the settlement for which these men died could visit such a spot as that. I wish that the thought that comes out of those graves could penetrate their consciousness. I wish that they could feel the moral obligation that rests upon us not to go back on those boys, but to see the thing through, to see it through to the end and make good their redemption of the world. For nothing less depends upon this decision, nothing less than liberation and salvation of the world.

87 You will say, "Is the League an absolute guaranty against war?" No; I do not know any

---

① "他们就像十字军战士。"威尔逊总统希望通过宗教的力量唤起民众的支持。crusader: a crusader for a cause is someone who does a lot in support of it.

② transcendent achievement: 卓越的成就。transcendent: extremely great。

③ （巴黎郊区的）叙雷讷墓园。

absolute guaranty against the errors of human judgment or the violence of human passions but I tell you this: With a cooling space of nine months for human passion, not much of it will keep hot.

88　I had a couple of friends who were in the habit of losing their tempers, and when they lost their tempers they were in the habit of using very unparliamentary language. Some of their friends induced them to make a promise that they never would swear inside the town limits.

89　When the impulse next came upon them, they took a street car to go out of town to swear, and by the time they got out of town they did not want to swear. They came back convinced that they were just what they were, a couple of unspeakable fools, and the habit of getting angry and of swearing suffered great inroads upon it by that experience.

90　Now, illustrating the great by the small, that is true of the passions of nations. It is true of the passions of men however you combine them. Give them space to cool off. I ask you this: If it is not an absolute insurance against war, do you want no insurance at all? Do you want nothing? Do you want not only no probability that war will not recur, but the probability that it will recur?

91　The arrangements of justice do not stand of themselves, my fellow citizens. The arrangements of this treaty are just, but they need the support of the combined power of the great nations of the world. And they will have that support. Now that the mists of this great question have cleared away, I believe that men will see the truth, eye to eye and face to face.

92　There is one thing that the American people always rise to and extend their hand to, and that is the truth of justice and of liberty and of peace. We have accepted that truth and we are going to be led by it, and it is going to lead us, and through us the world, out into pastures of quietness and peace such as the world never dreamed of before.

Vocabulary

homogeneity (para. 2)	*n.* the same type
hyphen (para. 5)	*n.* short written or printed line (-) that joins words or syllables
dagger (para. 5)	*n.* a short pointed knife used as a weapon
cluster (para. 7)	*v.* form a small group in that place
coterie (para. 10)	*n.* a small group of people who enjoy doing the same things together, and do not like including others
aggrandizement (para. 11)	*n.* when a person or country tries to increase their power or importance—used to show disapproval
impair (para. 13)	*v.* to damage something or make it not as good as it should be
tribunal (para. 13)	*n.* a type of court that is given official authority to deal with a particular situation or problem

haze (para. 14)	*n.* smoke, dust, or mist in the air which is difficult to see through, the feeling of being very confused and unable to think clearly
gallant (para. 33)	*adj.* brave
armistice (para. 62)	*n.* an agreement to stop fighting
fortify (para. 63)	*v. written* to make someone feel physically or mentally stronger
tentative (para. 68)	*adj.* not definite or certain, and may be changed later
prowess (para. 76)	*n. formal* great skill at doing something
errand (para. 77)	*n.* a short journey in order to do something for someone, for example delivering or collecting something for them
impenetrable (para. 79)	*adj.* impossible to get through, see through, or get into
palpable (para. 81)	*adj.* complete
halo (para. 80)	*n.* a circle of light or something bright
mantelpiece (para. 81)	*n.* a wooden or stone shelf which is the top part of a frame surrounding a fireplace
serried (para. 83)	*adj. literary* standing or arranged closely together in rows
deploy (para. 83)	*v.* to organize or move soldiers, military equipment, etc. so that they are in the right place and ready to be used
redemption (para. 86)	*n.* the state of being freed from the power of evil, believed by Christians to be made possible by Jesus Christ

Questions for discussion

1. What was Wilson's intention to deliver this speech?
2. What was Wilson's real purpose to promote the creation of the League of Nations?
3. What were the differences and conflicts among those Allies? And how did Wilson deal with them?
4. Why did Wilson put an emphasis on Articles 10 and 11 of the Covenant of the League of Nations?
5. Why did Wilson finally fail in his attempt to create the League of Nations?

Background

Wilsonianism was President Wilson's idea and practice of modifying American traditional foreign policy and of designing the new international order. It was characterized by the special international role of the United States — taking the commitment to international justice and being its embodiment. From then on, spreading American values has become the foreign policy aim of the United States. The principles of the new world order, such as collective security, self-determination, free trade, are all based on the moral leadership of the United States. Wilsonian foreign policy embodied the anti-power politics inclination at the beginning of the twentieth century. Power politics, which inhered in the European modern diplomacy, referred to the conduct of international relations by force and threat of force, without consideration of right and justice. It was once contained by the special conditions of laissez-faire capitalism, but spurred by imperialist expansion. In this context, President Wilson saw the big question that the whole twentieth century had to encounter: what is the just international order? And how to get it? In order to answer the question, Wilson equated the American values and the principles of its political institution with the universal ones. However, such equation had no legitimacy. And what Wilson said always contradicted his foreign policy practices: The role of "world mediator" was limited by the close economic relationship between the United States and the Allies. "Peace without victory" ultimately became the absolute victory over the Central Powers in the name of "democracy vs. autocracy." Moreover, Wilson betrayed his own just principles in order to get the support to League of Nations from other great powers. The unjust means to create League of Nations that Wilson actually adopted couldn't be justified by its aims. It was Wilson himself that must be responsible for the failure of his new world order. Although Wilson failed in Paris, Wilsonianism finally conquered. The United Nations works on the principle of collective security; the confrontation with the Soviet Union cannot be understood without considering Wilsonian ideological dimension. And the dominance of Wilsonianism after the Cold War implies something new in our time — the ideological aims have been the "realist" national interest of the United States.

The Fourteen Points were listed in a speech delivered by President Woodrow Wilson of the United States to a joint session of the United States Congress on January 8, 1918. In his speech, Wilson intended to set out a blueprint for lasting peace in Europe after World War I. The idealism displayed in the speech gave Wilson a position of moral leadership among the Allies, and encouraged the Central Powers to surrender.

Wilson spent 1914 through the beginning of 1917 trying to keep America out of the war in Europe. Wilson won the support of the U.S. peace element by arguing that an army buildup would provoke war. He vigorously protested Germany's use of submarines as illegal.

While German submarines were sinking allied ships, Britain had declared a blockade of Germany, preventing neutral shipping carrying "contraband" goods to Germany. Wilson protested this violation of neutral rights by London. However, his protests to the British were not viewed as being as forceful as those he directed towards Germany. Re-nominated in 1916, Wilson's major campaign slogan was "He kept us out of the war" referring to his administration's avoiding open conflict with Germany or Mexico while maintaining a firm national policy. Wilson, however, never promised to keep out of war regardless of provocation. In his acceptance speech on September 2, 1916, Wilson pointedly warned Germany that submarine warfare that took American lives would not be tolerated.

When Germany resumed unrestricted submarine warfare in early 1917 and made a clumsy attempt to enlist Mexico as an ally, Wilson took America into World War I as a war to make "the world safe for democracy." He did not sign a formal alliance with Great Britain or France but operated as an "Associated" power. Woodrow Wilson had decided by then that the war had become a real threat to humanity. Unless the U.S. threw its weight into the war, as he stated in his declaration of war speech, Western civilization itself could be destroyed. His statement announcing a "war to end all wars" meant that he wanted to build a basis for peace that would prevent future catastrophic wars and needless death and destruction. This provided the basis for Wilson's Fourteen Points which intended to resolve territorial disputes, ensure free trade and commerce and establish a peacemaking organization, which later emerged as the League of Nations.

The Points were the only war aims clearly expressed by any belligerent nation and thus became the basis for the Treaty of Versailles following World War I. The speech was highly idealistic, translating Wilson's progressive domestic policy of democracy, self-determination, open agreements, and free trade into the international realm. It also made several suggestions for specific disputes in Europe. But the speech was controversial in America, and even more so with their Allies. France wanted high reparations from Germany as French agriculture, industry, and lives had been so demolished by the war, and Britain, as the great naval power, did not want freedom of the seas. Wilson compromised with Clemenceau, Lloyd George, and many other European leaders during the Paris Peace talks to ensure that the fourteenth point, the League of Nations, would be established. In the end, Wilson's own Congress did not accept the League and only four of the original Fourteen Points were implemented fully in Europe.

Although the speech was delivered over 10 months before the Armistice with Germany ended World War I, the Fourteen Points became the basis for the terms of the German surrender, as negotiated at the Paris Peace Conference in 1919 and documented in the Treaty of Versailles.

While the First World War was still underway, a number of governments and groups had already started developing plans to change the way international relations were carried out in order to prevent a repetition of the war. United States President Woodrow Wilson and his advisor Colonel Edward M. House enthusiastically promoted the idea of the League as a means of avoiding any repetition of the bloodshed seen in World War I, and the creation of the League was a centerpiece of Wilson's Fourteen Points for Peace. Specifically the final point provided: "A general association of nations must be formed under specific covenants for the purpose of affording mutual guarantees of political independence and territorial integrity to great and small states alike."

Before drafting the specific terms of his peace deal, Wilson recruited a team led by Colonel House to compile whatever information deemed pertinent in assessing Europe's geopolitical situation. In early January, 1918, Wilson summoned House to Washington and the two began hammering out, in complete secrecy, the President's first address on the League of

Nations which was delivered to an unsuspecting Congress on January 8, 1918.

Wilson's final plans for the League were strongly influenced by the South African Prime Minister, Jan Christiaan Smuts. In 1918 Smuts had published a treatise entitled The League of Nations: A Practical Suggestion. According to F.S. Crafford's biography on Smuts, Wilson adopted "both the ideas and the style" of Smuts.

On July 8, 1919, Woodrow Wilson returned to the United States and embarked on a nation-wide campaign to secure the support of the American people for their country's entry into the League. On July 10, Wilson addressed the Senate declaring that "a new role and a new responsibility have come to this great nation that we honour and which we would all wish to lift to yet higher levels of service and achievement." Positive reception, particularly from Republicans, was scarce at best.

The Paris Peace Conference, convened to build a lasting peace after World War I, approved the proposal to create the League of Nations (French: Société des Nations, German: Völkerbund) on 25 January 1919. The Covenant of the League of Nations was drafted by a special commission, and the League was established by Part I of the Treaty of Versailles. On 28 June 1919, 44 states signed the Covenant, including 31 states which had taken part in the war on the side of the Triple Entente or joined it during the conflict. Despite Wilson's efforts to establish and promote the League, for which he was awarded the Nobel Peace Prize in October 1919, the United States did not join the League. Opposition in the U.S. Senate, particularly from Republican politicians Henry Cabot Lodge and William E. Borah, together with Wilson's refusal to compromise, ensured that the United States would not ratify the Covenant.

The League held its first council meeting in Paris on 16 January 1920, six days after the Treaty of Versailles came into force. In November, the headquarters of the League moved to Geneva, where the first General Assembly was held on 15 November 1920 with representatives from 41 nations in attendance.

威尔逊主义是伍德罗·威尔逊总统对美国传统对外政策的改造和国际新秩序的构想，影响了第一次世界大战前后美国的对外政策。它的根本特征是，以美国的价值观和制度标准作为国际秩序的原则，把美国塑造成国际正义的化身和担当者。正因如此，威尔逊主义带有强烈的美国式的理想主义色彩。从威尔逊主义开始，传播美国的价值观、确立美国在国际政治中的道德领导地位，成为美国明确的政策目标。威尔逊主义把集体安全、大小国家一律平等、自决

（逐渐演变为民族自决）、自由贸易等作为国际新秩序的基本原则。威尔逊的政策是对20世纪初世界强权政治的直接反映。近代欧洲国际秩序由于受到自由资本主义时代特有的经济和道德条件约束，秘密外交手段和有限战争基本上没有影响普通资产阶级的利益；主要依赖于跨国市场的经济交往，即使在战争时期也能正常进行。

从19世纪后期开始，随着帝国主义的不断扩张，自由资本主义经济政治对国际秩序的约束条件逐渐崩溃，近代外交手段的强权性质充分暴露出来。帝国主义国家的全面总体竞争，卷入了社会的一切阶层，国际关系成为空前赤裸裸的实力政治争夺，其中起作用的仅仅是暴力的逻辑。威尔逊主义产生于这样的背景，它试图回答当时面临的重大问题，也是整个20世纪国际政治的重大问题——何为公正的国际秩序，如何建立公正的国际秩序？威尔逊通过把美国的价值观和制度普遍化来回答这个问题。但是这样做既无合法依据，又与美国的实际政策选择时常发生矛盾：改善与拉美国家关系的良好愿望受到美国在该地区固有利益的制约；以"世界调停者"的身份尽快结束第一次世界大战、建立以公正为基础之持久和平的目标，受制于美国与协约国的传统密切关系，并在对抗专制、推进民主的意识形态要求面前演变为对德国不公正的彻底胜利；以"十四点计划"为代表的国际新秩序构想不仅具有内在矛盾，而且在建立过程中的手段严重违背了目的：威尔逊为了获得大国对国际联盟（简称国联）的支持，不惜背离自己提出的道义原则。威尔逊的失败是必然的。在巴黎和会上，他自己打败了自己。然而，威尔逊主义却在第二次世界大战后获得了成功。罗斯福的联合国规划和杜鲁门的欧洲政策，是威尔逊主义不同方面的体现。

1914年夏，欧洲的同盟国（德国和奥匈帝国）与协约国（英国、法国和俄国）之间爆发了战争。美国人从未参与欧洲的战争，而且威尔逊总统宣称，美国人应当"名副其实地保持中立……表里一致地保持公正。"华盛顿和杰斐逊的这一重要规定经门罗主义得到进一步强调，即美国应避免卷入国际政治斗争。但事实证明，保持中立是十分困难的。1915年5月，一艘德国潜艇击沉了英国客轮"露西塔尼亚"号，包括128名美国人在内共有约1200人丧生，舆论一片哗然。

1916年威尔逊依赖"他使我们避开了战争"这一口号在总统竞选中再次获胜。威尔逊认为他能够促使交战双方和解，因此将助手派往欧洲，试图找到可能结束战争的条件。1917年1月，威尔逊对国会发表讲话，谈及他正努力寻找一个方案以达到"没有胜利的和平"，即既无赢家也无输家的解决办法，一个将由国际"和平联盟"确保的解决办法。威尔逊颇有远见地警告说，一种带惩罚性质的和平会给另一场欧洲冲突种下祸根。

德国保证不再突袭非武装船只，但在1917年初重新开始了毫无节制的潜艇进攻，击沉了好几艘美国商船。威尔逊对德国的政策忍无可忍，于1917年4月2日请求国会批准宣战。这里选录的威尔逊关于宣战的演讲，将一百多万美军投入世界历史上最血腥的冲突之一。

1918年威尔逊提出结束第一次世界大战的纲领及战后世界的蓝图。为了对抗俄国十月革命和苏维埃政权的影响，为美国战后称霸创造条件，1918年1月8日威尔逊在国会发表演说，提出"十四点计划"作为"建立世界和平的纲领"，主要内容是：（1）签订公开和约，杜绝秘密外交；（2）平时和战时海上航行绝对自由；（3）取消一切经济壁垒，建立贸易平等条件；（4）裁减军备到同国内安全相一致的最低点；（5）公正处理殖民地问题，在决定一切有关主权问题时，应兼顾当地居民的利益和殖民政府之正当要求；（6）外国军队撤出俄国，并保证俄国独立决定其政治发展和国家政策，欢迎它在自己选择的制度下，进入自由国家的社会；（7）德军撤出比利时，并恢复其主权；（8）德军撤出法国，阿尔萨斯和洛林归还法国；（9）根据民族分布情况，调整意大利疆界；（10）允许奥匈帝国境内各民族自治；（11）罗马尼亚、塞尔维亚和门的内哥罗的领土予以恢复；（12）承认奥斯曼帝国内的土耳其部分有稳固的主权，但土耳其统治的其他民族有在"自治"的基础上不受干扰的发展机会，达达尼尔海峡在国际保证下永远开放为自由航道；（13）重建独立的拥有出海口的波兰，以国际条约保证其政治经济独立和领土完整；（14）根据旨在国家不分大小、相互保证政治独立和领土完整的特别盟约，设立国际联合机构。1918年10月，美国官方对"十四点"作了注解，将美国的意图说得更加明确。

"十四点计划"表面上标榜"民族自决"，反对"秘密外交"，倡导建立"公正而持久的和平"，实际上是美国企图利用战争中增长的实力，削弱竞争对手英、法帝国主义，重新瓜分世界。也反映其敌视苏俄、反对被压迫民族争取独立解放的立场。威尔逊为了反对英、法、俄撇开美国秘密分割世界，提出反对秘密外交；为了取代英国的海上霸权，主张海上自由；为了确立美国的商业霸权，要求废除经济壁垒；在欢迎俄国进入"自由"国家社会的招牌下，反对苏维埃政权，在注解中明确表示要承认并援助若干临时政府，与苏俄政府对抗；以同等重视殖民地人民与帝国主义的要求来否认被压迫民族的民族独立，以"自治"为名反对奥斯曼帝国内的阿拉伯民族的独立；为了使美国成为世界盟主，建议创立国际联合机构。

威尔逊的"十四点计划"实质上是一个不折不扣的建立美国世界霸权的纲领。威尔逊曾经讲过："战争一结束，我们就能迫使他们（指英、法）附和我们的意见，因为到那时它们在财务上将被我们所控制。""十四点计划"就是在这样的思想指导下制定的。巴黎和会的召开，对美国是一个有利时机。美国的如意算盘是：在西半球继续巩固和发展在战争中取得的对拉美国家的控制；在西欧竭力扶植德国对抗英、法；在东南欧要建立由它支配的巴尔干联盟；在东半球，美国则要利用门户开放政策，争夺在中国和太平洋地区的霸权。通过这次会议，美国试图争得西欧领导权，进而称霸世界。

1918年8月，德国在战败前夕向美国提出愿在"十四点计划"的基础上和谈。10月，英、法同意以"十四点计划"为和谈基础。但在1919年的巴黎和会上，英、法操纵会议进程，猛烈反对美国旨在建立世界霸权的纲领。所议定的和约条款大多不符合

"十四点计划"的初衷,新创立的国际联盟也成为推行英、法两国政策的工具。美国国会拒绝批准《凡尔赛和约》,不参加国际联盟。这标志着"十四点计划"的失败。

威尔逊外交政策长期以来是一个激起研究者兴趣也引起热烈争论的题目。究其原因,其中最重要的一点是他1912—1920年间担任总统期间,美国正处于需对内外政策做出重大抉择的转折时代。这一时期的特征在外交与国际关系领域中可简单概括为:美国正在实力上成为世界上最强大的国家,外交政策也要发生相应变化。但是20世纪的世界既不是美国建国之初还处于弱小时期的世界,也不是英、法等老牌帝国主义当年称霸一时的世界。世界在进入20世纪时出现了新的特点:世界开始了走向多元化的进程。这是一个复杂而又需要重新认识的世界。处于这样一个时代的威尔逊政府需要为美国制定一个与时代相适应的外交战略。威尔逊为美国选择的外交战略是以自己强大的经济实力加入角逐世界霸主的行列,威尔逊毫不含糊地认为美国应是世界的领袖。但他同时也不可能摆脱历史的束缚,美国的外交传统也为他的政策打下了深深的烙印。在传统与时代发生冲突时,威尔逊试图从传统中找到依据来解决冲突。在威尔逊之前,美国基本上没有参与世界事务的经历,因此也没有固定、明确的政策,在美国向老牌帝国主义的霸主地位挑战时,威尔逊只能从美国历史的经验中寻找办法来改造世界。这是威尔逊外交决策思维的重要特征。

威尔逊外交活动中最重要的也是最具代表性的应是他倡导并促成其建立的国际联盟。他在巴黎和会上的有形成果中最突出的也是国际联盟。虽然后来这一政策由于参议院拒绝批准《凡尔赛和约》,美国将自己排除在国际联盟之外而成为历史的讽刺,但是国际联盟作为威尔逊外交政策的一个重要部分,以及作为国联基础的集体安全原则应是研究威尔逊外交的重要内容。因为它的影响超过了威尔逊的时代,它是美国在国际关系格局的转变期,在美国外交重大抉择时期的产物,至今仍影响着美国的外交与国际关系。威尔逊外交的一些特征:利用美国独特的地缘政治地位及强大的经济实力,推行以集体安全为旗帜的政策,以一种貌似中间立场而实为超越欧洲列强之上的政策,来达到主宰世界的外交战略目标。但是威尔逊在推行其外交政策时并没有取得希望的结果,原因是:美国要以自己强大的实力凌驾于国际事务及欧洲各列强之上,即使美国放弃了中立政策,也并没有放弃"美国例外"与美国超然于其他国家之上的思维方式。但是当美国想要以自己的实力来使世界都服从于自己的目标时却发现多元化的国际环境与多元化的国内因素使美国心有余而力不足。这也是整个20世纪美国外交的特征。

Further reading

Bailey, Thomas A., *Woodrow Wilson and the Lost Peace*, Encounter Paperbacks, 1963.

Baker, Ray S. (ed.), *Woodrow Wilson and World Settlement*, 3 Vols., New York: Doubleday Page & Company, 1922.

Calhoun, Frederick S., *Power and Principle: Armed Intervention in Wilsonian Foreign Policy*, Kent: The Kent State University Press, 1986.

Clements, Kendrick A, "Woodrow Wilson and World War I", *Presidential Studies Quarterly* 34: 1, 2004.

Ginsberg, Benjamin. J., Lowi Theodore & Weir Margaret, *We the People*, New York: W.W. Norton & Company, 2001.

Hoover, Herbert, *The Ordeal of Woodrow Wilson*, New York: McGraw-Hill, 1958.

Johnson, Myron M., *League of Nations: A Review of American Foreign Policy from 1914 to 1946*, Boston, Mass.: House of Edinboro, 1946.

Lawrence, David, *The True Story of Woodrow Wilson*, New York: George H. Doran Company, 1924.

Link, Arther S., *Wilson the Diplomatist: A Look at His Major Foreign Policy*, Baltimore: The John Hopkins Press, 1974.

Tumulty, Joseph P., *Woodrow Wilson As I Know Him*, Los Angeles, CA: Hardpress Publishing, 2012.

Wilson, Woodrow, *A History of the American People*, New York: Harper and Brothers, 1902.

丹尼尔·E.哈蒙:《伍德罗·威尔逊》,孟祥德译,北京:现代教育出版社,2005年。

邓蜀生:《伍德罗·威尔逊》,上海:上海人民出版社,1982年。

韩莉:《新外交·旧世界——伍德罗·威尔逊与国际联盟》,北京:同心出版社,2002年。

任李明:《威尔逊主义研究》,北京:中国社会科学出版社,2013年。

王玮、戴超武:《美国外交思想史:1775—2005年》,北京:人民出版社,2007年。

王晓德:《梦想与现实:威尔逊理想主义外交研究》,北京:中国社会科学出版社,1995年。

杨生茂主编:《美国外交政策史:1775—1989》,北京:人民出版社,1991年。

张瑞德:《第一次世界大战》,北京:商务印书馆,1973年。

Chapter 6

Four Freedoms

（四大自由）

Pre-reading questions

1. How did the United States give up the policy of isolationism in WWII?
2. Why did President Roosevelt propose the Four Freedoms?

About the author

Franklin D. Roosevelt (1882—1945), often referred to by his initials FDR, is the 32nd president of the United States (1933—1945). Roosevelt served longer than any other president. He was regarded as one of the three greatest presidents in US history, along with George Washington and Abraham Lincoln. He was elected for four terms of presidency. His unprecedented election to four terms in office will probably never be repeated. The 22nd Amendment to the Constitution of the United States, passed after his death, denies the right of any person to be elected president more than twice.

Roosevelt was born in Hyde Park, New York, to a family made well known by Theodore Roosevelt, the 26th president of the United States. FDR attended Groton School, Harvard College, and Columbia Law School, going on to practice law in New York City. In 1905, he married his fifth cousin once removed, Eleanor Roosevelt. They had six children. He won election to the New York State Senate in 1910, and then served as Assistant Secretary of the Navy under President Woodrow Wilson during World War I. Roosevelt was James M. Cox's running mate on the Democratic Party's 1920 national ticket, but Cox was defeated by Warren G. Harding. In 1921, Roosevelt contracted a paralytic illness, believed at the time to be polio, and his legs became permanently paralyzed. While attempting to recover from his condition, Roosevelt founded the treatment center in Warm Springs, Georgia, for people with poliomyelitis. In spite of being unable to walk unaided, Roosevelt returned to public office by winning election as Governor of New York in 1928. He was in office from 1929 to 1933 and served as a reform Governor, promoting programs to combat the economic crisis besetting the United States at the time.

In the 1932 presidential election, Roosevelt defeated Republican President Herbert Hoover in a landslide. Roosevelt took office while the United States was in the midst of The Great Depression, the worst economic crisis in the country's history. During the first 100 days of the 73rd United States Congress, Roosevelt spearheaded unprecedented federal legislation and issued a profusion of executive orders that instituted the New Deal — a variety of programs designed to produce relief, recovery, and reform. He created numerous programs to provide relief to the unemployed and farmers while seeking economic recovery with the National Recovery Administration and other programs. He also instituted major regulatory reforms related to finance, communications, and labor, and presided over the end of Prohibition. The economy having improved rapidly from 1933 to 1936, Roosevelt won a landslide reelection in 1936. Even so, the economy then relapsed into a deep recession in 1937 and 1938. After the 1936 election, Roosevelt galvanized opposition by seeking passage of the Judiciary Reorganization Bill of 1937, which would have expanded the size of the Supreme Court of the United States. The bipartisan Conservative Coalition that formed in 1937 prevented passage of the bill and blocked the implementation of further New Deal programs and reforms. Major surviving programs and legislation implemented under Roosevelt include the Securities and Exchange Commission, the National Labor Relations Act, the Federal Deposit Insurance Corporation, and Social Security. His leadership of the Democratic Party transformed it into a political vehicle for American liberalism. Both in peacetime and in war his impact on the office of president was enormous. Although there had been strong presidents before him, they were the exception. In Roosevelt's 12 years in office, strong executive leadership became a basic part of United States government. He made the office of president the center of diplomatic initiative and the focus of domestic reform.

During the Second World War, the US adopted the non-interference policy. However, it adopted strict measures towards Hitler. Roosevelt led the Allies in collaboration with Churchill. Following the Japanese attack on Pearl Harbor on December 7, 1941, an event he famously called "a date which will live in infamy," Roosevelt obtained a declaration of war on Japan the next day, and a few days later, on Germany and Italy. Assisted by his top aide Harry Hopkins and with very strong national support, he worked closely with British Prime Minister Winston Churchill and Soviet leader Joseph Stalin in leading the Allies against the Axis Powers. Roosevelt supervised the mobilization of the U.S. economy to support the war effort and implemented a Europe first strategy, making the defeat of Germany a priority over that of Japan. He also initiated the development of the world's first atomic bomb and worked with the other Allied leaders to lay the groundwork for the United Nations and other post-war institutions. Roosevelt won reelection in 1944 but with his physical health seriously and steadily declining during the war years, he died in April 1945, just 11 weeks into his fourth term. The Axis Powers surrendered to the Allies in the months following Roosevelt's death, during the presidency of Roosevelt's successor, Harry S. Truman.

Text 1

The Four Freedoms Speech
Franklin D. Roosevelt, 6 January, 1941

Mr. President, Mr. Speaker, Members of the 77th Congress:

1   I address you, the members of this new Congress, at a moment unprecedented① in the history of the union. I use the word "unprecedented" because at no previous time has American security been as seriously threatened from without as it is today.

2   Since the permanent formation of our government under the Constitution in 1789, most of the periods of crisis in our history have related to our domestic affairs. And, fortunately, only one of these — the four-year war between the States② — ever threatened our national unity. Today, thank God, 130,000,000 Americans in 48 States have forgotten points of the compass in our national unity.

3   It is true that prior to 1914 the United States often has been disturbed by events in other continents. We have even engaged in two wars with European nations and in a number of undeclared wars in the West Indies, in the Mediterranean and in the Pacific, for the maintenance of American rights and for the principles of peaceful commerce.③ But in no case had a serious threat been raised against our national safety or our continued independence.

4   What I seek to convey is the historic truth that the United States as a nation has at all times maintained opposition — clear, definite opposition — to any attempt to lock us in behind an ancient Chinese wall while the procession of civilization went past.④ Today, thinking of our children and of their children, we oppose enforced isolation for ourselves or for any other part of the Americas.

5   That determination of ours, extending over all these years, was proved, for example, in the early days during the quarter century of wars following the French Revolution.⑤ While the Napoleonic struggles did threaten interests of the United States because of the French foothold in the West Indies and in Louisiana, and while we engaged in the War of 1812 to vindicate our right to peaceful trade, it is nevertheless clear that neither France nor Great Britain nor any other nation was aiming at domination of the whole world.

6   And in like fashion, from 1815 to 1914 — ninety-nine years — no single war in Europe or in Asia constituted a real threat against our future or against the future of any other

---

① 罗斯福用 unprecedented（前所未有的）这个词来形容当时形势的紧急，希望得到国会的支持。
② four-year war: 指美国南北战争（1861—1865），即美国内战。
③ 这里指美国和英国、法国发生的领土争端、1812 年第二次美英战争、1898 年美西战争，以及 1803 年杰斐逊总统曾派舰队到地中海打击勒索过往美国商船钱财的巴巴里海盗事件。
④ 指要以旧中国为鉴，不能闭关自守，像旧中国那样成为闭关锁国的国家。（闭关自守：close the country to the international intercourse）
⑤ 指从 1789 年法国大革命到 1814 年美国为扩大领土和英、法等国发生的战争。

American nation.

7 Except in the Maximilian interlude in Mexico,① no foreign power sought to establish itself in this hemisphere. And the strength of the British fleet in the Atlantic has been a friendly strength; it is still a friendly strength.

8 Even when the World War broke out in 1914, it seemed to contain only small threat of danger to our own American future. But as time went on, as we remember, the American people began to visualize what the downfall of democratic nations might mean to our own democracy.

9 We need not overemphasize imperfections in the peace of Versailles.② We need not harp on failure of the democracies to deal with problems of world reconstruction. We should remember that the peace of 1919 was far less unjust than the kind of pacification which began even before Munich,③ and which is being carried on under the new order of tyranny that seeks to spread over every continent today. The American people have unalterably set their faces against that tyranny.

10 I suppose that every realist knows that the democratic way of life is at this moment being directly assailed in every part of the world — assailed either by arms or by secret spreading of poisonous propaganda④ by those who seek to destroy unity and promote discord in nations that are still at peace. During 16 long months this assault has blotted out the whole pattern of democratic life in an appalling number of independent nations, great and small. And the assailants are still on the march, threatening other nations, great and small.

11 Therefore, as your President, performing my constitutional duty to "give to the Congress information of the state of the union," I find it unhappily necessary to report that the future and the safety of our country and of our democracy are overwhelmingly involved in events far beyond our borders.

12 Armed defense of democratic existence is now being gallantly waged in four continents.⑤ If that defense fails, all the population and all the resources of Europe and Asia, and Africa and Austral-Asia will be dominated by conquerors. And let us remember that the total of those populations in those four continents, the total of those populations and their resources greatly exceed the sum total of the population and the resources of the whole of the Western Hemisphere — yes, many times over.

13 In times like these it is immature — and, incidentally, untrue — for anybody to brag

---

① 指 1864—1867 年间。奥地利大公马克西米连（1832—1867）在此期间由墨西哥保守派和法国皇帝拿破仑三世扶持在墨西哥称帝，遭到各方反对，法军撤离墨西哥后他被击败处死。

② 1919 年第一次世界大战结束后交战各国在凡尔赛签订合约，对战后各国的领土划分和战争赔款等问题作出了规定。

③ 1938 年英国首相张伯伦为了避免战争几次飞往德国会见希特勒，承认希特勒占领苏台德地区，牺牲捷克的利益来换取"我们时代的和平"，集中体现了西欧国家在法西斯面前的软弱。

④ propaganda（宣传）这个词在第一次世界大战中成为虚假宣传的代名词，在美国的社会历史语境中，是一个贬义词。

⑤ "现在四大洲正在英勇地进行着以武力保卫民主生存的战争"，指参战国家最多、涉及范围最广、人员物资损耗最大的第二次世界大战。

that an unprepared America, single-handed and with one hand tied behind its back, can hold off the whole world.

14　No realistic American can expect from a dictator's peace international generosity, or return of true independence, or world disarmament, or freedom of expression, or freedom of religion — or even good business. Such a peace would bring no security for us or for our neighbors. Those who would give up essential liberty to purchase a little temporary safety deserve neither liberty nor safety.

15　As a nation we may take pride in the fact that we are soft-hearted; but we cannot afford to be soft-headed. We must always be wary of those who with sounding brass and a tinkling cymbal preach the "ism" of appeasement. We must especially beware of that small group of selfish men who would clip the wings of the American eagle in order to feather their own nests.①

16　I have recently pointed out how quickly the tempo of modern warfare② could bring into our very midst the physical attack which we must eventually expect if the dictator nations win this war.

17　There is much loose talk of our immunity from immediate and direct invasion from across the seas. Obviously, as long as the British Navy retains its power, no such danger exists. Even if there were no British Navy, it is not probable that any enemy would be stupid enough to attack us by landing troops in the United States from across thousands of miles of ocean, until it had acquired strategic bases from which to operate.③

18　But we learn much from the lessons of the past years in Europe — particularly the lesson of Norway, whose essential seaports were captured by treachery and surprise built up over a series of years. The first phase of the invasion of this hemisphere would not be the landing of regular troops. The necessary strategic points would be occupied by secret agents and by their dupes — and great numbers of them are already here and in Latin America. As long as the aggressor nations maintain the offensive they, not we, will choose the time and the place and the method of their attack.

19　And that is why the future of all the American Republics is today in serious danger. That is why this annual message to the Congress is unique in our history. That is why every member of the executive branch of the government and every member of the Congress face great responsibility, great accountability. The need of the moment is that our actions and our policy should be devoted primarily — almost exclusively — to meeting this foreign peril. For all our domestic problems are now a part of the great emergency.

20　Just as our national policy in internal affairs has been based upon a decent respect for the rights and the dignity of all our fellow men within our gates, so has our national policy in

---

① soft-hearted: 宽厚的，仁慈的；soft-headed: 愚蠢的，傻的。本段开头使用了押头韵（alliteration）和对比（contrast）的方法加强演讲效果，在段中还使用了借代（metonymy）和暗喻（metaphor）增加演讲的生动性。
② 罗斯福总统意指现代战争节奏很快，孤立主义无法抵挡。
③ 这里罗斯福总统实际上提到了马汉的海权理论，根据海权理论，美国必须要有海外战略基地。

foreign affairs been based on a decent respect for the rights and the dignity of all nations, large and small. And the justice of morality must and will win in the end.

21 Our national policy is this:

22 First, by an impressive expression of the public will and without regard to partisanship, we are committed to all-inclusive national defense.①

23 Secondly, by an impressive expression of the public will and without regard to partisanship, we are committed to full support of all those resolute people everywhere who are resisting aggression and are thereby keeping war away from our hemisphere. By this support we express our determination that the democratic cause shall prevail, and we strengthen the defense and the security of our own nation.②

24 Third, by an impressive expression of the public will and without regard to partisanship, we are committed to the proposition that principles of morality and considerations for our own security will never permit us to acquiesce in a peace dictated by aggressors and sponsored by appeasers. We know that enduring peace cannot be bought at the cost of other people's freedom.③

25 In the recent national election there was no substantial difference between the two great parties in respect to that national policy. No issue was fought out on this line before the American electorate. And today it is abundantly evident that American citizens everywhere are demanding and supporting speedy and complete action in recognition of obvious danger.

26 Therefore, the immediate need is a swift and driving increase in our armament production. Leaders of industry and labor have responded to our summons. Goals of speed have been set. In some cases these goals are being reached ahead of time. In some cases we are on schedule; in other cases there are slight but not serious delays. And in some cases — and, I am sorry to say, very important cases — we are all concerned by the slowness of the accomplishment of our plans.

27 The Army and Navy, however, have made substantial progress during the past year. Actual experience is improving and speeding up our methods of production with every passing day. And today's best is not good enough for tomorrow.

28 I am not satisfied with the progress thus far made. The men in charge of the program represent the best in training, in ability, and in patriotism. They are not satisfied with the progress thus far made. None of us will be satisfied until the job is done.

29 No matter whether the original goal was set too high or too low, our objective is quicker and better results.

---

① "在明确表达公众意愿以及排除党派偏见的情况下，我们致力于全面的国防。"
② "在明确表达公众意愿以及排除党派偏见的情况下，我们决定对于任何地方反抗侵略致使战火没有燃到我们西半球来的所有英勇民族，予以全力支持。我们用这种支持，来表示我们对民主事业必胜的决心；我们要加强我国本身的防御和安全。"
③ "在明确表达公众意愿以及排除党派偏见的情况下，我们决定声明，道德的基本原则和我们对本身安全的考虑，将永不容许我们默认由侵略者所支配和'和解'主义者所赞许的和平。我们知道，持久和平是不能以他人的自由为代价买来的。" appeaser: n. 劝解人。

30   To give you two illustrations:

31   We are behind schedule in turning out finished airplanes. We are working day and night to solve the innumerable problems and to catch up.

32   We are ahead of schedule in building warships, but we are working to get even further ahead of that schedule.

33   To change a whole nation from a basis of peacetime production of implements of peace to a basis of wartime production of implements of war is no small task. And the greatest difficulty comes at the beginning of the program, when new tools, new plant facilities, new assembly lines, new shipways must first be constructed before the actual material begins to flow steadily and speedily from them.

34   The Congress of course, must rightly keep itself informed at all times of the progress of the program. However, there is certain information, as the Congress itself will readily recognize, which, in the interests of our own security and those of the nations that we are supporting, must of needs be kept in confidence.

35   New circumstances are constantly begetting new needs for our safety.① I shall ask this Congress for greatly increased new appropriations and authorizations to carry on what we have begun.

36   I also ask this Congress for authority and for funds sufficient to manufacture additional munitions and war supplies of many kinds, to be turned over to those nations which are now in actual war with aggressor nations. Our most useful and immediate role is to act as an arsenal for them as well as for ourselves. They do not need manpower, but they do need billions of dollars' worth of the weapons of defense.②

37   The time is near when they will not be able to pay for them all in ready cash. We cannot, and we will not, tell them that they must surrender merely because of present inability to pay for the weapons which we know they must have.

38   I do not recommend that we make them a loan of dollars with which to pay for these weapons — a loan to be repaid in dollars. I recommend that we make it possible for those nations to continue to obtain war materials in the United States, fitting their orders into our own program. And nearly all of their material would, if the time ever came, be useful in our own defense.③

39   Taking counsel of expert military and naval authorities, considering what is best for our own security, we are free to decide how much should be kept here and how much should be sent abroad to our friends who, by their determined and heroic resistance, are giving us time

---

① 罗斯福对国会陈述了美国对正在不断扩大的国际冲突的反应。仅在几个月之前，法国落入希特勒之手；就在罗斯福发表演讲的同时，英国正坚决抵抗纳粹的空袭。在那几个扣人心弦的月份中，英国一直存在着现实而可怕的军事崩溃的可能性。在这篇演说中，罗斯福为积极援助美国的盟国作了舆论准备。

② 罗斯福发出号召，美国必须实施向关系到美国安全的国家租借或转让武器的计划，号召美国人以全部的道义力量支持《租借法》，支持英、法等国的反法西斯战争。

③ "我建议由我们设法使那些国家继续从美国取得作战物资，并使他们的定单与我们自己的计划配合起来。一旦时刻到来，他们的几乎全部军用物资都会有利于我们自己的防卫。"

in which to make ready our own defense.

40   For what we send abroad we shall be repaid, repaid within a reasonable time following the close of hostilities, repaid in similar materials, or at our option in other goods of many kinds which they can produce and which we need.

41   Let us say to the democracies, "We Americans are vitally concerned in your defense of freedom. We are putting forth our energies, our resources, and our organizing powers to give you the strength to regain and maintain a free world. We shall send you in ever-increasing numbers, ships, planes, tanks, guns. That is our purpose and our pledge."

42   In fulfillment of this purpose we will not be intimidated by the threats of dictators that they will regard as a breach of international law or as an act of war our aid to the democracies which dare to resist their aggression.① Such aid — Such aid is not an act of war, even if a dictator should unilaterally proclaim it so to be.

43   And when the dictators — if the dictators — are ready to make war upon us, they will not wait for an act of war on our part.

44   They did not wait for Norway or Belgium or the Netherlands to commit an act of war. Their only interest is in a new one-way international law, which lacks mutuality in its observance and therefore becomes an instrument of oppression. The happiness of future generations of Americans may well depend on how effective and how immediate we can make our aid felt. No one can tell the exact character of the emergency situations that we may be called upon to meet. The nation's hands must not be tied when the nation's life is in danger.

45   Yes, and we must prepare, all of us prepare, to make the sacrifices that the emergency — almost as serious as war itself — demands.② Whatever stands in the way of speed and efficiency in defense, in defense preparations of any kind, must give way to the national need.③

46   A free nation has the right to expect full cooperation from all groups. A free nation has the right to look to the leaders of business, of labor, and of agriculture to take the lead in stimulating effort, not among other groups but within their own group.

47   The best way of dealing with the few slackers or trouble-makers in our midst is, first, to shame them by patriotic example, and if that fails, to use the sovereignty of government to save government.

48   As men do not live by bread alone, they do not fight by armaments alone.④ Those who man our defenses and those behind them who build our defenses must have the stamina and the courage which come from unshakable belief in the manner of life which they are defending. The mighty action that we are calling for cannot be based on a disregard of all the

---

① "我们不会因独裁者的威胁而退缩不前，这些人认为我们对那些胆敢抵抗他们侵略的民主国家进行支持，是违反国际公法，是战争行为。" intimidate: to make timid; to coerce or inhibit by or as if by threats 恐吓，胁迫，通过威胁或近乎威胁的手段强制或禁止。
② "我们全体都必须准备为那种和战争本身一样严重的非常时期的要求，作出牺牲。"
③ "任何阻碍迅速而有效地进行防卫准备的事，都必须为国家的需要让路。"
④ 罗斯福想告诉美国人，武器固然重要，但是勇气和精神更重要。

things worth fighting for.①

49 The nation takes great satisfaction and much strength from the things which have been done to make its people conscious of their individual stake in the preservation of democratic life in America. Those things have toughened the fiber of our people, have renewed their faith and strengthened their devotion to the institutions we make ready to protect.

50 Certainly this is no time for any of us to stop thinking about the social and economic problems which are the root cause of the social revolution which is today a supreme factor in the world.② For there is nothing mysterious about the foundations of a healthy and strong democracy.

51 The basic things expected by our people of their political and economic systems are simple. They are:

Equality of opportunity for youth and for others.

Jobs for those who can work.

Security for those who need it.

The ending of special privilege for the few.

The preservation of civil liberties for all.

The enjoyment — The enjoyment of the fruits of scientific progress in a wider and constantly rising standard of living.③

52 These are the simple, the basic things that must never be lost sight of in the turmoil and unbelievable complexity of our modern world. The inner and abiding strength of our economic and political systems is dependent upon the degree to which they fulfill these expectations.

53 Many subjects connected with our social economy call for immediate improvement. As examples:

54 We should bring more citizens under the coverage of old-age pensions and unemployment insurance.

55 We should widen the opportunities for adequate medical care.

56 We should plan a better system by which persons deserving or needing gainful employment may obtain it.

57 I have called for personal sacrifice, and I am assured of the willingness of almost all Americans to respond to that call. A part of the sacrifice means the payment of more money in taxes. In my budget message I will recommend that a greater portion of this great defense program be paid for from taxation than we are paying for today. No person should try, or be allowed to get rich out of the program, and the principle of tax payments in accordance with ability to pay should be constantly before our eyes to guide our legislation.

---

① "我们所号召的伟大行动的基础是重视所有值得奋斗的东西。"
② 美国在罗斯福新政的指引下，刚刚从一场经济大萧条的浩劫中恢复过来。罗斯福在此提到："现在并非停止考虑各种社会和经济问题的时候，这些问题都是社会革命的根本原因，而这种革命则是今天世界的一个主要因素。"
③ "给青年和其他人以均等机会；给能工作的人以工作；给需要保障的人以保障；终止少数人享有的特权；保护所有人的公民自由权；在生活水平更普遍和不断提高的情况下，享受科学进步的成果。"

58　If the Congress maintains these principles the voters, putting patriotism ahead pocketbooks, will give you their applause.

59　In the future days, which we seek to make secure, we look forward to a world founded upon four essential human freedoms.①

60　The first is freedom of speech and expression — everywhere in the world.

61　The second is freedom of every person to worship God in his own way everywhere in the world.

62　The third is freedom from want, which, translated into world terms, means economic understandings② which will secure to every nation a healthy peacetime life for its inhabitants — everywhere in the world.

63　The fourth is freedom from fear, which, translated into world terms, means a world-wide reduction of armaments to such a point and in such a thorough fashion that no nation will be in a position to commit an act of physical aggression against any neighbor — anywhere in the world.

64　That is no vision of a distant millennium.③ It is a definite basis for a kind of world attainable in our own time and generation. That kind of world is the very antithesis of the so-called "new order" of tyranny which the dictators seek to create with the crash of a bomb.

65　To that new order we oppose the greater conception — the moral order.④ A good society is able to face schemes of world domination and foreign revolutions alike without fear.

66　Since the beginning of our American history we have been engaged in change, in a perpetual, peaceful revolution, a revolution which goes on steadily, quietly, adjusting itself to changing conditions without the concentration camp or the quicklime in the ditch⑤. The world order which we seek is the cooperation of free countries, working together in a friendly, civilized society.

67　This nation has placed its destiny in the hands and heads and hearts of its millions of free men and women, and its faith in freedom under the guidance of God. Freedom means the supremacy of human rights everywhere.⑥ Our support goes to⑦ those who struggle to gain those rights and keep them. Our strength is our unity of purpose.

68　To that high concept there can be no end save victory.⑧

---

① 罗斯福的"四大自由"：在全世界任何地方发表言论和表达意见的自由；在全世界任何地方以自己的方式来崇拜上帝的自由；免于匮乏的自由；免于恐惧的自由。
② "这种自由，就世界范围来讲，就是一种经济上的融洽关系……"
③ "这并不是对一个渺茫的黄金时代的憧憬。" millennium: *n.* 太平盛世，一千年。
④ 1940 年大选时，两位候选人均表示美国不介入国外战争。然而 1940 年法国战败，罗斯福积极作防御准备，决定用参战以外的一切方式援助英国，暗示着美国将用道义援助和经济援助支持盟友。
⑤ the concentration camp or the quicklime in the ditch: 集中营或万人冢。
⑥ "自由意味着在任何地方人权都是至高无上的。" supremacy: *n.* 至高无上；最高权力。
⑦ 相当于"We support…"，此句的意思是："凡是为了取得或保持这种权利而斗争的人，我们都予以支持。"
⑧ "为了实现这一崇高的观念，我们是不获全胜绝不停止。"

Vocabulary

unprecedented (para. 1)	*adj.* having no previous example 史无前例的
isolation (para. 4)	*n.* the act of separating sb. or sth. or the state of being separated
domination (para. 5)	*n.* mastery or supremacy over another or others
interlude (para. 7)	*n.* an intervening episode, feature, or period of time
visualize (para. 8)	*v.* to form a mental image of; envisage
assail (para. 10)	*v.* to assault or to attack verbally; to trouble, beset
gallantly (para. 12)	*adv.* bravely; grandly; stately
single-handed (para. 13)	*adj.* done by one person with no help from others
wary (para. 15)	*adj.* on guard, watchful; characterized by caution
appeasement (para. 15)	*n.* act or policy making concessions to a possible enemy
phase (para. 18)	*n.* a distinct stage of development; a temporary manner, attitude, or pattern of behavior; an aspect, a part
acquiesce (para. 24)	*v.* to consent or comply passively or without protest
electorate (para. 25)	*n.* all the qualified electors as a group
munitions (para. 36)	*n.* (*pl.*) war materiel, especially weapons and ammunition *v.* to supply with munitions
arsenal (para. 36)	*n.* place where weapons and ammunition are made or stored
pledge (para. 41)	*n.* vow; a binding commitment to do or give or refrain from sth.
stamina (para. 48)	*n.* physical or moral strength to resist or withstand illness, fatigue, or hardship; endurance
abiding (para. 52)	*adj.* lasting for a long time; enduring
attainable (para. 64)	*adj.* that can succeed in getting or achieving
antithesis (para. 64)	*n.* direct contrast or exact opposite; opposition

Questions for discussion

1. According to FDR, to what extent was American national security in great danger?
2. How did FDR illustrate to Congress?
3. According to FDR, what was the basis of American policy?
4. According to FDR, was it easy to change a whole nation from a basis of peacetime production of implements of peace to a basis of wartime production of implements of war?
5. What should be the role played by the U.S. in the war according to FDR?
6. How did FDR justify lend-lease in regard to American relations with aggressor nations?
7. How did FDR call for defense preparations?

About the author

1. Franklin D. Roosevelt (Please refer to Text 1)

2. Winston Churchill (1874—1965), a British politician known chiefly for his leadership of the United Kingdom during World War II, served as Prime Minister from 1940 to 1945 and again from 1951 to 1955. A noted statesman and orator, Churchill was also an officer in the British Army, historian, writer, and artist. He was the only British Prime Minister to have received the Nobel Prize in Literature and the first person to be recognized as an Honorary Citizen of the United States.

Before the First World War, he served as President of the Board of Trade, Home Secretary and First Lord of the Admiralty as part of the Asquith Liberal government. During the war he continued as First Lord of the Admiralty until the disastrous Gallipoli Campaign caused his departure from government. He returned as Minister of Munitions, Secretary of State for War and Secretary of State for Air. In the interwar years, he served as Chancellor of the Exchequer in the Conservative government.

After the outbreak of the Second World War, Churchill was again appointed First Lord of the Admiralty. Following the resignation of Neville Chamberlain on 10 May 1940, he became Prime Minister of the United Kingdom and led Britain to victory against the Axis powers. Churchill was always noted for his speeches, which became a great inspiration to the British people and embattled Allied forces.

After losing the 1945 election, he became Leader of the Opposition. In 1951, he again became Prime Minister before finally retiring in 1955. Upon his death, the Queen granted him the honor of a state funeral, which saw one of the largest assemblies of statesmen in the world.

Text 2

Atlantic Charter[①]
Franklin D. Roosevelt & Winston Churchill, August 14, 1941

1   The President of the United States of America and the Prime Minister, Mr. Churchill, representing His Majesty's Government in the United Kingdom, being met together, deem it right to make known certain common principles in the national policies of their respective countries on which they base their hopes for a better future for the world.[②]

2   First, their countries seek no aggrandizement, territorial or other;

3   Second, they desire to see no territorial changes that do not accord with the freely expressed wishes of the peoples concerned[③];

4   Third, they respect the right of all peoples to choose the form of government under which they will live; and they wish to see sovereign rights and self government restored to those who have been forcibly deprived of them;

5   Fourth, they will endeavor, with due respect for their existing obligations, to further the enjoyment by all States, great or small, victor or vanquished, of access, on equal terms[④], to the trade and to the raw materials of the world which are needed for their economic prosperity;

6   Fifth, they desire to bring about the fullest collaboration between all nations in the economic field with the object of securing, for all, improved labor standards, economic advancement and social security;

7   Sixth, after the final destruction of the Nazi tyranny[⑤], they hope to see established a

---

① 《大西洋宪章》最初由丘吉尔起草，确定了民主国家抵抗德国侵略的原则。丘吉尔在1941年9月9日议会上宣称："在大西洋会议上，我们始终记得恢复此刻处于纳粹奴役下的国家主权。"对丘吉尔而言，《大西洋宪章》仅限于打败纳粹主义。罗斯福对宪章有不同的理解。他将这看成是结束英国殖民地进程的机遇。罗斯福和美国整个民族对英国的帝国主义动机非常不信任。他对丘吉尔说："我无法相信我们能为对抗法西斯而战，同时却无法让全世界的人民脱离落后的殖民制度。和平不包括任何专制……民族平等是指竞争贸易的最大自由。"罗斯福对丘吉尔的宪章进行了增补，扩充了对它的解释。他成功迫使英国同意其殖民地独立。丘吉尔很不愿意做出这种让步，他对宪章的措辞提出了不同意见。罗斯福想加入一个条款，内容为："一视同仁地努力促使所有国家，不分大小，战胜者或战败者，都有机会在同等条件下……参加世界贸易和获得世界的原料 (without discrimination to further the enjoyment by all States, great or small, victor or vanquished, of access, on equal terms, to the trade and to the raw materials of the world ....)。"丘吉尔要求将 "一视同仁地（without discrimination）"改成 "在尊重他们现有义务下（with due respect to their existing obligations）"。

② "美利坚合众国总统和代表联合王国的丘吉尔首相，经过会商，觉得把他们两国政策的若干共同原则（对更美好未来世界的希望即以此为基础）在此时向世界宣布，是合适的。"

③ "他们不希望看见发生任何与有关人民自由表达的意志不相符合的领土变更。"指不承认法西斯通过侵略造成的领土变更。

④ 在平等的基础上。

⑤ 纳粹暴政。

peace① which will afford to all nations the means of dwelling in safety within their own boundaries, and which will afford assurance that all the men in all lands may live out their lives in freedom from fear and want;

8   Seventh, such a peace should enable all men to traverse the high seas and oceans without hindrance;

9   Eighth, they believe that all of the nations of the world, for realistic as well as spiritual reasons must come to the abandonment of the use of force. Since no future peace can be maintained if land, sea or air armaments continue to be employed by nations which threaten, or may threaten, aggression outside of their frontiers, they believe, pending the establishment of a wider and permanent system of general security, that the disarmament of such nations is essential②. They will likewise aid and encourage all other practicable measure which will lighten for peace-loving peoples the crushing burden of armaments③.

Franklin D. Roosevelt (Signature)
Winston S. Churchill (Signature)

Vocabulary

aggrandizement (para. 2)	*n.* the act of increasing the wealth or prestige or power or scope of something
sovereign (para. 4)	*adj.* independent of outside authority
victor (para. 5)	*n.* the winner of a battle, competition, game, etc.
vanquish (para. 5)	*v.* to defeat or overcome in a battle, contest, etc.; conquer
collaboration (para. 6)	*n.* the act of working with another or others on a joint project
dwell (in) (para. 7)	*v.* to live (in a specified state)
traverse (para. 8)	*v.* to pass or go over or back and forth over (something); cross
hindrance (para. 8)	*n.* an obstruction or snag; impediment
pending (para. 9)	*prep.* while waiting for or anticipating
disarmament (para. 9)	*n.* the reduction of offensive or defensive fighting capability, as by a nation

Questions for discussion

1. To what extent are the Four Freedoms reflected in the *Atlantic Charter*?

---

① 本句结构为 see a peace which...established, see sth. done 的结构, 由于 which 引导的定语从句太长, 所以置于句末。
② "所以他们相信, 在一个更普遍和更持久的全面安全体系建立之前, 解除这些国家的武装是必要的。"
③ "来减轻爱好和平的人民在军备上的沉重负担。"原句序为: lighten the crushing burden of armaments for peace-loving peoples, 由于宾语过长, 置于句末, 以保持句子平衡。

2. What was the significance of the *Atlantic Charter* both during and after World War II?
3. Was Roosevelt and Churchill's "hope for a better future for the world" fulfilled after World War II?

 Text 3

The United Nations Fight for the Four Freedoms①
The Office of War Information, 1942

The Rights of All Men — Everywhere

The four freedoms of common humanity are as much elements of man's needs as air and sunlight, bread and salt. Deprive him of all these freedoms and he dies — deprive him of a part of them and a part of him withers. Give them to him in full and abundant measure and he will cross the threshold of a new age, the greatest age of man.

These freedoms are the rights of men of every creed and every race, wherever they live. This is their heritage, long withheld. We of the United Nations have the power and the men and the will at last to assure man's heritage.

The belief in the four freedoms of common humanity — the belief in man, created free, in the image of God — is the crucial difference between ourselves and the enemies we face today. In it lies the absolute unity of our alliance, opposed to the oneness of the evil we hate. Here is our strength, the source and promise of victory.

Franklin D. Roosevelt

The Four Freedoms

1   Beyond the war lies the peace. Both sides have sketched the outlines of the new world toward which they strain. The leaders of the Axis countries have published their design for all to read. They promise a world in which the conquered peoples will live out their lives in the service of their masters②.

2   The United Nations, now engaged in a common cause, have also published their design, and have committed certain common aims to writing③. They plan a world in which men stand straight and walk free, free not of all human trouble but free of the fear of despotic power, free to develop as individuals, free to conduct and shape their affairs. Such a world has been more dream than reality, more hope than fact④; but it has been the best hope men have had and the one for which they have most consistently shown themselves willing to die.

---

① 《联合国为四大自由而战》是一本宣传册,1942 年由华盛顿特区战情办公室制作发行。
② "被征服的民族将过一种为其主人(即纳粹德国)服务的生活。"
③ "将一些共同目标写了下来。"
④ "这样的一个世界更多的是梦想而非现实,是希望而非事实。"

3   This freeness, this liberty①, this precious thing men love and mean to save, is the good granite ledge② on which the United Nations now propose to raise their new world after victory. The purpose of this pamphlet is to examine and define the essential freedoms.

4   To talk of war aims, shouting over the din of battle while the planet rocks and vibrates, may seem futile to some③. Yet the talk must go on among free peoples. The faith people have in themselves is what the free have to build upon. Such faith is basic to them — man's hot belief in man, a belief which suggests that human beings are capable of ordering their affairs. This is a high compliment paid by man to himself, an evidence or gesture of self-respect, of stature, of dignity, and of worth, an affidavit of individual responsibility④.

5   The freedoms we are fighting for, we who are free: the freedoms for which the men and women in the concentration camps and prisons and in the dark streets of the subjugated countries wait, are four in number.⑤

"The first is freedom of speech and expression everywhere in the world.

"The second is freedom of every person to worship God in his own way everywhere in the world.

"The third is freedom from want — which, translated into world terms, means economic understandings which will secure to every nation a healthy peacetime life for its inhabitants — everywhere in the world.

"The fourth is freedom from fear — which, translated into world terms, means a world-wide reduction of armaments to such a point and in such a thorough fashion that no nation will be in a position to commit an act of physical aggression against any neighbor — anywhere in the world."

6   These freedoms are separate, but not independent. Each one relies upon all the others. Each supports the whole, which is liberty. When one is missing, all the others are jeopardized. A person who lives under a tyrant, and has lost freedom of speech, must necessarily be tortured by fear. A person who is in great want is usually also in great fear — fear of even direr want and greater insecurity. A person denied the right to worship in his own way has thereby lost the knack of free speech⑥, for unless he is free to exercise his religious conscience, his privilege of free speech (even though not specifically denied) is meaningless. A person tortured with fears has lost both the privilege of free speech and the strength to supply himself with his needs. Clearly these four freedoms are as closely related, as dependent one upon

---

① freeness: 指更小范围的自由，可以翻译为无拘无束，无顾虑；freedom: "自由"的涵义比较广泛，包括社会政治经济意义上的自由，以及个体内心的无拘无束。liberty 可以与 freedom 互换，但 liberty 更强调自由选择的权利。
② granite ledge: 坚固的基础。granite: 花岗岩；ledge: 平台，壁架，窗台。
③ "对一些人来说，在整个地球摇动战栗之时，透过战斗的喧嚣去谈论战争的目的，似乎是一种徒劳。"
④ 个人责任的宣誓书。affidavit: a written statement which someone makes after they have sworn officially to tell the truth, and which might be used as proof in a court of law 宣誓作证书。
⑤ "我们（自由的人）所为之斗争的自由——那些在集中营、监狱、战败国黑暗街道上的男男女女所等待的自由——共有四条。"
⑥ "一个被剥夺了自由信仰权利的人也就失去了言论自由的能力。"

another, as the four seasons of the natural year, whose winter snows irrigate the spring, and whose dead leaves, fermenting, rebuild the soil for summer's yield.

7　The first two freedoms — freedom of speech and freedom of religion — are cultural. They are prerogatives of the thinking man, of the creative and civilized human being. Sometimes, as in the United States, they are guaranteed by organic law①. They are rather clearly understood, and the laws protecting them are continually being revised and adjusted to preserve their basic meaning. Freedom from fear and from want, on the other hand, are not part of our culture but part of our environment — they concern the facts of our lives rather than the thoughts of our minds. Men are unafraid, or well-fed, or both, according to the conditions under which they live.

8　To be free a man must live in a society which has relieved those curious pressures which conspire to make men slaves: pressure of a despotic government, pressure of intolerance, pressure of want②. The declaration of the four freedoms, therefore, is not a promise of a gift which, under certain conditions, the people will receive; it is a declaration of a design which the people themselves may execute.

9　Freedom, of whatever sort, is relative. Nations united by a common effort to create a better world are obviously not projecting a Utopia③ in which nobody shall want for anything. That is not the point — nor within the range of human possibility. What unites them is the purpose to create a world in which no one need want for the minimum necessities of an orderly and decent life, for cleanliness, for self-respect and security. It is an ambitious design, perhaps too ambitious for the cynic or the faithless; but it is supported by the sure knowledge that the earth produces abundantly and that men are already in possession of the tools which could realize such a purpose if men chose to use them④.

10　This, then, is a credo to which the representatives of 28 nations have subscribed — not a promise made by any group of men to any other group. It is only the people themselves who can create the conditions favoring these essential freedoms which they are now repurchasing in the bazaar of war and paying for with their lives.⑤ Nothing is for sale at bargain prices, nor will the house be built in three days with cheap labor. From a world in ruins there can rise only a slow, deliberate monument. This time, conceived by so many peoples of united purpose, it will rise straight upward and rest on good support.

Freedom of Speech

11　To live free a man must speak openly: gag him and he becomes either servile or full

---

① organic law: law determining the fundamental political principles of a government, 基本法；组织法。
② "要想自由，我们生存的社会必须消除那些变人为奴的困扰：专制政府的困扰，不宽容的困扰，匮乏的困扰。"
③ 乌托邦（理想中美好的社会）。
④ "但是有确凿的知识证明地球物产丰富，人类已掌握工具，只要他们利用这些工具，这个目标就能实现。"
⑤ "只有人类自己能创造出有利于这些基本自由的条件，他们此刻正在战争的市场中重新购买，并用自己的生命去支付。"

of cankers①. Free government is then the most realistic kind of government for it not only assumes that a man has something on his mind, but concedes his right to say it. It permits him to talk — not without fear of contradiction, but without fear of punishment.

12 There can be no people's rule unless there is talk. Men, it turns out, breathe through their minds as well as through their lungs, and there must be a circulation of ideas as well as of air. Since nothing is likely to be more distasteful to a man than the opinion of someone who disagrees with him, it does the race credit② that it has so stubbornly defended the principle of free speech. But if a man knows anything at all, he knows that that principle is fundamental in self-government, the whole purpose of which is to reflect and affirm the will of the people.③

13 In America, free speech and a free press were the first things the minds of the people turned to after the fashioning of the Constitution. Farsighted men, in those early days, readily understood that some sort of protection was necessary. Thus when the first amendment to the Constitution was drawn (part of what the world now knows as the Bill of Rights), it prohibited the Congress from making any law which might abridge the freedom of speech or of the press, or the right of the people peaceably to assemble and to petition the Government for a redress of their grievances.

14 In the Nazi state, freedom of speech and expression have been discarded — not for temporary military expediency, but as a principle of life. Being contemptuous of the individual, and secretly suspicious of him, the German leader has deprived him of his voice. Ideas are what tyrants most fear. To set up a despotic state, the first step is to get rid of the talkers — the talkers in schools, the talkers in forums, the talkers in political rallies and in trade union meetings, the talkers on the radio and in the newsreels, and in the barber shops and village garages. Talk does not fit the Nazi and the Fascist scheme, where all ideas are, by the very nature of the political structure, the property of one man.

15 Talk is death to tyranny, for it can easily clarify a political position which the ruler may prefer to becloud, and it can expose injustices which he may choose to obscure.

16 Our Bill of Rights specifically mentioned the press. Today the press is one of many forms of utterance. Talk and ideas flow in ever-increasing torrents through books, magazines, schools, the radio, the motion picture. The camera has created a whole new language of its own.

17 All these new forms are safeguarded with the ancient guarantees, but the essential danger of not being allowed to speak freely remains. Today the privilege is challenged

---

① "堵住一个人的嘴，他会变得屈从或长满溃疡。"
② do ...credit：使……感到光荣。
③ "唯一的目标就是反映并肯定人民的意愿。"

more gravely than ever before; in the countries dominated by the Axis books are burned, universities are shut down, men are put to death for listening to a radio broadcast. Hitler's New Order① seeks to prove that unity and efficiency are achieved most readily among people who are prevented from reading, thinking, talking, debating. This new anesthesia is a subtle drug. Under its quick influence men sleep a strange sleep.

18 The right to speak, the right to hear, the right of access to information carry with them certain responsibilities. Certain favorable conditions are necessary before freedom of speech acquires validity.

19 The first condition is that the individual have something to say. Literacy is a prerequisite of free speech, and gives it point. Denied education, denied information, suppressed or enslaved, people grow sluggish; their opinions are hardly worth the high privilege of release. Similarly, those who live in terror or in destitution, even though no specific control is placed upon their speech, are as good as gagged②.

20 Another condition necessary for free speech is that the people have access to the means of uttering it — to newspapers, to the radio, the public forum. When power or capital are concentrated, when the press is too closely the property of narrow interests③, then freedom suffers. There is no freedom, either, unless facts are within reach, unless information is made available. And a final condition of free speech is that there be no penalties attached to the spread of information and to the expression of opinion, whether those penalties be applied by the Government or by any private interests whatsoever.

21 The operation of a free press and the free expression of opinion are far from absolute rights. The laws of libel and slander④ set limits on what men may say of other men. The exigency of war sets limits on what information may be given out, lest it give aid and comfort to the enemy. Good taste sets limits on all speech.

22 Freedom of speech, Justice Holmes has warned, does not grant the right to shout fire in a crowded theatre. When ideas become overt acts against peace and order, then the Government presumes to interfere with free speech. The burden of proof, however, is upon those who would restrict speech — the danger must be not some vague danger but real and immediate.

23 We are not so much concerned with these inevitable limitations to free speech as with the delight at the principle in society and how greatly it has strengthened man's spirit, how

---

① 1936年3月，希特勒在进军莱茵非军事区后宣称"欧洲应该出现一种新秩序"。随着大战爆发，德国在战场上节节胜利，欧洲大部分地区沦入纳粹德国之手。为了控制占领区人民，掠夺占领区的财产，纳粹政权推行了一系列措施，着手建立"欧洲新秩序"。综观纳粹政权在占领区的行为，所谓"欧洲新秩序"可概括为：改变欧洲原有版图，合并所有德意志人居住区，建立"大德意志国"；以"大德意志国"为中心，建立一个统一的、由纳粹政权控制的欧洲；以德意志人为主宰，将各民族按人种划分等级；设立集中营，消灭犹太人，在占领区实行恐怖统治；控制占领区经济，掠夺其财产；强制推广德语，摧残各国文化和民族语言，等等。

② "几乎等同于嘴被堵上了。" as good as：几乎，实际上。

③ "当新闻近乎成为狭隘的利益群体的财产时。"

④ laws of libel and slander：污蔑诽谤法。

steadily it has enlarged his culture and his world.① We in America know what the privilege is because we have lived with it for a century and a half. Talk founded the Union, nurtured it, and preserved it. The dissenter, the disbeliever, the crack-pot②, the reformer, those who would pull down as well as build up — all are free to have their say.

24　Talk is our daily fare — the white-bosomed lecturer regaling the Tuesday Ladies' Club, the prisoner at the bar testifying in his own behalf, the editorial writer complaining of civic abuses, the actor declaiming behind the footlights, the movie star speaking on the screen, the librarian dispensing the accumulated talk of ages, the professor holding forth to his students, the debating society, the meeting of the aldermen, the minister in the pulpit, the traveler in the smoking car, the soap-box orator with his flag and his bundle of epigrams, the opinions of the solemn magistrate and the opinions of the animated mouse — words, ideas, in a never-ending stream, from the enduring wisdom of the great and the good to the puniest thought troubling the feeblest brain. All are listened to, all add up to something and we call it the rule of the people, the people who are free to say the words.

25　The United States fights to preserve this heritage, which is the very essence of the Four Freedoms. How, unless there is freedom of speech, can freedom of religion or freedom from want or freedom from fear be realized? The enemies of all liberty flourish and grow strong in the dark of enforced silence.

26　For the right to be articulate the inarticulate airman climbs to his fabulous battleground. For this fight the grim-lipped soldier; the close-mouthed sailor; the marine.③

Freedom of Religion

27　That part of man which is called the spirit and which belongs only to himself and to his God, is of the very first concern in designing a free world. It was not their stomachs but their immortal souls which brought the first settlers to America's shores, and they prayed before they ate. Freedom of conscience, the right to worship God, is part of our soil and of the sky above this continent.

28　Freedom of worship implies that the individual has a source of moral values which transcends the immediate necessities of the community, however important these may be. It is one thing to pay taxes to the state — this men will do; it is another to submit their consciences to the state — this they politely decline. The wise

---

① "我们所关注的不是这些言论自由必然的限制性，而是对社会中的这个原则高兴不已，它大大地增强了人类的意志，稳步地拓展了人类的文化和世界。"
② crack-pot：不切实际的狂想家。
③ "为了清楚表达这种权利，沉默的飞行员加入了战斗。严肃的士兵、抿着嘴唇的水手，还有海军都在为此战斗。" 句序应为：the grim-lipped soldier; the close-mouthed sailor; the marine fight for this. 此处倒装强调战斗的目的。

community respects this mysterious quality in the individual, and makes its plans accordingly.

29　The democratic guarantee of freedom of worship is not in the nature of a grant — it is in the nature of an admission①. It is the state admitting that the spirit soars in illimitable regions beyond the collectors of customs. It was Tom Paine②, one of the great voices of freedom in early America, who pointed out that a government could no more grant to man the liberty to worship God than it could grant to God the liberty of receiving such worship.

30　The miracle which democracy has achieved is that while practicing many kinds of worship, we nevertheless achieve social unity and peace. And so we have the impressive spectacle, which is with us always here in America, of men attending many different churches, but the same town meeting, the same political forum.③

31　Opposed to this democratic conception of man and of the human spirit is the totalitarian conception.④ The Axis powers pretend that they own all of a man, including his conscience. It was inevitable that the Nazis should try to deny the Christian church, because in virtually every respect its teachings are in opposition to the Nazi ideal of race supremacy and of the subordination of the individual. Christianity could only be an annoyance and a threat to Hitler's bid for power and his contempt for the common man.

32　Today the struggle of Man's spirit is against new and curious shackles. Today a new monstrosity has shown itself on earth, a seven days' wonder, a new child of tyranny — a political religion in which the leader of the state becomes, himself, an object of worship and reverence and in which the individual becomes a corpuscle in the blood of the community, almost without identity.⑤ This Nazi freak must fail, if only because men are not clods, because the spirit does live. In the design for a new and better world, religious freedom is a fundamental prop.

33　We of the nations united in war, among whom all the great religions are represented, see

---

① "信仰自由的民主保证不在于一份同意书——而在于一份认可。"
② 托马斯·潘恩（1737—1809），英裔美国思想家、作家、政治活动家、革命家。潘恩对美国历史的贡献巨大。1774年，37岁的潘恩离开伦敦来到北美英属殖民地。13个月后，适逢北美独立战争，潘恩发表了著名的小册子《常识》。潘恩出身于工人阶层，有着强烈的亲工人反贵族的进步主义意识，这在《常识》中有所体现。这本小册子仅84页；语言简单、通俗易懂；内容激进、大胆，"像一道闪电，瞬间照亮了黑暗的天空，给美国人民指明了斗争的方向"。潘恩在书中提出殖民地独立并建立一个向人民负责而不是向国王负责的政府。这种革命精神，大大鼓舞了殖民地的人民，为殖民地精英阶层和决策者指明了方向，在美国历史上具有转折性、变革性的意义，对美国独立战争影响深远。但是潘恩对奴隶制度的反对，对战争中腐败现象的抨击，使他遭到建国时许多精英的憎恨，以至于战争结束后，他不得不因为找不到合适的工作而重返欧洲。1789年，他参与了法国大革命的政治辩论。在欧洲期间，潘恩出版了另外3本书：《人的权利》（*Rights of Man*）、《理性时代》（*The Age of Reason*）和《农业正义》（*Agrarian Justice*）。
③ "因此我们能看到一个令人难忘的景象（在美国我们总是能看到这样的景象）：去不同教堂做礼拜的人却在参加同一个镇民大会或参与同一个政治论坛。"
④ "与民主的人和人类精神的观念相对的是极权主义观念。" totalitarian: 极权主义的。
⑤ "当今，一种新的恐怖恶行在七天奇迹诞生的地球上出现，这是暴政的一个新生儿——这是一个政治宗教，国家领导人自己成为信仰和崇拜的对象，而个人则成为社会血液中的一粒血球，几乎失去身份。" monstrosity: 畸形，恐怖恶行。

a triumphant peace by which all races will continue the belief in man, the belief in his elusive and untouchable spirit, and in the solid worth of human life.

Freedom from Want

34   The proposal that want be abolished from this world would be pretentious, or even ridiculous, were it not for two important recent discoveries.①

35   One is the discovery that, beyond any doubt, men now possess the technical ability to produce in great abundance the necessities of daily life — enough for everyone. This is a revolutionary and quite unprecedented condition on earth, which stimulates the imagination and quickens the blood.

36   Another is the discovery (or rather the realization) that the earth is one planet indivisible that one man's hunger is every other man's hunger. We know now that the world must be looked at whole if men are to enjoy the fruits they are now able to produce, and if the inhabitants of the globe are to survive and prosper.

37   Freedom from want, everywhere in the world, is within the grasp of men. It has never been quite within their grasp before. Prosperous times have been enjoyed in certain regions of the world at certain periods in history, but local prosperity was usually achieved at the expense of some other region, which was being impoverished, and the spectre of impending war hung over all. Now the industrial changes of the last 150 years and the new prospect implicit in the words "United Nations" have given meaning to the phrase "freedom from want" and rendered it not only possible but necessary.

38   It was in the year 1492 that the earth became round in the minds of men — although it had been privately globular for many centuries. Now in the year 1942, by a coincidence which should fortify astrologers, the earth's rotundity again opens new vistas, this time not of fabulous continents ready to be ransacked, but of a fabulous world ready to be unified and restored.② War having achieved totality, against men's wishes but with their full participation, our great resolve as we go to battle must now be that the peace shall be total also. The world is all one today. No military gesture anywhere on earth, however trivial, has been without consequence everywhere; and what is true of the military is true, also, of the economic. A hungry man in Cambodia is a threat to the well-fed of Duluth③.

39   People are worried about the period which will follow this war. Some fear the peace

---

① "如果没有最近两项最重要的发现，从这个世界消除匮乏的提议则显得言过其实，甚而荒谬。"
② "现在，在1942年，令占星家更感巧合的是，圆形的地球再次向我们揭开新的未来，当然这次不是伟大的各洲将被掠夺，而是这个伟大的世界将联合起来恢复重建。" fortify: 增强，加强; rotundity: 球状，圆形; vista: （未来可能发生的）一系列情景，一连串事情; ransack: 抢劫；掠夺。
③ "柬埔寨任何饥饿的人对丰衣足食的德卢斯都是一种威胁。" 这句话的意思是世界是统一的，任何地方的情况都会对其他地区造成影响，军事上如此，经济上也如此。Duluth: 德卢斯，美国明尼苏达州东北部港口城市，位于苏必利尔湖畔。

more than they fear the war. But the picture is neither hopeless nor is it black. Already, in this country and abroad, agencies are at work making preliminary studies and designing machinery to stabilize the peacetime world which will follow the war. They are preparing to reemploy the returning soldier, to maintain buying power at a high level, to stand behind industry while it is changing back to peaceable products, to guarantee a certain security to the groups which need such guarantees. The fact that these plans are being drawn is itself encouraging, for when trouble is anticipated and fairly faced, it is less likely to ensue.

40 The tools of production and the skills which men possess are tremendous in the present war emergency, and when the peace comes, the world will contain more skilled people than ever before in history. Those who are at work planning broadly for a better human society propose to equip this enormous productive manpower with new ideas to fit new conditions.

41 The pattern is already beginning to become apparent. Once, the soil was regarded as something to use and get the most from and then abandon. Now it is something to conserve and replenish. Once it was enough that a man compete freely in business, for the greatest possible personal gain; now his enterprise, still free, must meet social standards and must not tend toward concentration of power unfavorable to the general well-being of the community. Once, an idle man was presumed to be a loafer; now it is realized he may be a victim of circumstances in which all share, and for which all are responsible.

42 The great civilizations of the past were never free from wide-spread poverty. Very few of them, and these only during short periods, produced enough wealth to make possible a decent living standard for all their members, even if that wealth had been equally divided. In the short space of a few decades we have changed scarcity to abundance and are now engaged in the experiment of trying to live with our new and as yet unmanageable riches. The problem becomes one not of production but of distribution and of consumption; and since buying power must be earned, freedom from want becomes freedom from mass unemployment, plus freedom from penury for those individuals unable to work.

43 In our United States the Federal Government, being the common meeting ground of all interests and the final agency of the people, assumes a certain responsibility for the solution of economic problems. This is not a new role for the Government, which has been engaged since the earliest days of our history in devising laws and machinery and techniques for promoting the well-being of the citizen, whether he was a soldier returning from a war, or a new settler heading west to seek his fortune, or a manufacturer looking for a market for his goods, or a farmer puzzled over a problem in animal husbandry.

44 The beginning has been made. The right to work. The right to fair pay. The right to adequate food, clothing, shelter, medical care. The right to security. The right to live in an atmosphere of free enterprise. We state these things as "rights" — not because man has any natural right to be nourished and sheltered, not because the world owes any man a living, but because unless man succeeds in filling these primary needs his only development is backward and downward, his only growth malignant, and his last resource war.

45   All of these opportunities are not in the American record yet, and they are not yet in the world's portfolio in the shape of blueprints. Much of America and most of the world are not properly fed, clothed, housed. But there has never been a time, since the world began, when the hope of providing the essentials of life to every living man and woman and child has been so good, or when the necessity has been so great.

46   It can be done. The wealth exists in the earth, the power exists in the hills, men have the tools and the training. What remains to be seen is whether they have the wit and the moral character to work together and to lay aside their personal greed.

47   We and our allies are fighting today not merely to defend an honorable past and old slogans and faiths, but to construct a still more honorable and rewarding future. Fighting men, coming back from the war, will not be satisfied with a mere guarantee of dull security — they will expect to find useful work and a vigorous life. Already moves are being made to meet this inescapable challenge.

48   The first step, obviously, will be to prevent the sort of slump which has usually followed a great war. War is tremendously costly, in terms of money. Billions are being spent in order that we may win. The peace, too, will be costly, and nothing is gained by evading the fact. But a democracy which can organize itself to defeat one sort of enemy is capable of sustaining the effort through the days that follow. Work, in vast quantity and in infinite variety, will be waiting to be done. We will have the capacity to produce the highest national income ever known, and the jobs to keep men at work.

49   Freedom from want is neither a conjurer's trick nor a madman's dream. The earth has never known it, nor anything approaching it. But free men do not accept the defeatist notion that it never will. The freeing of all people from want is a continuing experiment, the oldest and most absorbing one in the laboratory, the one that has produced the strangest gases and the loudest explosions[①]. It is a people's own experiment and goes on through the courtesy of chemists and physicists and poets and technicians and men of strong faith and unshakable resolve.

Freedom from Fear

50   Fear is the inheritance of every animal, and man is no exception. Our children fear the tangible dark, and we give them what reassurance we can, so that they will grow and develop normally, their minds free from imaginary terrors. This reassurance, this sense of protection and security, is an important factor in their lives.

51   The new dark which has settled on the earth with the coming of might and force and evil has terrified grown men

---

① "使人类不虞匮乏是一个持久的实验,是实验室最久远最吸引人的实验,这个实验产出了最奇怪的气体,发出了最响亮的爆炸声。"意思是使人类不虞匮乏是一件长期的事情,以此为目的衍生出众多发明和发现。

and women. They fear the dark, fear fire and the sword; they are tormented by the dread of evils which are only too real. They fear the conqueror who places his shackles on the mind. Above all else they are tortured by that basic political fear: fear of domination of themselves by others — others who are stronger, others who are advancing, others who have the weapons and are destroying and burning and pillaging. This is the fear which haunts millions of men and women everywhere in the world. It is the fear of being awakened in the night, with the rapping on the door.

52 No structure of peace, no design for a good world, will have any solidity or strength or even any meaning unless it disperses the shadow of this fear and brings reassurance to men and women, not only for themselves but for their children and their children's children. Aggressive war, sudden armed attack, secret police, these must be forever circumvented.[①] The use of force, historically the means of settling disputes, must be made less and less feasible on earth, until it finally becomes impossible. Even though the underlying causes which foment wars may not be immediately eradicated from the earth, the physical act of war can be prevented when people, by their ingenuity, their intelligence, their memory, and their moral nature, choose to do so. Force can be eliminated as a means of political action only if it be opposed with an equal or greater force — which is economic and moral and which is backed by collective police power, so that in a community of nations no one nation or group of nations will have the opportunity to commit acts of aggression against any neighbor, anywhere in the world.

53 The machinery for enforcing peace is important and indispensable; but even more important is that there be established a moral situation, which will support and operate this machinery. As the last war ended, an attempt was made to construct an orderly world society capable of self-control. It was an idealistic and revolutionary plan. But like the first automobile, it moved haltingly and was more of a novelty than a success. For a while men's hopes focused on the plan; but it was never universally accepted. The faith was not there, nor the courage.

54 Today many nations are working together with unbelievable energy and with harmony of feeling and interest. They are united at the moment by the desire to win battles, but they are also united by common principles and by a conviction that their people ultimately want the same thing from life — freedom, peace, security, the chance to live as individuals.

55 Such collaboration has its origin in the democratic spirit, which infects men regardless of latitude or longitude[②], and it has been fed by the close association between nations which are geographically near neighbors as, for example, the inter-American powers. Canada has been a good neighbor to the United States for many years, and the Canadian border, never fortified, stands today as a symbol of what the world will be when men's faith becomes great enough and their heads become hard enough.

---

① "侵略战争，突然武装袭击，秘密警察，必须永远远离这些。" circumvent: 设法克服或避免（某事物）；回避。
② regardless of latitude or longitude: 无论何处。latitude: 纬度；longitude: 经度。

56 Still another answer to fear is found in the concept of the United Nations. For the first time in history, twenty-eight nations have been acting together, in the very midst of a mortal struggle, to set down the specifications of a peace settlement and the aims of war and post-war action. Their representatives, meeting in Washington on New Year's Day, 1942, signed a historic Declaration by United Nations, saying:

"The Governments signatory hereto,

"Having subscribed to a common program of purposes and principles embodied in the Joint Declaration of the President of the United States of America and the Prime Minister of the United Kingdom of Great Britain and Northern Ireland dated August 14, 1941, known as the *Atlantic Charter*,

"Being convinced that complete victory over their enemies is essential to defend life, liberty, independence and religious freedom, and to preserve human rights and justice in their own lands as well as in other lands, and that they are now engaged in a common struggle against savage and brutal forces seeking to subjugate the world,

Declare:

" (1) Each Government pledges itself to employ its full resources, military or economic, against those members of the Tripartite Pact① and its adherents with which such government is at war.

" (2) Each Government pledges itself to cooperate with the Governments signatory hereto and not to make a separate armistice or peace with the enemies.②

"The foregoing declaration may be adhered to by other nations which are, or which may be, rendering material assistance and contributions in the struggle for victory over Hitlerism."

57 The nations signing the Declaration by United Nations are: The United Kingdom of Great Britain and Northern Ireland, the Union of Soviet Socialist Republics, China, Australia, Belgium, Canada, Costa Rica, Cuba, Czechoslovakia, the Dominican Republic, El Salvador, Greece, Guatemala, Haiti, Honduras, India, Luxembourg, the Netherlands, New Zealand, Nicaragua, Norway, Panama, Poland, South Africa, Yugoslavia, and the United States of America. On June 14, Mexico and the Philippine Islands adhered to the Declaration by United Nations.

58 Can anyone be deaf to the sound of hope in this assemblage? Men have not achieved their goal, but at least they have collectively aspired to it, and have accepted a responsibility for it which is continuing and not merely fitful. The work is to go on. The new building will indeed be built, whatever its shape, whatever its appointments, whatever its defects.

59 Those are the goals of the peace and the hope of the world. But the specific and

---

① 《德意日三国同盟条约》于 1940 年 9 月 27 日由纳粹德国、法西斯意大利与军国主义日本在德国柏林签署。此项协定正式确立了上述三个轴心国的同盟关系,并被认为是对美国的警告:要么保持中立,要么两面受敌。条约中,三国同意在未来十年会"支持及与对方互相合作……以期实现它们建立与维持新秩序的目标,以期提倡互惠互利与有关人民之福祉"。

② "每一政府各自保证只与宣言签字国合作,不与敌人单独缔结停战协定或协约"。

immediate problem, the first move to free people from fear, is to achieve a peaceable world which has been deprived of its power to destroy itself. This can only be accomplished by disarming the aggressors and keeping them disarmed. Last time they were disarmed, but they were not prevented from rearming. This time they will be disarmed in truth.

....

60　It will be remembered that the inquisitive Ben Franklin[①], testing the lightning with his kite, found in the storm's noisy violence the glimmerings of a secret which later illuminated the world. His example suggests that good news is sometimes hidden in bad weather. Today, in the storm which rages across the whole earth, men are sending up their kites to the new lightning, to try its possibilities and to prepare for clearing skies.

61　The Four Freedoms guide them on. Freedom of speech and religion, freedom from want and from fear — these belong to all the earth and to all men everywhere. Our own country, with its ideas of equality, is an experiment which has been conducted against odds and with much patience and, best of all, with some success for most people. It has prospered and brought fresh hope to millions and new good to humanity. Even in the thick of war the experiment goes ahead with old values and new forms. Life is change. The earth shrinks in upon itself and we adjust to a world in motion, holding fast to the truth as we know it, confident that as long as the love of freedom shows in the eyes of men, it will show also in their deeds.

Vocabulary

despotic (para. 2)	*adj.* characteristic of an absolute ruler or absolute rule; having absolute sovereignty
futile (para. 4)	*adj.* having no effect or achieving nothing; unsuccessful
compliment (para. 4)	*n.* a remark or an action that expresses approval, admiration or respect
subjugate (para. 5)	*v.* to defeat people or a country and rule them in a way which allows them no freedom
jeopardize (para. 6)	*v.* to put something such as a plan or system in danger of being harmed or damaged
dire (para. 6)	*adj.* very serious or extreme
ferment (para. 6)	*v.* to (cause something to) change chemically through the action of

---

① 本杰明·富兰克林（1706—1790），18 世纪美国最伟大的科学家和发明家，著名的政治家、外交家、哲学家、文学家、航海家，以及美国独立战争中的伟大领袖之一。据称在 1752 年夏季，在天空乌云密布时，富兰克林和儿子威廉用风筝进行了一项实验，证明闪电实际上就是大量的静电。富兰克林的理论后来被法国人证实，也奠定了他的科学家地位。从此，人类历史上诞生了一句名言："他从天空抓到了雷电，从专制统治者手中夺回了权力。"

	living substances, such as yeast or bacteria
prerogative (para. 7)	*n.* something which some people are able or allowed to do or have, but which is not possible or allowed for everyone
execute (para. 8)	*v.* to do or perform something, especially in a planned way
cynic (para. 9)	*n.* a person who believes that people are only interested in themselves and are not sincere
subscribe (to) (para. 10)	*v.* to agree with or support an opinion, belief or theory
gag (para. 11)	*v.* to stop up (a person's mouth), esp. with a piece of cloth, etc. to prevent him or her from speaking or crying out
servile (para. 11)	*adj.* submissive or fawning in attitude or behavior
contradiction (para. 11)	*n.* when something is the complete opposite of something else or very different from something else, so that one of them must be wrong
amendment (para. 13)	*n.* a change made to the words of a text
abridge (para. 13)	*v.* to make a book, play or piece of writing shorter by removing details and information that is not important
petition (para. 13)	*v.* to make a formal request for something, especially in a court of law
redress (para. 13)	*n.* money that someone has to pay to someone else because they have injured them or treated them badly
grievance (para. 13)	*n.* a complaint or a strong feeling that you have been treated unfairly
expediency (para. 14)	(also expedience) *n.* when something is helpful or useful in a particular situation, but sometimes not morally acceptable
contemptuous (para. 14)	*adj.* expressing a strong feeling of disliking and having no respect for someone or something
becloud (para. 15)	*v.* to cover or obscure with a cloud, to confuse or muddle
anesthesia (para. 17)	*n.* loss of bodily sensation with or without loss of consciousness
sluggish (para. 19)	*adj.* lacking energy; inactive; slow-moving
destitution (para. 19)	*n.* the state of being destitute; utter poverty, lack or deficiency
exigency (para. 21)	*n.* an urgent demand; pressing requirement, an emergency
fare (para. 24)	*n.* a range of food and drink; diet
dispense (para. 24)	*v.* to give out or issue in portions
regale (para. 24)	*v.* to give delight or amusement to
transcend (para. 28)	*v.* to go above or beyond (a limit, expectation, etc.), as in degree or excellence, to be superior to
subordination (para. 31)	*n.* the act of giving someone or something less importance or power
bid (para. 31)	*n.* an attempt to achieve or get something

shackle (para. 32)	*n.* a restraint that confines or restricts freedom (especially something used to tie down or restrain a prisoner) 枷锁，镣铐
triumphant (para. 33)	*adj.* having achieved a great victory (= winning a war or competition) or success, or feeling very happy and proud because of such an achievement
render (para. 37)	*v.* cause someone or something to be in a particular state
ensue (para. 39)	*v.* to happen after something else, especially as a result of it
replenish (para. 41)	*v.* to fill something up again
penury (para. 42)	*n.* the state of being extremely poor

Questions for discussion

1. How do you define the nature of the four freedoms?
2. In examining and defining the freedom of speech, what does the text mean by saying that "Men, it turns out, breathe through their minds as well as through their lungs"? (para. 12)
3. Why did the German leader deprive a person of his voice? (para. 14)
4. What conditions were necessary before freedom of speech took effect? (para. 18)
5. In the "Freedom of Religion" part, what does "new and curious shackles" mean in the sentence "Today the struggle of Man's spirit is against new and curious shackles"? (para. 32)
6. How does the text support the idea "Freedom from want, everywhere in the world, is within the grasp of men"? (para. 37)
7. What does a world free from want look like?
8. What is the first move to free people from fear according to the text?

Background

President Roosevelt made his Four Freedoms Speech almost a year before the United States entered World War II (1939—1945). In his address, Roosevelt envisioned a postwar world in which four freedoms would be guaranteed: freedom of speech and expression, freedom of worship, freedom from want, and freedom from fear. In a world society based on these principles, he said, no nation would be able to commit aggressions. War and tyranny would be replaced by the friendly cooperation of free countries. Roosevelt also stated that the United States should help democratic governments fighting in the war, and he asked Congress to send ships, planes, tanks, and arms to those nations. Much of the spirit of the Four Freedoms was later expressed in the *Atlantic Charter*, a joint declaration of principles made on August 14, 1941, by Roosevelt and British Prime Minister Winston Churchill.

Chapter 6 Four Freedoms（四大自由）

Before Pearl Harbor, few speeches stirred Americans more deeply than United States president Franklin D. Roosevelt's statement of wartime objectives, delivered as part of his annual message to Congress in 1941. In this address he argued that America must uphold certain basic human principles that have come to be known as the Four Freedoms. Roosevelt also called for concrete actions, such as the Lend-Lease program, to provide military and economic aid to nations fighting Axis powers.

In 14 August 1941, President Franklin D. Roosevelt and Prime Minister Winston Churchill of Great Britain signed *Atlantic Charter* at a meeting in Argentina Bay off the coast of Newfoundland. The *Atlantic Charter* was perceived by the Axis powers as the beginnings of a United States and Great Britain alliance. This had the impact of strengthening the militaristic government in Japan. Though the *Atlantic Charter* pledged no military support for the war in Europe it had the impact of signaling the United States as a major player on the world stage. This was a position that the United States would firmly hold after World War II in its efforts to rebuild a war torn Europe. The *Atlantic Charter* was a significant first step towards the United Nations. On 1 January 1942, twenty-six countries (including the United States and Great Britain) signed the *United Nations Declaration*, which included among its provisions formal endorsement of the charter.

Roosevelt's insistence on human dignity, an economic bill of rights, and on the need for security around the globe was further reflected in his plan for a United Nations to keep the peace among nations and to guarantee basic human rights for all humankind, not just for Americans.

1941年12月8日，罗斯福总统签署对日宣战令

153

1941年8月10日—12日，罗斯福和丘吉尔在大西洋会议上

1945年2月4日—11日，罗斯福与丘吉尔、斯大林在雅尔塔会议上

20世纪30年代，美国民众普遍反对政府介入外部事务。第一次世界大战中美国的盟友在战后未能向美国赔偿战争债务，使美国人大失所望。在他们看来，战争中收获最大的是少数几个武器制造商。公众和美国政界对外部事务的厌恶导致美国国会从1935年到1937年制定了一系列《中立法》，禁止美国向交战双方出售武器、贷款，甚至禁止美国人乘坐交战国的轮船，反对武装美国商船。

此时，世界局势日趋紧张。日本全面侵略中国，希特勒攫取了苏台德地区，英、法推行绥靖政策，以牺牲弱小国家的利益来换取暂时的和平。苏、德签定互不侵犯条约。独裁国家的步步紧逼威胁到美国在世界各地的切身利益。这一切都表明，国际联盟形同虚设，第一次世界大战后建立起来的集体安全原则已被希特勒、墨索里尼和日本军国主义分子打碎。尽管大多数美国人对日益猖獗的极权主义感到悲哀，同情那些独裁国家的受害者，但美国民众依然不赞同政府介入外部事务。1939年9月，德军入侵波兰，英、法随即向德宣战，第二次世界大战正式爆发。然而美国在相当一段时间内做出的反应只限于废除《中立法》规定的武器禁运原则，以"现款自运"方式向交战各国出售武器。1940年春天，丹麦、挪威、比利时、荷兰、卢森堡、法国相继沦陷，美国人一下子意识到自己的安全受到了前所未有的威胁。

1940年9月，美国国会通过《和平时期征兵法》。这时候，大部分美国人已同意"让美国成为民主国家的大兵工厂"。同年，罗斯福第三次当选为美国总统，他力排众议，继续实施对外援助计划。次年，罗斯福向国会提出，美国必须实施向关系到美国安全的国家租借或转让武器的计划。同年，罗斯福发表《四大自由演说》，号召美国人以全部的道义力量支持《租借法》，支持英、法等国的反法西斯战争，同时向世界宣布，美国的目标是在战后建立一个享有四大自由的世界新秩序。罗斯福于1941年3月签署《租借法》，向与德、意、日作战的国家提供物资。8月14日，罗斯福与英国首相丘吉尔发表《大西洋宪章》，声称"两国不追求领土或其他方面的扩张；尊重各民族自由选择其政府形式的权利；赞同摧毁德国纳粹暴政和解除侵略国家的武装"等，把"使全世界所有人类悉有自由生活，无所恐惧，亦不虞匮乏的保证"列为目标，并宣布战后"被剥夺主权和自治的人民，得以恢复主权与自治"；9月24日，苏联政府声明同意其基本原则，接着召开莫斯科三国会议，奠定了美、英、苏战时合作的基础。

1941年底，美国参战。罗斯福代表美国两次参加同盟国"三巨头"会议。1943年1月14日到23日，罗斯福和丘吉尔及两国高级将领在摩洛哥卡萨布兰卡举行了战略会议，罗斯福政府提出了轴心国必须无条件投降的原则并得到了实施。在德黑兰会议上，罗斯福详细地向丘吉尔和斯大林介绍了他对联合国的构想；1944年早秋，四大参战国家（美国、英国、苏联和中国）在美国首都华盛顿郊区的敦巴顿橡树园召开会议，会上讨论了战后将怎样维持和平的提案（即联合国机构组织草案），最终确立建立一个国际组织即联合国的目标，以便维持安全和促进繁荣。

罗斯福提出的四大自由思想是美国历史上最重要的思想之一。它阐述了美国人所认为的世界秩序应遵守的几项基本原则，被认为是关于美国人民准备为之奋斗的原则的最简要声明，同时也是《联合国宪章》和《世界人权宣言》的重要思想来源，对此后世界的发展产生了巨大影响。《四大自由演说》也因此成为美国希望成为世界领袖的一份宣言和声明。这份宣言既是现实主义的，也是理想主义的。

Further reading

Barlett, Ruhl J., *The Record of American Diplomacy: Documents and Readings in the History of American Foreign Relations*, Alfred A. Knopf, Inc., 1947.

Borgwardt, Elizabeth, *A New Deal for the World: America's Vision for Human Rights*, Cambridge: Belknap, 2005.

Cole, Wayne S., *Roosevelt and the Isolationists*, Nebraska: University of Nebraska Press, 1983.

Commager, Henry S., *Documents of American History*, New Jersey: Prentice-Hall Inc., 1973.

Dallek, Robert, *Franklin D. Roosevelt and American Foreign Policy, 1932—1945*, New York: Oxford University Press, 1979.

Farnham, Barbara R., *Roosevelt and the Munich Crisis*, Princeton, N.J.: Princeton University Press, 1997.

Gellman, Irwin F., *Good Neighbor Diplomacy: United States Policies in Latin America, 1933—1945*, Baltimore: The Johns Hopkins University Press, 1979.

Heinrichs, Waldo, *Threshold of War: Franklin D. Roosevelt and American Entry into World War II*, New York: Oxford University Press, 1988.

Jerel A. Rosati, *Readings in the Politics of United States Foreign Policy*, Beijing: Peking University Press, 2004.

Jonas, Manfred, *The United States and Germany, A Diplomacy History*, Cornell: Cornell University Press, 1984.

Marks, Frederick W., *Wind over Sand, the Diplomacy of Franklin Roosevelt*, Georgia: Georgia University Press, 1988.

Paterson, Thomas G., J. Garry Clifford, and Kenneth J. Hagan, *American Foreign Relations, Vol. 2: A History Since 1895*, 5th ed., Boston: Houghton Mifflin, 2000.

Reynolds, David, *From Munich to Pearl Harbor: Roosevelt's America and the Origins of the Second World War*, Chicago: Ivan R. Dee, Inc, 2001.

Robert, Axelrod, *The Evolution of Cooperation*, New York: Basic Books, 1984.

Schmitz, David F. & Richard D. Challener, *Appeasement in Europe: A Reassessment of U.S. Policies*, Westport: Greenwood Press, 1990.

C.A.戈尼昂斯基等：《外交史（第四卷）》，北京：生活·读书·新知三联书店，1980年。

戴安娜·拉维奇编：《美国读本：感动过一个国家的文字》，林本椿等译，北京：生活·读书·新知三联书店，1995年。

富兰克林·德·罗斯福：《罗斯福选集》，关在汉编译，北京：商务印书馆，1982年。

简·爱德华·史密斯：《罗斯福传》，李文婕译，武汉：长江文艺出版社，2016年。

李道揆：《美国政府和美国政治》，北京：商务印书馆，1990年。

罗伯特·达莱克：《罗斯福与美国对外政策1932—1945》（上册），伊伟等译，白自然校，北京：商务印书馆，1984年。

迈克尔·H.亨特：《意识形态与美国外交政策》，北京：世界知识出版社，1999年。

欧阳静雯编著：《勇者无敌：罗斯福》，北京：北京师范大学出版社，2015年。

让-巴蒂斯特·迪罗塞尔：《外交史（1919—1978年）》（下），李仓人等译，上海：上海译文出版社，1982年。

任东来、王波等：《当代美国——一个超级大国的成长》，贵阳：贵州人民出版社，2001年。

W.兰斯·班尼特：《新闻：政治的幻象》，杨晓红等译，北京：当代中国出版社，2005年。

杨生茂主编：《美国外交政策史：1775—1989》，北京：人民出版社，1991年。

岳西宽、张卫星译：《美国历届总统就职演说》，北京：中央编译出版社，2001年。

詹姆斯·麦格雷戈·伯恩斯：《罗斯福》，孙天义等译，北京：国际文化出版公司，2003年。

参考书目

Bailey, Thomas A., *Woodrow Wilson and the Lost Peace*, Encounter Paperbacks, 1963.

Baker, Ray S. (ed.), *Woodrow Wilson and World Settlement*, 3 Vols., New York: Doubleday Page & Company, 1922.

Barlett, Ruhl J., *The Record of American Diplomacy: Documents and Readings in the History of American Foreign Relations*, Alfred A. Knopf, Inc., 1947.

Beveridge, Albert J., *The Meaning of the Times, and Other Speeches*, Indianapolis: Bobbs-Merrill, 1908.

Bickerton, Ian James, Bankers, *Businessmen, and the Open Door Policy, 1899—1911*, Ann Arbor, Mich.: UMI, 1975.

Borgwardt, Elizabeth, *A New Deal for the World: America's Vision for Human Rights*, Cambridge: Belknap, 2005.

Bowers, Claude, *Beveridge and the Progressive Era*, Boston: Houghton-Mifflin Company, 1932.

Braeman, John, *Albert J. Beveridge: American Nationalist*, Chicago: University of Chicago Press, 1971.

Calhoun, Frederick S., *Power and Principle: Armed Intervention in Wilsonian Foreign Policy*, Kent: The Kent State University Press, 1986.

Campbell, Charles. S., *Special Business Interests and the Open Door Policy*, New Haven: Archon Books, 1951.

Clements, Kendrick A, "Woodrow Wilson and World War I", *Presidential Studies Quarterly* 34, 2004.

Cole, Wayne S., *Roosevelt and the Isolationists*, Nebraska: University of Nebraska Press, 1983.

Commager, Henry S., *Documents of American History*, New Jersey: Prentice-Hall Inc., 1973.

Crutchfield, James A., *George Washington: First in War, First in Peace*, New York: Forge Books, 2005.

Dallek, Robert, *Franklin D. Roosevelt and American Foreign Policy, 1932—1945*, New York: Oxford University Press, 1979.

Doenecke, Justus D., "American Isolationism, 1939—1941", *Journal of Libertarian Studies*, Summer/Fall 1982, 6 (3), pp.201—216.

Dulles, Foster Rhea, *The Old China Trade,* Boston and New York: Houghton Mifflin Company, 1930.

Farnham, Barbara R., *Roosevelt and the Munich Crisis*, Princeton, N.J.: Princeton University Press, 1997.

Gaddis, John Lewis, *Strategies of Containment: A Critical Appraisal of Postwar American National Security Policy*, New York: Oxford University Press, 1982.

Gellman, Irwin F., *Good Neighbor Diplomacy: United States Policies in Latin American, 1933—1945*, Baltimore: The Johns Hopkins University Press, 1979.

Gilderhus, Mark T., "The Monroe Doctrine: Meanings and Implications", *Presidential Studies Quarterly*, Blackwell Publishing Ltd., 2006.

Ginsberg, Benjamin. J., Lowi Theodore & Weir Margaret, *We the People*, New York: W.W. Norton & Company, 2001.

Grackel, Theodore, *The Papers of George Washington*, Charlottesville: University of Virginia Press, 2006.

Griswold, A.W., *The Far Eastern Policy of the United States*, New Haven: Yale University Press, 1962.

Haynes, Sam W. and Christopher Morris (ed.), *Manifest Destiny and Empire: American Antebellum Expansionism*, College Station: The University of Texas at Arlington, 1997.

Heinrichs, Waldo, *Threshold of War: Franklin D. Roosevelt and American Entry into World War II*, New York: Oxford University Press, 1988.

Henriques, Peter R., *Realistic Visionary: A Portrait of George Washington*, Charlottesville: University of Virginia Press, 2006.

Hoover, Herbert, *The Ordeal of Woodrow Wilson*, New York: McGraw-Hill, 1958.

Horsman, Reginald, *Race and Manifest Destiny: The Origins of American Racial Anglo-Saxonism*, Cambridge, Massachusetts: Harvard University Press, 1981.

Jerel A. Rosati, *Readings in the Politics of United States Foreign Policy*, Beijing: Peking University Press, 2004.

Johnson, Myron M., *League of Nations: A Review of American Foreign Policy from 1914 to 1946*, Boston, Mass.: House of Edinboro, 1946.

Jonas, Manfred, *The United States and Germany, A Diplomacy History*, Cornell: Cornell University Press, 1984.

Koo, V. K. Wellington, *The Open Door Policy and World Peace*, London; New York: Toronto: Oxford University Press, 1939.

Lawrence, David, *The True Story of Woodrow Wilson*, New York: George H. Doran Company, 1924.

Lewis, James E., Jr., *John Quincy Adams: Policymaker for the Union*, Scholarly Resources, 2001.

Link, Arther S., *Wilson the Diplomatist: A Look at His Major Foreign Policy*, Baltimore: The John Hopkins Press, 1974.

Marks, Frederick W., *Wind over Sand, the Diplomacy of Franklin Roosevelt*, Georgia: Georgia University Press, 1988.

May, Ernest R, *The Making of the Monroe Doctrine*, Cambridge, Mass.: Harvard University Press, 1975.

Miller, Robert J., *Native America, Discovered and Conquered: Thomas Jefferson, Lewis & Clark, and Manifest Destiny*, Westport, Connecticut: Praeger Publishers, 2006.

Moore, Gregory, *Defining and Defending the Open Door Policy: Theodore Roosevelt and China, 1901—1909*, Lanham, Maryland: Lexington Books, 2015.

Mountjoy, Shane, *Manifest Destiny: Westward Expansion*, New York: Infobase Publishing, 2009.

Paterson, Thomas G., J. Garry Clifford, and Kenneth J. Hagan, *American Foreign Relations*, Vol. 2: *A History Since 1895*, 5th ed., Boston, 2000.

Preston, Daniel (ed.), *The Papers of James Monroe*, Westport, Connecticut: Greenwood Press, 2003.

Remini, Robert V., *John Quincy Adams*, New York: Times Books, 2002.

Reynolds, David, *From Munich to Pearl Harbor: Roosevelt's America and the Origins of the Second World War*, Chicago: Ivan R. Dee, Inc, 2001.

Robert, Axelrod, *The Evolution of Cooperation*, New York: Basic Books, 1984.

Sampson, Robert D., *John L. O'Sullivan and His Times*, Kent, Ohio: Kent State University Press, 2003.

Schmitz, David F. & Richard D. Challener, *Appeasement in Europe: A Reassessment of U.S. Policies*, Westport: Greenwood Press, 1990.

Tumulty, Joseph P., *Woodrow Wilson As I Know Him*, Los Angeles, CA: Hardpress Publishing, 2012.

Wilson, Woodrow, *A History of the American People*, New York: Harper and Brothers, 1902.

Yen, En Tsung, *The Open Door Policy*, Boston, Mass.: The Stratford Co., 1923.

Zinn, Howard, *A People's History of the United States*, New York: Harper Collins, 2003.

阿伦·米利特、彼得·马斯洛斯金：《美国军事史》，军事科学院外国军事研究部译，北京：军事科学出版社，1989年。

B.阿瓦林：《帝国主义在满洲》，北京对外贸易学院俄语教研室译，北京：商务印书馆，1980年。

保罗·S.芮恩施：《一个美国外交官使华记》，李抱宏等译，游燮庭校，北京：商务印书馆，1982年。

保罗·约翰逊：《乔治·华盛顿传》，李蔚超译，南京：译林出版社，2016年。

C.A.戈尼昂斯基等：《外交史（第四卷）》，北京：生活·读书·新知三联书店，1980年。

陈乐民主编《西方外交思想史》，北京：中国社会科学出版社，1995年。

戴安娜·拉维奇编：《美国读本：感动过一个国家的文字》，林本椿等译，北京：生活·读书·新知三联书店，1995年。

丹尼尔·E.哈蒙：《伍德罗·威尔逊》，孟祥德译，北京：现代教育出版社，2005年。

邓蜀生：《伍德罗·威尔逊》，上海：上海人民出版社，1982年。

丁则民：《美国通史（第三卷）：美国内战与镀金时代 1861—19世纪末》，北京：人民出版社，2002年。

董小川：《关于美国对华门户开放政策的几个问题》，《美国研究》1998年第4期。

费正清：《美国与中国》（第四版），北京：世界知识出版社，1999年。

福森科：《瓜分中国的斗争和美国的门户开放政策（1895—1900）》，杨诗浩译，北京：生活·读书·新知三联书店，1958年。

富兰克林·德·罗斯福：《罗斯福选集》，关在汉编译，北京：商务印书馆，1982年。

哈尔·马科维奇：《詹姆斯·门罗》，席娟译，北京：现代教育出版社，2005年。

韩莉：《新外交·旧世界——伍德罗·威尔逊与国际联盟》，北京：同心出版社，2002年。

亨利·基辛格：《大外交》，顾淑馨等译，海口：海南出版社，1998年。

洪育沂：《1931—1939年国际关系简史》，北京：读书·生活·新知三联书店，1980年。

华盛顿·欧文：《华盛顿传》，吉灵娟译，武汉：长江文艺出版社，2016年。

黄安年：《二十世纪美国史》，石家庄：河北人民出版社，1989年。

黄安年：《美国的崛起》，北京：中国社会科学出版社，1992年。

加尔文·D.林顿编著：《美国两百年大事记》，谢延光等译，上海：上海译文出版社，1984年。

贾庆国：《美国外交思想与实践》，袁明主编：《美国文化与社会十五讲》，北京：北京大学出版社，2003年。

贾士毅：《华会见闻录》，台北：文海出版社，1975年影印版。

简·爱德华·史密斯：《罗斯福传》，李文婕译，武汉：长江文艺出版社,2016年。

蒋相泽、吴机鹏主编：《简明中美关系史》，广州：中山大学出版社，1989年。

克里斯托弗·希钦斯：《托马斯·杰斐逊》，彭娟等译，南京：译林出版社，2014年。

理查德·霍夫施塔特：《美国政治传统及其缔造者》，崔永禄等译，北京：商务印书馆，1994年。

李道揆：《美国政府和美国政治》，北京：商务印书馆，1990年。

李庆余：《美国外交史——从独立战争至2004》，济南：山东画报出版社，2008年。

李庆余：《美西战争》，北京：商务印书馆，1984年。

李庆余：《美西战争的研究成果概述》，《国外社会科学情况》1987年第3期。

李庆余编著：《美国外交——从孤立主义到全球主义》，南京：南京大学出版社，1990年。

李庆余等：《美国外交传统及其缔造者》，北京：商务印书馆，2010年。

罗伯特·达莱克：《罗斯福与美国对外政策 1932—1945》（上册），伊伟等译，白自然校，北京：商务印书馆，1984年。

罗伯特·V.雷明尼：《雄辩老将：约翰·昆西·亚当斯传》，饶涛等译，合肥：安徽教育出版社，2006年。

欧阳静雯编著：《勇者无敌：罗斯福》，北京：北京师范大学出版社，2015年。

乔伊斯·亚普雷拜：《美国民主的先驱：托马斯·杰斐逊传》，彭小娟译，叶桂革校，合肥：安徽教育出版社，2005年。

任东来、王波：《当代美国——一个超级大国的成长》，贵州：贵州人民出版社，2001年。

任李明：《威尔逊主义研究》，北京：中国社会科学出版社，2013年。
S.F. 比米斯：《美国外交史》（第一分册），叶笃义译，北京：商务印书馆，1985年。
汪凯：《从亚当斯到杰克逊——美国早期精英政治的兴衰》，北京：中央编译出版社，2016年。
王晓德：《美国外交的奠基时代（1776—1860）》，北京：中国社会科学出版社，2013年。
王晓德：《梦想与现实：威尔逊理想主义外交研究》，北京：中国社会科学出版社，1995年。
王雁：《"山东问题"与美国的门户开放政策（1914—1922）》，济南：山东人民出版社，2016年。
杨生茂编：《美西战争资料选辑》，上海：上海人民出版社，1981年。
杨生茂主编：《美国外交政策史：1775—1989》，北京：人民出版社，1991年。
杨卫东：《扩张与孤立——约翰·昆西·亚当斯外交思想研究》，北京：中国社会科学出版社，2006年。
杨卫东：《约翰·昆西·亚当斯与美国"大陆帝国"的构建》，《东北师范大学学报》2006年第1期。
余志森：《华盛顿评传》，北京：中国社会科学出版社，1990年。
袁明主编：《美国文化与社会十五讲》，北京：北京大学出版社，2003年。
岳西宽、张卫星译：《美国历届总统就职演说》，北京：中央编译出版社，2001年。
詹姆斯·麦格雷戈·伯恩斯：《罗斯福》，孙天义等译，北京：国际文化出版公司，2003年。
张江河：《美西战争与美国向东南亚地缘政治扩张的历史脉络》，《东南亚研究》2013年第5期。
张瑞德：《第一次世界大战》，北京：商务印书馆，1973年。
张友伦主编：《美国通史（第二卷）：美国的独立和初步繁荣 1775—1860》，北京：人民出版社，2002年。
钟月强：《美国"门罗主义"外交政策实践研究》，《人民论坛》2015年总第36期。